# AFTER THE MIRACLE

# BY MAURY ALLEN

# AFTER THE MIRACLE

## *The 1969 Mets Twenty Years Later*

## MAURY ALLEN

FRANKLIN WATTS

1989

*New York · Toronto*

Library of Congress Cataloging-in-Publication Data

Allen, Maury, 1932–
    After the miracle.

    Includes index.
        1. New York Mets (Baseball team)—History.
I. Title.
GV875.N45A44  1989    796.357'64'097471      88-33940
    ISBN 0-531-15100-X

For Janet, my love, my life, my wife
And for Jennifer and Ted, my beloved
babies of 1968 and 1969

AND

For the Miracle Mets of 1969
And the 2,175,373 who paid to see them at Shea

# Contents

# Acknowledgments

The odyssey of the 1969 Mets twenty years later was born out of a historic, joyful summer. In more than two decades of covering sports, I had never fallen so in love with a team. Those of us who recorded the deeds of Gil Hodges and Tom Seaver and Ron Swoboda and Tug McGraw and all the rest in that last year of the turbulent 1960s have no shame in our deep affection. They were all talented and tough, brave and bright, open and enthusiastic. We, the sportswriters who brought them to the fans, were lucky to be part of their team and part of their time. It was a mythic age, so unlike working in the media mass of today, covering the huge-salaried players and burdened with the cynicism of the players and fans.

For nearly twenty years I nurtured the idea that I could investigate their lives, discover their joys, share with them yesterday's triumphs, and see them deal with today's realities. As I visited with them, I noticed that in middle age they remain open and articulate, friendly and opinionated, interesting and interested. It was as much a joy to record their present as it was to remember their past.

This book consists, mostly, of the valued reminiscences of the 1969 Mets. It must, however, include the recorded words and deeds of their earlier days. For that, I thank all my talented sportswriting colleagues for the accuracy and elegance of their stories, which helped to balance my own memories of those days and nights.

Many thanks, as always, go to super agent Julian Bach, who steered this project through from its conception, and to Kent Oswald, my editor at Franklin Watts, who always saw the charm in this romantic idea.

We shared that summer of '69 with all the Mets. We share it still.

# AFTER THE MIRACLE

# 1

# *In the Beginning*

The doorman looked like a Turkish general. He was tall and erect with a thick brush mustache and steely eyes. There were several loops of braids over the shoulders of his heavy blue trench coat. Unsmiling, he opened one of the glass double doors of New York governor Nelson Rockefeller's Manhattan apartment building at 812 Fifth Avenue. When I identified my wife and myself he quickly scanned his list.

His tone turned cordial as he discovered our names. He pressed a button and the inside glass doors magically opened to the sprawling lobby. The elevator took us quickly to the fifth-floor apartment of Nelson and Happy Rockefeller.

The 1969 National League Champion New York Mets—and those of us in the press who had been links to their uproarious past—had been feted all day. There had been cocktails and hors d'oeuvres at Mayor John Lindsay's Gracie Mansion home. Then the players and their wives were taken by bus downtown to the governor's apartment. Lindsay, who had been credited with keeping the peace in the city during the racial and antiwar turmoil that summer, was engaged in a bitter reelection campaign. He saw only good resulting from an association with the Mets and their triumph. Rockefeller, not facing reelection but ever mindful of the enormous following of the Mets, quickly scheduled a visit to his apartment across from Central Park. Neither man was a fan of long standing.

Happy Rockefeller, a charming and ebullient woman, was at the door to greet her visitors. Little Nelson Rockefeller, the governor's five-year-old son, came up to Art Shamsky and asked for his autograph on a baseball. Shamsky signed and said, "I'd better be nice to this kid. He's got millions."

Happy Rockefeller noticed that my wife, Janet, was large with child. "When do you expect?" she asked. "About three weeks," Janet said. "It will be a boy," Happy Rockefeller said. "I always carried that way with my boys." As the parents of an eighteen-month-old daughter, we were bemused. "Let me know," Mrs. Rockefeller said.

Some three weeks later when our son, Ted, would be born, we would send her a birth announcement. An outfit would arrive a week later for our baby boy from Bloomingdale's with a sweet note from the governor's wife.

The players, their wives and the press had been going hard all evening. The noise level in the governor's apartment was high. There was a clanging of glass. The governor was now standing on top of a large coffee table. "A toast," he said, in that familiar, friendly voice. "To Mrs. Payson (not in attendance) and the New York Mets. The greatest thing since the moon landing."

"This is better than the moon landing," shouted coach Joe Pignatano.

"Better than the moon landing. I amend that," said the governor.

There were more drinks served by uniformed waitresses, more laughs, more food offered by tuxedoed waiters. The players ambled through the apartment. Relief pitcher Ron Taylor, a graduate engineer, studied some of the fine paintings on the wall. "I'd like to see the Picassos," he said.

My wife and I and Ron Taylor asked Mrs. Rockefeller if that would be possible. "Certainly," she said, "follow me."

We walked down a flight of stairs in the duplex to a large room. There were several Picassos hung as if in a gallery. We studied them carefully. Tug McGraw, the frenetic relief pitcher, had sauntered down the same stairs. He stared at the Picasso, studied the antiques in the room, and surveyed the sculpture. This witty twenty-five-year-old son of a Vallejo, California, fireman, a little giddy with success and wine, walked over to his pitching buddy, thrust his face up towards the magnificent painting, and asked loudly, "What in the world are we doing here?"

It all began, really, in those dreadful days of September in 1957. With each passing day it became more certain that the legendary Brooklyn Dodgers and the ever so less loved New York Giants would vacate the city. The Dodgers had been in Ebbets Field since 1913, and the Giants had been in the Polo Grounds on Manhattan's West Side even longer. The two old ball parks were structurally damaged, and their neighborhoods were decaying. The owners of both teams—the energetic, articulate, creative Walter O'Malley of the Dodgers, and the less flamboyant, more pliable Horace Stoneham of the Giants—had often suggested in their private moments that they saw no future for their teams in this withering environment.

O'Malley, of course, was the leader of the move west. He had acquired the territory formerly controlled by the Chicago Cubs minor-league team in Los Angeles, had surveyed the area to his pleasure, and had gained much political support from California politicians. The Dodgers were moving west to a little-known area of Los Angeles called Chavez Ravine. O'Malley chose to relocate rather than seriously entertain plans for a new Dodger park in Queens ("The Brooklyn Dodgers in Queens?" he rightfully asked) or at the Atlantic Avenue connection of the Long Island Railroad.

Stoneham, equally desirous of moving out of New York's Harlem and essential to the economic viability of the westward plan, was relocating in San Francisco. He had visited the site in the early morning of a still, sunny day and found it magnificent. The city fathers left him unaware of the howling winds of San Francisco Bay. They erupt about three in the afternoon, making Candlestick Park the most uncomfortable playground for professional players in baseball history. One Giant relief pitcher, Stu Miller, would be blown from the mound there during an All-Star game and Willie Mays would say, "Once you can get the peanut shells to stop blowing in your eyes, you can hit."

O'Malley moved the Dodgers without dissent from his fellow investors. The Giants had a bit more trouble. A stockholder named Donald Grant, representing some shares of his own and a client named Joan Whitney Payson, a bon vivant millionaire sportswoman, art connoisseur, and patron of creative artists, opposed the move. Gaining some measure of fame and appreciation from their stand, they would surface in three years as significant personalities in the New York baseball scene.

Outside New York few cared when the Dodgers announced officially that they were now the Los Angeles Dodgers, and the Giants, that they were now the San Francisco Giants.

"Who needs New York? bellowed National League president Warren Giles, when reporters badgered him on the moves. The Boston Braves had moved to Milwaukee successfully in 1953, and the St. Louis Browns had moved to Baltimore with some degree of success in 1954. The Giants and especially the Dodgers may have been wedged deeper into the hearts of their fans, but business was business. The country would survive, a billion Chinese didn't care, and O'Malley's gorgeous Dodger Stadium became one of baseball's most enviable showplaces.

New York City mayor Robert F. Wagner, a colorless executive, responded admirably, after the fact. Restaurant owners, hotel managers, taxi-fleet owners and department store executives informed him their businesses were suffering from the absence of the baseball teams. The games had not only enlivened the city for more than half a century, they added to the financial well-being of many millions. The absence was felt realistically in pocketbooks and emotionally in hearts. Brooklyn without the Dodgers was no longer a very warm, funny joke. Comedians who were guaranteed a laugh by mentioning "Dem Bums" were anguished and empty. There was nothing warm or amusing about the Yankees. "Rooting for the Yankees," it was said, "was like rooting for U.S. Steel."

In 1958, sensing the melancholy of the city and aware of the economic downturn, Wagner appointed a committee to investigate the possibility of bringing another baseball franchise to New York. Chairman of the committee was William A. Shea, a well-connected, politically active, highly intelligent New York attorney. Many of Shea's clients were Washington pols, offering him the ear of some of the country's most influential men.

Things heated up in 1959. Using his legal skills and reminding baseball officials at every meeting that antitrust laws, which protected baseball franchises, were legally shaky at best, Shea pushed his ball park idea. More teams seemed interested. They wanted what O'Malley and Stoneham were getting out west, new stadiums built by public funds.

While Organized Baseball continued to stonewall expansion, Shea, urged on by Wagner, made contact with Branch Rickey. The founder of baseball's farm system, at St. Louis, the builder of the great Brooklyn Dodger teams of the 1940s and early 1950s, and the man who made history by signing Jackie Robinson in 1945, Rickey was the out-front man for a new league. The Continental League had been incorporated in early 1959, and Rickey was hired to lead it.

Teams would be suggested for Denver, Houston, Toronto,

Minneapolis–St. Paul, Atlanta, Dallas–Fort Worth and Buffalo as well as New York. A New York franchise in this nebulous league was awarded to Joan Payson and Donald Grant, the saddened owners of New York Giants stock. The Continental League's New York franchise took office space on Fifth Avenue.

From the days of Commissioner Kenesaw Mountain Landis, baseball had paid lawyers large sums of money to keep it out of court. And they succeeded again in the accustomed manner. The Continental League was swallowed up in expansion. Minnesota and Los Angeles were admitted to the American League for play in 1961, and Houston and the New York Metropolitan Baseball Club, Inc., would be admitted as full-fledged members, for the price of 1.8 million dollars, for play in 1962.

On March 14, 1961, at the Shamrock Isle Hotel in Miami Beach, Donald Grant announced that the New York Metropolitan Baseball Club had signed George Weiss to run the team. Weiss's retirement contract from the Yankees prevented him from working for any other team as general manager. The title Weiss received from the new team was president.

On May 6, 1961, a group of New York sportswriters assembled in the Fifth Avenue apartment of Joan Payson. The purpose of the meeting was to select a nickname for the new National League New York franchise.

"The first thing I remember is that Tom Meany [the team's public relations man] spilled a drink on Mrs. Payson's fifty-thousand-dollar rug," said Harold Rosenthal, a sportswriter for the *New York Herald Tribune*.

"Gentlemen," Mrs. Payson began, "what shall we call this team?"

"Young yelled Subways and everybody booed," said Rosenthal of Dick Young's suggestion. It would be Young, the *Daily News* columnist, who would become most identified with the team, as he had been with the Brooklyn Dodgers. Names were floated by everybody, the Skyliners, the Giogers (a combination of the two former teams' names), Blue Birds, Rens, Robins, Gamecocks, Bushwackers, Meadowlarkers (for Flushing Meadow, site of the new proposed stadium), Brooklyns, and assorted other combinations.

"We drank a lot of Mrs. Payson's booze, but I don't think we came to any decision," said Rosenthal. "It was an enjoyable experience. I got to look at Mrs. Payson's art collection close up."

The paintings on Mrs. Payson's apartment wall included Vincent Van Gogh's famed *Irises*, which would be sold by her son in 1987 for fifty-four million dollars. It had been purchased some forty years earlier for ten thousand dollars.

"Nothing was resolved that night," Rosenthal said, "but the next day a press announcement came in the mail. 'The New York Metropolitan Baseball team today announced the name of the team is Mets.' I think that's what the lady wanted all along. That's how it works."

On May 8, 1961, the Mets were formally christened at a party in the Savoy-Hilton Hotel. Mrs. Charles Shipman Payson (Joan Whitney Payson) broke a bottle of champagne over a bat to symbolize the christening. In attendance were Commissioner Ford Frick, National League president Warren Giles, Mets president George Weiss, board chairman Donald Grant, and executive vice-president Herbert Walker.

Casey Stengel went to work as usual that day as a vice-president of the Toluca Lake branch of the Valley National Bank in California. He received a call there early that morning from George Weiss. The president of the Mets only wanted to know how his old friend was feeling. "Except for this bad back I got from the fall," he told Weiss, "I'm fine." Weiss hung up. Stengel forgot about the call quickly and prepared to go to the Dodger game that night as Walter O'Malley's guest.

Casey Stengel celebrated his seventy-first birthday on July 30, 1961. His wife of thirty-seven years, Edna Lawson Stengel, arranged for a small party at their home at 1663 Grandview Avenue, Glendale. Stengel, born in Kansas City (hence, KC and later Casey), had purchased the Glendale home shortly after his marriage to Edna. It was filled with many of the memories of his long career as a player with the Dodgers and Giants and his incredibly successful career as a manager with the New York Yankees. George Weiss, who had first met Stengel in the early 1920s while operating a semipro team in New Haven, called to congratulate Stengel on his birthday.

"How's that new team of yours doing?" Stengel asked.

"We don't have a manager and we don't have any players, but we will be on the field next year," said Weiss.

"Let me know if I can help you, George," said Stengel.

Weiss had known from the beginning whom he wanted as the manager of the Mets. He also knew Stengel well enough to know he couldn't be pushed. The whole thing had to sort of be Casey's idea.

Weiss remained in contact with Stengel through August and September, calling him to ask about a player, informing him of the flow of money available from the deep pockets of Mrs. Payson, floating the idea carefully that Stengel might just be interested in coming back to New York, back to the town where he only so recently had been let go when, as Stengel put it, "My services were no longer required."

Weiss was suggesting, by God, that his services were required by the Mets.

More importantly, Weiss recognized that Stengel would draw fans. Yankee attendance had incredibly decreased from 1957 to 1958 when they were the only team in town. It had increased again only marginally in the next two seasons while the Dodgers and Giants played in California. Stengel could win the war of the words. Only he could help the Mets dominate the press and the ever more significant television time in a battle for the baseball dollar against the Yankees. Weiss was a zero with the press. "You can buy any of them with a steak," was his standard reference as to the worth and integrity of the press. Stengel called traveling reporters "My writers." Charles Dillon (Casey) Stengel had been part of the New York sports fabric for four decades. He arrived first in 1912 as a brash twenty-one-year-old outfielder for the Brooklyn Dodgers just before play began in newly opened Ebbets Field in 1913. He would endear himself to Dodger fans with his play, his personality, and his pugnacity. He would play for the New York Giants, hit two game-winning home runs against the Yankees in the 1923 World Series, go on to minor-league managing, return as a big-league manager in Brooklyn and Boston, return to the minors again, and resume his big-league managerial time with the New Yankees from 1949 through 1960. He won ten pennants in those twelve seasons. His arrival with the Yankees was scandalous. This sedate, conservative baseball organization hired the talkative manager with the floppy ears. His reputation preceded him.

"The common feeling around the Yankees when he was hired," said Lee MacPhail, then the team's farm director, "was that they had hired a clown."

Casey Stengel was a clown all right. He could ham it up with the facial contortions of an Emmett Kelly. He could entertain "my writers" with Stengelese. He could close down bars in dozens of towns and talk the ears off a corn. This was a distinct aspect of his personality.

More importantly, he loved baseball and life, in that order. He saw the competition as all-consuming and the joys of winning as unmatchable. He knew every dimension of the game, led men, motivated, taught, and controlled teams with tyrannical strength.

His arrival was front-page news and pushed the World Series between the Yankees and the Cincinnati Reds into a secondary position.

There were few straight answers as the Mets announced the hiring of Stengel at a riotous press conference.

"What about your health?"

"My health is good enough above the shoulders and I didn't say I'd stay fifty years or five," he rasped.

Four days later, the Mets signed a thirty-year lease with the City of New York to play in the new Municipal Stadium at Flushing Meadow. The target date was the 1963 season but it would be 1964 before the Stadium—finally named Shea Stadium for the man who pushed the plan—would open. Many years later, Shea would be walking out of the Stadium after a hectic Mets game and overhear two youngsters talking about the park.

"The first kid asked the second kid who this guy Shea was that they named the park after. The second kid was huffy," said Shea. "He berated the other kid for being so dumb. 'You don't know who Shea is and you're a Mets fan. He's the guy who was killed in World War Two fighting in one of them islands.' I had to laugh."

Now Mets fans know that Bill Shea is the guy who provides a flowered wreath of roses as good luck at the team's home opener each year.

There was one more piece of business for the Mets before they became a real team. They had to have players. The draft was held in Cincinnati. The Mets chose twenty-two players from the other eight National League teams. The first selection was a journeyman catcher named Hobie Landrith. Stengel was asked immediately why Landrith was selected. "If you don't have a catcher," he said, "you have a lot of passed balls."

Leaning heavily to players popular in New York, the Mets chose Dodger first baseman Gil Hodges, Dodger pitcher Roger Craig, and former Dodger shortstop Don Zimmer in the first group. The expensive selections, at a hundred and twenty-five thousand dollars each, were Jay Hook, Bob Miller, Zimmer, and Lee Walls. The next group cost seventy-five thousand each and included Craig Anderson, Roger Craig, Ray Daviault, Al Jackson, Chris Cannizzaro, Choo Choo Coleman, Landrith, Ed Bouchee, Elio Chacon (Mrs. Payson ordered that draft since she was fascinated when Chacon stole home for the Reds in the 1961 Series), Sammy Drake, Hodges, Felix Mantilla, Gus Bell, Joe Christopher, John DeMerit, and Bobby Gene Smith. For fifty-thousand dollars the Mets selected Sherman Jones and Jim Hickman. Hickman had worked on a cotton farm in his native Tennessee but had to give up farming because "the cotton lint got in my nose." He was the last of the twenty-two Original Mets—to some, more famous than the thirteen Original Colonies—to leave the team.

On that October afternoon a skinny sixteen-year-old high school pitcher named George Thomas Seaver played catch with his brother in the backyard of their Fresno, California, home. An eighteen-year-old farm boy named Jerry Martin Koosman cleaned out a hay loft. A seventeen-year-old Baltimore high school football player named Ronald Alan Swoboda practiced until it was dark on his pass catching. A twenty-four-year-old graduate engineer named Ronald Wesley Taylor returned from pitching with the Cleveland Indians Triple A farm team in Salt Lake City and went to work for a Toronto engineering firm. A nineteen-year-old junior college miler in San Antonio named Gerald Wayne Grote practiced for the state track meet. A twenty-six-year-old first baseman for the Pittsburgh Pirates named Donn Alvin Clendenon returned to his Atlanta home after lingering for a few days in Pittsburgh after finishing nine games with the Pirates. A twenty-five-year-old pitcher named Donald Eugene Cardwell went quail hunting near his Winston-Salem, North Carolina, home upon returning south from Chicago, where he recorded his biggest winning season ever with a 15–14 record with the Cubs. A sixteen-year-old James Monroe High basketball player named Edward Emil Kranepool scored 19 points for his Bronx, New

York, school in a neighborhood game. A seventeen-year-old boy named Frank Edwin McGraw drove through the streets of Vallejo, California, in his brother's car.

Not one of them noticed the Mets draft.

It would be Stengel, through that late fall and winter of 1961, who would send the message forth: The Mets are coming, the Mets are coming, the Mets are coming. He would speak at banquets and dinners, give print and television interviews, ride in a Thanksgiving Day Parade float down Broadway, announce to the world that his Mets, yet unborn as a team on the field, would be "amazin'," and spread the gospel of his team at every street corner.

He was vibrant, rejuvenated after the discouraging way he left the Yankees, enthusiastic, determined to succeed, pushing forward as fast as he could. He commuted regularly from his California home with Edna always at his side, met with prospective players, talked with other league officials, gave interviews in person and by phone, and counted the days anxiously until he could be in uniform again.

One afternoon he sat by his pool in the back of his Glendale home. He shared a drink with his pal, Babe Herman, the former Brooklyn Dodger hero, and they reminisced about teams of old and players long gone. He suddenly bolted up and announced, "I'm back in the ball game."

The Mets players, such as they were, assembled at Miller Huggins Field for the first time on February 19, 1962. The Yankees sold the Mets their old training headquarters in St. Petersburg, Florida, and built new quarters across Florida in Fort Lauderdale. All was in readiness. A day before the expected arrival of the manager, the coaches, and the players, George Weiss ordered that two new benches be placed at the entrance to the clubhouse. They were painted with the names of the chief figures on this team, Stengel and Weiss. When the manager arrived that first afternoon, he immediately sat on the one named Weiss.

"George won't be needing this," Stengel said. "He'll be too busy in the office getting me Stan Musial."

Weiss wouldn't succeed in getting Musial. He did get enough players for Stengel to open a spring camp, play the exhibition games, create a legend, and plant the seeds that would grow into the 1969 championship team.

# 2

# *Marvelous Marv to Tom Terrific*

$St$. Petersburg, Florida, was called by comics the Land of the Living Dead. It was a retirement community for thousands of Northerners who escaped the snow for the soft breezes, mild temperatures, and gentle waters of Tampa Bay. The shuffleboard courts seemed always filled, and the baseball games between the Kids and Cubs, those geriatric retirement wonders who still craved the thrill of a sharply hit line drive, provided exciting leisure. The bench traffic in front of Maas Brothers department store was always heavy, and the occupants would turn away when the devilish sound of ambulances or hearses creased the calm. Funeral parlors, often the most attractive building on a street, abounded.

On February 18, 1962, Casey and Edna Stengel stepped out of a limousine into the bright sun of Florida. Lou Niss, a veteran sportswriter and editor now turned traveling secretary for the Mets, had driven them joyously from the airport.

"When I got to the airport they had already arrived," said Niss. "I got a porter to get their baggage to the car. Edna had about twelve bags. Casey was carrying his hat and a small attaché case. He said he had his lineups in there. We got the car loaded and started to go. I didn't realize Casey was still outside the car talking to fans."

Niss would serve the Mets and Casey faithfully for many

years. Before he died, in 1987, Niss said he would like to write a book about the Mets. He wanted to call it *The Team That Didn't Cost a Dime and Wasn't Worth a Nickel.* He never got past the title.

It was Niss who demanded that any hotel which wanted to house the Mets in St. Petersburg—and be forever linked with the publicity of this event—would have to be integrated. The Colonial Inn, a sprawling low-slung row of motel rooms and apartments, agreed to house the team on that basis. As late as 1962 few Florida hotels would house blacks and whites. For years the St. Louis Cardinals and the Yankees had trained there. Many of their black players, including Bob Gibson, Bill White and Elston Howard, stayed in the homes of local black citizens. Niss would put an end to that kind of arrangement with the Mets.

"They did make us agree to one condition," he said. "They asked us to keep the black players out of the front part of the dining room. They said it was in consideration of the feelings of some of their long-standing, elderly full-time residents. I questioned our black players, Al Jackson, Joe Christopher, Sammy Drake, Choo Choo Coleman, and they accepted the conditions. It lasted about two days. Then the novelty of seeing blacks in the dining room wore off. The players sat where they wanted."

Stengel and Edna were given two connecting rooms facing the swimming pool. Edna Stengel would sit by the pool for hours on end, a practice she was familiar with from her own California home. Casey would show up after a workout in those early days, stand by the bar and chat with hotel guests. No one could ever remember seeing the manager of the Mets in a swimsuit. If Casey was to be found at the Colonial Inn during his waking hours, it was at the bar. He was selling the Mets, telling stories, recruiting fans, expounding on his life in the game, and constantly enjoying the conviviality, not to say the bourbon.

Early February 19, an unusually chilly Florida dawn, Casey

Stengel sat in the offices of the new New York Mets. It was shortly before seven o'clock in the morning.

"I had just gotten up to make myself some coffee," said Herb Norman, the clubhouse man who was lodged inside the building. "I heard this pounding on the door. The players weren't expected for more than two hours. I was in my underwear and walked to the door to see this little old guy in a felt hat. I had met Casey several times before, but he looked so different, so bouncy, so damn young for a guy his age. I opened the door and he rushed in. 'Gotta work on my lineup.' I gave him a cup of coffee, showed him to his office, helped him with his equipment, and went about my business. For an hour I could hear him in there rattling on about this player or that. Some of the names were awfully strange. I was sure I heard the name Ruth more than once."

Casey Stengel had faced Babe Ruth, then a Boston Red Sox pitcher, in the 1916 World Series, and never tired of talking of him. It would not be unusual.

Shortly before ten o'clock, dressed in his new Mets white uniform with orange and blue trim with the large numeral 37 on the back, Stengel pulled on a windbreaker, checked himself out in the mirror one last time, and walked onto the field.

The players, conscious of their part in this baseball saga, jogged on to the field. Stengel awaited them near home plate. He opened up his lecture by saying, "Now if you get to first base you can make a living in New York because everybody wants to support a new team and the public expects their best and the Polo Grounds is an old field which I played in but a new one is being built."

He continued in that vein for several minutes, moved his team past first, walked to second, spoke eloquently about opportunity and environment, sauntered to third, reminded one and all that it was now only ninety feet to that Promised Plate, strolled home and twinkle-toed the plate with a forceful punctuation mark that sounded something like, "For crissakes, why wouldn't ya when you could."

Richie Ashburn, the witty, wonderful Mets center fielder that season, said no one who heard that greeting could forget it.

"I couldn't recite the text," he said. "No one could. But I will always recall that experience, hear Casey's voice in my head, and remember that face."

Stengel's rubbery, animated face would remain a joyful reminder of a life well lived. In some ways the old man had a thousand faces and could put on a new one befitting the occasion. "I had a good change of face," in his own words.

With help from Ashburn and Roger Craig and a minor-leaguer turned media darling named Rod Kanehl, with the clever reporting of dozens of reporters, with the anticipation of National League baseball back again in New York, with the enormous resources of goodwill being constantly called upon, the Mets became beloved before they played a game. There was a hunger for them to succeed. Young soon tagged their fans the New Breed, and their public acceptance would be exemplified by a youngster unfurling a banner on opening day at the Polo Grounds reading, "I've been a Met fan all my life."

Human-interest stories were everywhere. George Weiss and Stengel argued over the relative merits of many players. One of their most bitter battles was over the skills of Rod Kanehl. Stengel won that fight and Kanehl came north with the team. He would help solidify the lovable image with his clubhouse panache. Ashburn was the team funnyman. He began his Mets career by parking his antique car in the only available spot opening day, a space clearly marked WEISS. When asked why he would drive into the GM's reserved place he answered, "Because it was there."

The ex-Dodger group, led by Gil Hodges and Roger Craig, would add professionalism to the scene even though their playing skills were diminishing. Each Original Met, in his way, would contribute to the legend and the lore of the most beloved team in town. The Yankees were admired, respected, envied—rarely loved. The Yankees were wealthy warriors; the Mets were delightful urchins.

Their finest hour that spring would come in the late afternoon of March 22. The Yankees played a meaningless spring exhibition game that day. The Mets played the seventh game of the World Series. The Mets beat the Yankees, 4–3, with a run in the bottom of the ninth on a triple by Joe Christopher and a pinch-single by Richie Ashburn. That hit transformed Ashburn from villain to hero in New York. He was the Phillies center fielder who had thrown Cal Abrams out at home in the last game of the 1950 season. It kept the Dodgers from winning the game and the pennant. Dick Sisler homered in the tenth inning to win the pennant for Philadelphia.

Stengel was bouncy and giddy as he talked up the win after the game in the first contest ever played between his old team and his new one. It would be a game he would often recall in the next thirteen years of his life.

The regular season opened in St. Louis on April 11. The game had been scheduled for the previous night but was postponed by rain. The opening game was played. Ashburn and Gus Bell, two veteran outfielders, messed up a fly ball. There were two other errors. Craig pitched poorly. St. Louis won, 11–4. Gil Hodges and Charley Neal homered. The Mets would lose eight more before Jay Hook would pitch them to their first victory on April 23.

After that first loss the team flew home. The next day, an open day in the schedule, a parade down Broadway and a reception at City Hall were given to a team that had not yet played a single game in the city.

The home opener was played Friday, the thirteenth of April. In a mixture of rain and snow and cold and fog, Pittsburgh beat the Mets, 4–3. There were 12,446 in attendance, most of them youngsters under twenty. They roared all game long. A good time was had by all. Banners made out of bedsheets were hung everywhere. The one for "Hot Rod" flew

from left field, "Walnut Ridge loves the Mets" was another,
and "Ashburn for president," read a third. This was the early
stages of participatory baseball-watching and -rooting.
On May 9 the Mets were 5–16. They were already thirteen
games out of first place. Stengel called the writers into his
office and announced, "We've tried to make the Mets look
better with distance hitting so we brought this here new fella."
Today he is a television celebrity, the foil in some clever
Miller Lite commercials, a well-paid guest at many business
conventions, and a successful performer. He is still Marvelous
Marv.

If any player came to represent the Mets in those early
days it was Marvin Eugene Throneberry, initials M.E.T. He
had been a burly Yankee farmhand in Stengel's days with the
American League team, a renowned minor-league hitter and
the most promising slugger in the organization. He failed in
every Yankee chance, drifted to several teams, and finally was
traded to the Mets for Hobie Landrith. He was a moon-faced,
bald Tennesseean with rippling muscles, a slow gait and a
thick cigar ever propped in his mouth. He admired Mickey
Mantle, whom he somewhat resembled. Many observers suggested his constant imitations of Mantle at bat and in the
clubhouse destroyed whatever chance he might have had for
baseball stardom.

Throneberry, a failed thirty-year-old when he joined the
Mets, lockered next to Ashburn. Ashburn understood that
Marvelous Marv—a name hung on him in derision by sportswriter Leonard Shecter—would not appreciate the humor of
the Mets. He would be frustrated rather than understanding.
Laconic and introverted by nature, a deadly serious man,
Throneberry soon became a Met pet. No game could be
played without Throneberry impact. If another player had a
poor day or committed an error, Marv, egged on by Ashburn,
would drawl, "What are you trying to do, steal my fans?" He
once pinch-hit a ball that looked like a triple. He was called

out at second for failing to touch the base. Stengel, incensed at the umpires, raced toward the field. "Don't argue too loudly," warned coach Cookie Lavagetto. "He also missed first."

"He had this huge, sexy photo of a scantily clad woman inside his wall locker," remembered Ashburn. "I looked at it every day. One day we were playing in Chicago. I was coming back to the dugout after flying out and looked into the stands. I recognized a pretty woman's face but couldn't place her. I urged Marv to take a look. He bounced up and said, 'Oh, that's my wife.' I realized why I recognized her. That was the woman in the huge, sexy photo in his wall locker."

He did hit sixteen homers for the Mets that season. He also had enormous trouble catching thrown balls or picking up batted ones. It was once said of him, "Marv's glove fields better without Marv in it." He would finish that year and last through fourteen games of the next season. A contract dispute with Weiss would end his time with the Mets. When he was released to the minor leagues, only to surface as a television darling twenty years later, he said, "I ain't gave up yet."

The Mets lost 120 games. They had 40 victories, none without bountiful excitement from their fans.


Shea Stadium opened in 1964. The Mets were beginning to find some young players who might help fill it. They signed Ed Kranepool, a kid out of James Monroe High School in the Bronx, on June 27, 1962. Eight days later they signed a notable Mobile, Alabama, football player named Cleon Joseph Jones. On June 7, 1963, they signed Derrel McKinley Harrelson, a 135-pound three-sport high school star from Hayward, California, out of his freshman year at San Francisco State. Frank Edwin McGraw was signed by scout Roy Partee on June 12, 1964. An Army veteran named Jerry Martin Koosman was signed by scout Red Murff on August 27, 1964. George

Thomas Seaver graduated from Fresno High School, served a six-month hitch in the Marines early that year, and spent the rest of that summer of 1964 playing baseball for the Alaska Goldpanners.

Casey Stengel raved about the new stadium, the second he had helped inaugurate in New York. He had been there when the first game was played at Brooklyn's Ebbets Field on April 9, 1913. He had made a memorable catch that day of a screeching line drive hit by Hans Lobert. Now he was excited mostly about the bathrooms (fifty-four of them) at Shea, the proximity to the World's Fair across the street in Flushing Meadow, and the huge scoreboard. Still, the Mets continued to lose at a discouraging rate in 1964. In 1965 Stengel was back again. The manager was approaching the age of seventy-five. His enthusiasm never waned, but his stamina was giving out. He was more prone to catnaps on the bench and rambled longer and deeper into Stengelese—a double-talk devised for simultaneously holding listeners and avoiding tough questions. He had had several bouts with illness. He had broken his wrist after a fall on a rainy walk at West Point during an exhibition game. He seemed more tired. In his earlier Met days, delayed plane flights had forced Stengel and the Mets to remain awake all night in an airport lounge. The plane finally arrived in Houston from Los Angeles about eight o'clock. "If the writers are looking for me," growled Stengel to Lou Niss, "tell them I'm being embalmed."

On July 25, Stengel, in his cups, slipped in the men's room at Toots Shor's Manhattan restaurant. He fractured his hip. Team physician Dr. Peter La Motte, an orthopedic specialist, performed a medical procedure that placed a metal ball inside Stengel's hip casing. Stengel was one of the oldest patients La Motte had ever performed this complicated surgery on. He recovered well but still was limping more than a month later. On August 30 it was announced to the press that Stengel had officially retired and interim manager Wes Westrum would assume his duties. Stengel's number 37 was retired at Shea ceremonies on September 2. "If I can't walk out to the mound to take out a pitcher, I can't manage."

Stengel would retire to his Glendale home, live pleasantly for the next ten years, attend many baseball events, draw a salary from the grateful Mets as a vice-president, and pass into history on September 29, 1975, at the age of eighty-five. As cancer eroded his body, Stengel watched one last baseball game on television that night. The recording of the national anthem was being played. Suddenly Stengel, wretched with pain, swung his legs over the edge of the bed, pushed his body to the floor, and stood up. He placed his right hand over his heart and looked at the set.

"I might as well do this for the last time," he said.

Westrum, a soft-spoken, intense personality, was not the answer. A fine receiver with the old New York Giants, he was not an effective speaker, teacher, or leader. Never a phrase-maker, he repeated a trusted description of his team after each horrendous loss. "Oh my God," he would say, "wasn't that awful?" It usually was. If there was one consolation that would encourage Mets fans, it was Leo Durocher and his Chicago Cubs. The flashy Durocher had assumed control of the Cubs in 1966 after the college-of-coaches idea that owner Phil Wrigley had installed had proven to be a distinct failure. Chicago had finished eighth in 1965. Durocher bellowed at his inauguration press conference, "We're not an eighth-place club." He was right. The Cubs beat the Mets out for tenth in 1966. It gave the Mets, with their 66–95 mark, a ninth-place finish, their first escape from the National League basement. They finished 28½ games out of first place.

There was an air of excitement about the 1967 spring-training program for the Mets. Some of the younger players—

Swoboda, Harrelson, Jones, Kranepool, infielder Ken Boswell, pitcher Danny Frisella, and a catcher obtained from Houston named Jerry Grote—seemed close to realizing big-league potential. The Mets had been searching for a center fielder ever since Ashburn retired after his one and only Met season. New general manager Bing Devine thought he had the answer when he made a deal with Pittsburgh for outfielder Don Bosch. He had come from the Bucs with veteran pitcher Don Cardwell. Devine suggested Bosch was Willie Mays' fielding equal.

The day of reckoning came the afternoon of the first spring game. Bosch had arrived in camp a week earlier after a season of winter ball in Venezuela. He was a small man as ballplayers go, maybe five feet, nine inches tall, weighing perhaps 155 pounds. He had light-blue eyes and hair that was shockingly gray for a twenty-four-year-old. His arrival was greeted by more than a dozen sportswriters, each intent on exploring the psyche of this heralded new outfielder. Bosch was puzzled when the press horde surrounded him in front of his locker at newly named Huggins-Stengel Field. He seemed extremely shy, nervous and clearly uncomfortable.

"I don't know if I can play in the big leagues. I don't even know why I'm here," he said.

Florida spring-training games have elements of anxiety not associated with regular season games. Players often complain of what they call the high sky. Looking up into that clear blue, especially in parks built near water such as Al Lang Field, where the Mets played, is not an easy chore for the most confident of professional outfielders. Dangerous for any youngster trying to impress a new manager, it is fraught with peril for insecure youngsters acquired for the express purpose of catching every fly ball hit in their direction, especially balls similar to so many not caught for five years.

Curt Flood led off for the Cardinals in the first spring game against the Mets. He hit a fly ball to center. Bosch went back. That was his first mistake. He came in. That was his second error. The ball sailed over his head as he tumbled backwards. In the press box high above the field, a dozen sportswriters giggled. Bosch was finished; his image, such as it was, was destroyed. Bosch was chagrined, Westrum was embarrassed, the fans were discouraged.

When last heard from, Don Bosch was driving a cement truck in California.

Much attention was paid to Bosch that spring. It allowed a young pitcher to go through a good part of spring training without undue pressure. When he was hit hard in his next to last spring start against the Detroit Tigers at Lakeland, it seemed likely he would be returned to the minor leagues for another year of seasoning. Still, he did show promise. Clubhouse man Herb Norman, after getting a list from the manager, told the young man to bring his personal equipment to the park the next day for shipment north by truck. It is baseball's traditional way of telling a youngster he has made the team and would be starting the big-league season. With such matters of little consequence are Hall of Fame careers begun.

George Thomas Seaver—George to his family and new bride, Nancy; Tom to teammates and friends—was a handsome twenty-two-year-old right-handed pitcher from Fresno, California. He came from comfortable middle-class circumstances. His father owned a raisin-packing company and was a golfer of some note. He had played on the United States Walker Cup golf team in the 1930s. The Cup had been donated by wealthy philanthropist G. Herbert Walker. His son, G. Herbert Walker, Jr., was a friend of Mrs. Payson, Donald Grant, and other Met executives. He held a small share of the team. He was always especially fond of Tom Seaver. Why not?

Seaver had not been drafted out of high school; he attended the University of Southern California and pitched for the baseball team there in 1965. He was drafted by the hometown Los Angeles Dodgers after his freshman season. The Dodgers offered a ten-thousand-dollar bonus to the thin, unpolished pitcher with a modest fastball. Seaver declined the offer and instead joined the Marines for six months. Returning from the service, he enrolled at USC and pitched in an Alaskan summer with the Goldpanners. By now he was some thirty pounds heavier and had increased the hop on his fastball. In January of 1966 he was selected by the Atlanta Braves in the second phase of the big-league draft. Negotiations continued into March. Seaver pitched two games for USC before signing with the Braves for fifty thousand dollars and preparing to report to their minor-league camp.

A few days later he was informed by the office of the baseball commissioner, William D. Eckert, that his signing violated baseball rules. Since his college season had already begun, he was ineligible for a professional contract. He was then informed by USC coach Rod Dedeaux that since he had signed a professional contract he was ineligible for college ball. He was between a rock and a hard place. His father called the commissioner's office. Eckert, who knew little of the baseball rules (he had been hired as a compromise commissioner candidate and forever known as the Unknown Soldier since his public personna was so minimal), turned the matter over to his qualified aide, Lee MacPhail. MacPhail spoke several times with Seaver and his father. "We'll work something out," he told them. A lottery was set up. Each club was allowed to have a chance at Seaver if they were willing to match the fifty-thousand-dollar bonus contract the Braves had offered. The Phillies, the Cleveland Indians, and the New York Mets, urged by head scout Whitey Herzog, decided to enter the sweepstakes. All other clubs declined to bid, for reasons best known to themselves. "Remember," said MacPhail, "the single most difficult thing to do in baseball is evaluate young talent. Seaver had been an undistinguished high school player and a modest college pitcher."

On April 1, 1966, Commissioner Eckert reached into Lee

MacPhail's hat at the Fifth Avenue offices of the baseball commissioner. He pulled out a folded slip of paper. The name on the paper, in MacPhail's scrawled hand, was METS in large block letters. A few hours later Mets West Coast scout Nelson Burbrink arrived at Seaver's Fresno home with a contract already made out, including a fifty-thousand-dollar bonus upon signing and a salary of a thousand dollars a month for six months for the Mets Triple A team in Jacksonville, Florida. Seaver signed and was given a check, a Mets cap, and a pair of baseball shoes. The following morning he flew to Florida.

Seaver started slowly at Jacksonville, established himself as a quality pitcher in mid-season, finished with a 12–12 mark in 34 games, and impressed the Mets no end with 188 strikeouts in 210 innings. This was clearly a kid to be watched.

In 1967 Bosch hit .140 for the Mets. Seaver was 16–13 and named the National League Rookie of the Year. His manner, his professionalism, his dedication to excellence seemed to infuse a new tone into the team. This young man, exceptional in every way, saw nothing funny in losing. The writers always searched for the humorous angle in reporting the adventures of the Mets. It had been Stengel's way of protecting his poor teams from undue criticism. Followed in Westrum's time, it ended in Seaver's time. He took defeat hard, and he urged that attention to winning upon his teammates. At the age of twenty-two he had clearly become the leader of the pitching staff, the leader of the team, the hope for the future. "The Franchise."

Veteran Don Cardwell pitched the opening game for the Mets in the 1967 season, an honor reserved for the team's best pitcher. "I wasn't the best pitcher," said Cardwell. "Seaver clearly was. It was just that Wes couldn't believe a rookie could be that good."

Looking back years later, Westrum seemed to agree. "I remember when I first saw him, I wondered if he could really be that good."

Despite Seaver's presence and the renewed optimism, the Mets fell backwards. After finishing ninth in 1966, they fell to tenth again. They won five fewer games than the year before and finished at 61–101. Westrum announced his resignation on September 21. Salty Parker, a veteran coach, finished out the dismal season as manager.

There would be only one man that new general manager Bing Devine would search out as the manager of the Mets for 1968. His name was Gilbert Ray Hodges, the big first baseman of the Brooklyn Dodgers, the Los Angeles Dodgers, and the Mets.

Hodges had left the Mets with knee trouble to become the Washington Senators' manager on May 22, 1963. He led the Senators, another expansion team, into sixth place by 1967. His wife, the former Joan Lombardi of Brooklyn, spent the home schedule with him in a Shoreham Hotel suite. When the Senators went on the road, she flew home. That routine was unpleasant. Joan wanted Hodges home. She yearned for his return to New York.

It all became official just before the third game of the 1967 World Series in Devine's Boston hotel suite. Gil Hodges was the new manager of the Mets. Six weeks later Devine resigned to return to St. Louis, and Johnny Murphy, the former Yankee pitcher and Mets farm director, was named general manager. The Mets would have a rookie management team in place for the 1968 season.


Hodges went about his business quietly and efficiently all spring. He studied his players. He made few demands. He offered small suggestions. Two important acquisitions were Tommie Agee, a swift outfielder from the White Sox who had been the American League Rookie of the Year in 1966, and Art Shamsky from the Reds, a thin power hitter who had slugged four homers in four straight at bats for Cincinnati.

Then he didn't play the next day because he was a left-handed hitter facing a left-handed pitcher. A couple of kid pitchers, Jerry Koosman and Nolan Ryan, were impressive in camp. Both made the team.

"Things are starting fresh here," Hodges said. "I don't know anything about what went on here before. We're starting clean."

Met fans were hopeful. Hodges, a big favorite in New York from his Dodger days, received friendly press and warm greetings when the team returned north from spring training. There had been some setbacks—Agee was hit in the head by a Bob Gibson fastball during his first Met at bat in spring training and never recovered his confidence that year—but the pitching was impressive. Seaver was 16–12 in his second season with a 2.20 ERA. Koosman was 19–12, a Met high for victories, and had a 2.08 ERA. He lost the rookie award to a young Cincinnati catcher, Johnny Bench. Ryan, bothered by control trouble and tender fingers (he regularly kept his hand in a jar of pickle brine to toughen the skin), was only 6–9 but he struck out 133 hitters in 134 innings, a strikeout ratio of promise.

There were hopeful signs. Younger players were moving into the lineup. The pitching was becoming big league. There was a sense of improvement everywhere. Hodges was patient and careful. Then came a damaging blow.

On September 24, 1968, in Atlanta, Hodges suffered a major heart attack. He had been nursing a cold for several days. After spending a restless night, he awakened with sweats at 6 A.M. He thought the cold was breaking, but wore a heavy jacket during infield practice as protection against the chill air. He hit fungoes and pitched some batting practice. In the second inning of the game he turned to coach Rube Walker and said, "I don't feel well. I'm going inside. You handle it."

Trainer Gus Mauch came into the clubhouse. He suggested Hodges lie down.

"I have this ache right here," he said. "It's like a toothache in the chest."

The Braves called their team physician. He suggested it might only be indigestion. He thought it would be safer to have Hodges examined at Wadworth Long Hospital by a heart specialist, Dr. Linton Bishop. The doctor diagnosed a heart attack. The news was kept from the press until after the game, and many of the Mets were as confused by their manager's absence as the sportswriters. Lou Niss, the traveling secretary, finally confirmed the news while public relations director Harold Weissman fought to keep it a secret. He was concerned about Joan Hodges back in Brooklyn.

There was a period of convalescence. Hodges went to Florida after being released by the hospital and walked the beach. He was told to give up smoking (he was a two-pack-a-day smoker) and control his diet. He stopped smoking and started walking. By Christmas he was home again with his family, fifteen pounds lighter at about two hundred pounds and appearing fit. By the middle of January he was working again on plans for the 1969 season. In early February he spoke to the press for the first time since the attack.

"I'll be managing the Mets again come February 20, the opening of spring training. I feel fine. The doctors have assured me I can do everything I ever did before. I'll have to cut down on my smoking and fungo hitting."

Again, as he had so many times in his long career, Hodges showed he was a man of courage. He prepared to head south for the 1969 spring-training season.

His return, less than five months after a serious heart attack, was considered by many a miracle. It would be the first of many in that year of 1969.

# 3

# *Relief on the Way*

---

Americans looked back fitfully at 1968 as the new year dawned. Trauma was everywhere. Civil rights demonstrations and antiwar demonstrations filled the city streets. Eugene McCarthy led a children's crusade through the snows of New Hampshire. Martin Luther King had been killed on the balcony of a Memphis motel. Bobby Kennedy had been shot to death in the pantry of a Los Angeles hotel. President Lyndon Johnson had decided he would not seek reelection. Richard Nixon defeated Hubert Humphrey in a bitter national election. In Southeast Asia, Americans were being killed every day in a tangled, bloody conflict. Not since the Civil War, more than a hundred years earlier, had the country been so divided, so torn asunder, so bewildered by national purpose, conduct, or morality.

January 15, 1969: The United States and North Vietnam reached full agreement on enlarged peace talks in Paris. After a White House meeting, President Johnson and President-elect Nixon reached agreement on methods for breaking the deadlock in negotiations with the North Vietnamese. In Los Angeles, jury selection continued in the trial of Sirhan Bishara Sirhan, the accused assassin of Robert F. Kennedy. In London, John Lennon said he and fellow Beatles would be broke in six months if Apple goes on losing money at the present rate. "We haven't got half the money people think we have," said the twenty-eight-year-old musician. Among the casualties in Southeast Asia were Pfc. Garfield M. Langhorn, twenty years old, of Riverhead, New York, 1st Lt. Nicholas John Swidonovich, twenty-three, of New York City, and Col. Michael Melvin Spark, forty-one, of New York City—all killed in an aircraft crash. In Vallejo, California, Frank Edwin McGraw mailed his signed contract calling for a fourteen-thousand-dollar salary in 1969 to the New York Mets office at Shea Stadium. He had serious doubts about his career.

Twenty years later that handsome, boyish Kirk Douglas smile was still there. There were some creases around Tug McGraw's eyes, deeper lines in his forehead, and wrinkles in his face. He walked with that same jaunty bounce, and his eyes were electric with excitement. I almost expected him to tap his thigh in that familiar sign of greeting as we met one fall afternoon at the Pennsylvania Railroad War Memorial statue in Philadelphia's 30th Street Station. We had not seen each other in the four years since he retired from pitching.

"It's been a tough adjustment," he was saying now as we rode in his Bronco to his Delaware Valley office. "I was ready to change speeds when I got out of baseball. I only changed lanes. I had to find out if I could make it outside the game. I'm still finding out."

Tug does some television work for WPVI in Philadelphia, specializing in light, human interest, nonsports features. He is a spokesperson for the First Pennsylvania Bank, invests in real estate, and runs a counseling office for senior citizens, mid-life crisis job-changers and new-career seekers.

"I worked every off-season I was in baseball," he said. "Getting up early in the morning wasn't a problem."

McGraw was born in Martinez, California, the birthplace

of Joe DiMaggio, and was raised in blue-collar surroundings in Vallejo. His parents had a troubled, bitter marriage, and he and his brother, Hank, spent most of their youth with their father, a city fireman. "He would be away twenty-four hours at a time," said McGraw. "That's why I became such a good cook." He developed as a pitcher at Vallejo Junior College. Less than three weeks after he signed with the Mets, on June 12, 1964, he pitched a no-hitter for their rookie team in Cocoa, Florida to earn a promotion to the Auburn, New York, Class A farm club. He was clearly a comer.

The following spring he impressed manager Casey Stengel and pitching coach Warren Spahn enough to make the 1965 Mets. "Why wouldn't ya go with the Youth of America," shouted Stengel when asked about the wisdom of a twenty-year-old pitcher on the team. Although there were some occasional flashes of excellence, he was in over his head in 1965 and 1966 as a Met, with season records of 2–7 and 2–9. His most memorable early Met win was a victory over the Dodgers and Sandy Koufax on August 26, 1965, the first time the Mets had ever beaten the Hall of Fame left-hander. Nineteen sixty-eight was spent playing Triple A ball at Jacksonville, but he returned to the Mets in 1969 and had a 9–3 season with 12 saves. His playing days ended after the 1984 season with Philadelphia, leaving him with a lifetime mark of 96–92 and 179 saves.

"As a pitcher I had confidence and turned it into positive energy. I would leave the house for the ball park and feel the flow of adrenalin. I missed that when I left baseball. I had gone from having a hundred percent confidence on the field to having one percent outside. I tried to compensate. I was drinking a lot more. I started craving sweets. I had a bag of jelly beans with me at all times, and I would eat pounds of the stuff for no reason."

There were strains on his marriage. He and his wife, Phyliss, a former airline stewardess he married in 1968, were the parents of two handsome teenage children. They lived in a big house in Delaware Valley. There were constant guests, including McGraw's brother, an unrepentant hippie and former minor-league catcher, his ailing father, Phyliss's mother, and friends and relatives. Most of the burden fell on Phyliss. As his career wound down, they became less and less communicative.

"Being a baseball wife is the most difficult job in the world," McGraw said. "There is so much responsibility and so little reward. All my emotions were at the ball park. I had nothing left when I came home. Wives are just left out of things."

Earlier in his career, their youth and enthusiasm covered the weaknesses in the marriage. "Things seemed to work when I was playing ball because we lived together on a part-time basis. I was away so much. When my career was over, we discovered we weren't good enough friends to live together full-time.

"I remember that first year at Jacksonville. I won a game and walked off the field. I looked in the stands for Phyliss. I tipped my cap to her. When it was over she said, 'I'm not just another fan. I'm your wife. You tip your cap to everybody.' I had to come up with something special. I developed that thigh slap with my glove as our signal, our greeting. I started doing it every game whether she was there or not. The fans came to expect it. It was a great big slap if I had gotten out of a big jam, a smaller slap if maybe I only got a single hitter out. If I got hit I still gave a little slap, just to show the fans I would be back tomorrow."

When the marriage ended in 1986 McGraw was depressed and admits to hours spent by himself searching his soul. Today, he shares a small home in Delaware County with his brother. Although he and his children live apart, they are very much a family.

"The family structure just didn't last in those final years. I had some deep depression. I finally went to a therapist, got some help; I'm still getting help. I've learned to understand things better, understand myself. I have a new life now, new friends, new surroundings. Sure there are doubts. I always had doubts. Even when I was on the mound, even when I was winning world championships, there were doubts. As a ball player nobody wants to believe you have doubts. Nobody wants to appear weak. You are looked on as a role model. I think that's why I did better as a relief pitcher than a starter. When I started I would get a guy out two or three times and then have to face him again. He's seen everything I've got. He knows what I can do. I used to be filled with thoughts that he would get me. That all disappeared when I became a relief pitcher. I knew I had good stuff, four tough pitches to hit. I truly felt I was better than the hitter."

Few pitchers entered a game with more overt cockiness, a jauntier bounce, more energy for the assignment.

"I couldn't wait to get in. I used to tell myself this is what I wanted all my life, to be on the mound, to be facing Willie Stargell or Willie McCovey or Johnny Bench. Why should I be afraid?"

Gil Hodges deserves the credit for converting McGraw into a relief pitcher. He remains emotional when he talks of Hodges.

"I loved him. I loved him more than any man I have ever loved in my life. He understood me, he helped me, he guided me. I was a kid when he came to the Mets. He made me a man. I can't say it was a father-and-son relationship. That's too strong. We only had four years together before he died— damn—but I knew he cared about me, not just as a pitcher, as a person, me, the human being."

Hodges came to the Mets in 1968. McGraw was farmed out to Jacksonville. It did not shock him. He knew it was for his own good. He was sent down to develop another pitch and soon mastered the screwball, the reverse curve that would carry him to fame and fortune.

"There was this story in the spring of 1968 that I was sent out because my dog pooped on some of [GM] Johnny Murphy's flowers and chewed up the rest. That wasn't it. I just couldn't pitch. I hurt my elbow when I banged it against a doorknob in the Colonial Inn. I started favoring the arm, and my shoulder began bothering me. Gil was new and went on what he saw. He saw I couldn't pitch."

The National League had expanded to twelve teams in 1969. McGraw had been unprotected through the first two rounds of the expansion draft. Neither San Diego nor Montreal thought he was worthy enough to be selected. McGraw returned to the Mets with that new pitch and new incentive as a married man. He lived in a small, rented house just behind a house my wife and I rented that spring. There were several young players, Ed Kranepool, Danny Frisella, Ron Swoboda, Nolan Ryan, all living in the same area. There would be barbecues at one player's home or another's almost every night. Pam Frisella, the beautiful, ebullient wife of the swarthy relief pitcher, always seemed to have a social event planned for the group. We were invited a couple of times and could only see unbridled joy. Ballplayers are wonderful actors.

"Gil called me in the day before spring training ended. I was a little in awe of him. He was tough, an ex-Marine. I had been in the Marines. I was used to taking orders. I was ready to accept whatever marching orders he gave me. He told me there was no place on the roster for me as a starter. He had Koosman, Seaver, Gentry, Ryan, McAndrew, Cardwell, a couple of others. He needed a relief pitcher. He said I could have the choice of going back to Jacksonville as a starter and waiting for a new chance or staying as a relief pitcher. He told me I would at best be an average starter. I would never be a Koufax, a Spahn, a Whitey Ford. I could be a great relief pitcher, have a long career, and make as much money as a starter. When I walked out of his office I was a relief pitcher."

By late May, McGraw was about the best pitcher on the

team. He was 4–0 with a couple of starts because of injuries to Koosman, Ryan, and McAndrew. He started the second game of the season, the Mets' first win in 1969. By May 30, with the team seemingly headed nowhere (they were in fourth place, nine games out at 20–23), he had earned more important assignments.

"Gil's door was always open. He called me in that night and complimented me on the job I had done in the few starts and as a long relief man. 'I need a stopper. I am giving you that job.' I walked out without much emotion. My confidence had been high. Now it was just a bit higher," he said.

He and Phyliss rented an apartment on Ditmars Avenue in Queens, some twenty minutes from the park. McGraw would wake up late each morning, have a bullpen omelet (eggs and anything left over from dinner), read the morning papers, run some errands to the cleaners or the grocery, and drive to the park around three o'clock for the eight o'clock game. He played catch, ran a little, and then, with the possibility of pitching every night, he retired to the trainer's room an hour before the game and took what he calls "my power nap."

"Gil didn't like that very much. I thought it was important. He thought it meant you were out too late the night before. We had our disagreements."

He bounced around the clubhouse, talking to his teammates, giving endless amusing interviews to the press, telling bullpen tales, offering haircuts at bargain prices. He enjoyed the fraternity of the clubhouse as much as the pitching.

"I loved everything about it," he said wistfully. "I even got a lump in my throat standing for the national anthem each day."

Coach Joe Pignatano was in charge of the bullpen, and McGraw often enraged him with his antics.

"We had that bullpen phone and sometimes we would order ribs or a pizza sent in. That got him crazy. But he would eat like the rest of us. I almost made him cry when I ordered a birthday cake for him," McGraw said.

During the season, more and more reporters came to depend on him as one of the best wordsmiths on the club. He talked of his close relative Old Granddad and how he battled cold weather with coffee, Irish coffee, and when asked the difference once between the baseball playing surfaces of grass and Astroturf he replied, "I don't know. I never smoked Astroturf."

"I'm not going to say I never smoked marijuana," he says now. "I'll just say drugs never became a problem for me."

As he was entrusted with more important games, he responded magnificently. There was fear as he walked in from the bullpen; there was never fear once he faced the hitter.

"In the bullpen I would concern myself with getting loose, throwing strikes, concentrating on the catcher. I'd have butterflies coming in, sometimes so badly I thought I would lose my cookies on the way to the mound. My legs were so heavy I would think I had polio. Then I would reach the mound and look up at those fifty thousand people at Shea and I would feel like Superman. There was nothing to be afraid of. Let's get on with it."

The Mets began winning in July, had a small setback in August, and roared to the pennant in September. McGraw became the pitcher Hodges turned to when the game was close.

"I palled around with Swoboda and Kranepool, and we didn't talk much about winning until September. We had all been there a few years by then and we were tired of losing, tired of that Basement Bertha image. When the astronauts walked on the moon I figured we had a chance to win. Nothing seemed impossible after that."

The Mets went into first place on September 10 and never were behind again. They won the East division title by 8 games over the Cubs with a record of 100–62. McGraw pitched three scoreless innings of relief in the second game of the National League Championship Series against the Braves. He was not used in the World Series against Baltimore.

He had 25 saves and a record of 5–6 as the Mets rallied to the 1973 NL East title before beating Cincinnati in the NLCS and losing the World Series to Oakland in the seventh game. He made the 1973 season famous with his cry of "Ya gotta believe." Mets board chairman M. Donald Grant had suggested self-confidence could help the Mets win.

"Grant came in to the clubhouse for this meeting. He started telling us the front office was behind us, they thought we could still win and we could if we only believed we could. As he was leaving, I was all fired up. I screamed, 'Ya gotta believe.' He thought I was making fun of him; I wasn't. I was just overtaken by the emotion of the moment. Kranepool said to me, 'You better get your ass upstairs and explain it to Grant or you're gone.' I went up in uniform and told him I was just excited. He seemed to understand."

That became the rallying cry of the winning Mets under Yogi Berra. At the end of the following season, on December 3, 1974, McGraw was traded to the Philadelphia Phillies. Met fans were shocked.

"I had this growth on my back," he said. "I think they thought I had cancer. They got rid of me before I died. I went to Philadelphia, had the growth removed without any problems, and had ten pretty good years there."

He anchored the bullpen for the 1980 World Championship Phillies. With the field surrounded by angry mounted policemen and angry police dogs, he struck out Kansas City's Willie Wilson to end the final game. His jubilant leap into the air was captured on television screens across America.

"The 1969 Mets had to be special being the first. But 1980 was special too. The Phillies hadn't won in ninety-seven years.

I enjoyed them both. Hell, there was never a day in baseball I didn't enjoy."

It was raining as McGraw drove me back to the railroad station in the Bronco. There were papers scattered on the floor of the car and a half-eaten bag of jelly beans in the glove compartment. He talked to his office on the mobile phone. I remembered how much I always liked him, enjoyed watching him pitch, rooted so hard for him.

"Say hello to everybody in New York," he said. "Don't forget now."

The train pulled out of Philadelphia. I couldn't stop thinking about how much I hoped Tug McGraw could get another chance to slap his glove against his thigh.


There were 150 people rattling around the large Toronto house on December 13, 1987. This was the fiftieth birthday party of Doctor Ronald Wesley Taylor. As an old philosopher once said, "The grand thing about being fifty is that you know you won't die young." There was fellowship and good cheer, joyous laughter and raucous noise. Rona Taylor had succeeded in marking the event for her husband with elan. There were even calls and telegrams from North Carolina and Minnesota, New York and Texas, from friends who shared another life with the Toronto physician.

Surrounded by his wife and two small sons, by dozens of Toronto friends and medical colleagues, by grateful patients and business associates, this night was clearly a measure of how far Taylor had come, how dramatically life had changed since the day nearly twenty years earlier when he retired Brooks Robinson for the final out in Jerry Koosman's first World Series win over Baltimore.

Taylor had been one of the older Mets that summer of '69, a grizzly veteran of thirty-one, the only player on the team to have experienced previous World Series action. But he was a gamble with the downtrodden Mets when he arrived at their St. Petersburg spring training camp in 1967.

"I had back trouble and underwent surgery," he recalled. "Houston placed me on their Triple A roster at Oklahoma City over the winter. I was concerned about my baseball future. Bing Devine (the Met GM who had been the Cards GM when Taylor was there) called one day. He asked me if I could pitch. I told him I was sound. 'Get me outta here.' He said he thought he could make a deal. The next day he called back and said they had purchased my contract. I would train with the Mets big club. It was a great opportunity to pitch and I made the ball club."

Ronald Wesley Taylor, son of a Toronto rubber company salesman who had come to Canada from Wales, was a bright, shy boy. He had dark hair and dark eyes, spoke softly and respectfully to his elders, seemed sad so much of the time. At eighteen he accepted a four-thousand-dollar bonus contract from the Cleveland Indians to pitch in Daytona Beach, Florida. He returned home that fall and entered the University of Toronto. For four springs he reported late to his professional baseball team. He missed spring training, but he earned an electrical engineering degree.

"I was never emotionally committed to engineering," he said. "I think my father wanted me to be an engineer and I did it to please him."

He progressed through the Cleveland chain until he made the big club in 1962. He was traded to the Cardinals on December 15, 1962. He was 9–7 with the Cards in 1963, and 8–4 in the pennant-winning year. He pitched 4⅔ scoreless innings against the Yankees in the 1964 Series, won by St. Louis. He was traded to Houston on June 15, 1965.

"I had always been a starter until I got to St. Louis. They needed a relief pitcher after they traded Bobby Shantz, and I was given the job."

He started one game for Houston and never started with the Mets. He finished up in 1972 with San Diego.

Taylor was a droll man, capable of outrageous conduct. His travel reading was engineering texts or other serious nonfiction. However, he rarely discussed his nonbaseball interests with teammates or colleagues.

"I guess people thought I was as dumb as I looked." He never felt superior, intellectually arrogant, or uncomfortable around other professional athletes. On the team, his best friends were Jerry Koosman and Don Cardwell, a couple of good old farm boys from Minnesota and North Carolina. "I know a lot of Ph.D.'s I wouldn't let touch my car."

He often seemed alone around the team, clearly out of synch, so much older than his teammates. On occasion he would exhibit a dark side, grow testy or petulant upon questioning, push away when he felt you were zeroing in on a forbidden zone. He could be so articulate, so intelligent, so emotional that teammates and friends hungered to push through the reserve. Victory and defeat were handled equally with outward calm and maturity. Taylor was a complex man, remains so to this day, and seems most relaxed around his late-arriving family. He failed twice in marriage before meeting his present wife, Rona, a nurse. His first wife, Diane, was with him through his early baseball years, and his second wife, Paula, helped him through his medical school years before leaving him as he entered the practice of medicine. "That was when I was going through my early middle-aged menopause."

He had visited military hospitals in the Philippines and in Vietnam during the war there and began thinking of medicine as his career wound down. He was on a trip to Montreal with the Padres in 1972 when he appeared after a side trip to Toronto for a medical school interview.

"I had talked about medicine with some surgeon friends of mine. It seemed a little ridiculous. I was thirty-four years old and I was out of college twelve years. I must have suffered some brain damage hanging around Koosman but I decided to try it. I had an A average in college and when I presented my transcript at the University of Toronto Medical School the interviewer asked me what I had been doing the last twelve years. That was deflating. I had to present letters of recommendation, and one of the most important came from Donald Grant. He really went to bat for me. He was from Montreal, and that helped. Anyway, I was accepted. I had to take some undergraduate courses first and pass them. My first course was in molecular chemistry. I got a straight A. When I first entered the class the kids looked at me and figured I was the janitor."

The following year he was admitted to the medical school.

"I would start my day at eight in the morning, go to class until five, get home, sleep until eleven, then study from eleven until about nearly eight the next morning. I did that for four years."

He made straight A's and graduated with honors. He interned and did his residency at Mount Sinai Medical Center in Toronto before beginning the practice of medicine in 1979, at the age of forty-two. Today, he owns his own medical building, practices privately every day but Sunday, runs a sports-medicine clinic that has served some ten thousand patients, works as the Toronto Blue Jays team physician weekends in Florida during spring training, pitches occasional batting practice, and lectures at medical conventions.

"On Sundays we take the kids skating in the winter, or swimming or picnicking in the summer. It's a full life."

Taylor was 9–4 in the 1969 championship year with a club-leading 13 saves. He was unscored upon from May 30 through June 24 that season as the Mets identified themselves as a contending team. He remembers those years fondly.

"Sometimes I dream of coming back as a pitcher," he said, "and not making it."

He is a serious man now engaged in serious pursuits. It does not stop him from enjoying those rare moments at old-timer reunions with his former teammates.

"They still treat me as a flaky relief pitcher. Nobody is impressed with anything that has happened since. It's a time warp, as if it all stopped still in 1969 with nothing ever changing from that day. I can only think of that with pleasure. I don't envy ballplayers of today or the money they make. If I made that much money I might not be here."

Ron Taylor's life has moved in a different direction from most of his 1969 teammates. Most of the Toronto Blue Jays do not know he even played baseball in some earlier life. "When they find out they usually say, 'Did you know Tom Seaver?' I tell them I even saved a lot of his games. That impresses them."

His face glowed and his thin lips seemed to purse with some emotion when he recited his fondest memory of that championship season.

"It was after we won and we were riding down Broadway in that ticker-tape parade and the crowds were cheering and the paper was floating down from high above those office buildings. I couldn't stop thinking this was the path that MacArthur had ridden and Eisenhower and Kennedy. I never felt so euphoric."


Only twenty-eight years old that summer of 1969, Calvin Lee Koonce, the textbook advertisement of a Southern gentleman, appeared so much older. He was completely bald.

"The only hair I've grown since then," he said, "is down the back of my neck."

Cal Koonce, a right-hander from Fayetteville, North Carolina, threw a sinking fastball, had a good curve and excellent control. He was not a star on that team, but he was a vital asset, always willing to pitch, a good influence on younger players, a good soldier under the unquestioned leadership of Gil Hodges.

"Gil was the dominant personality. I always had every confidence in Gil. I think everybody did. I never questioned any move of his."

Koonce was raised in the tobacco farm country of Fayetteville. He attended Southview High in Hope Mills and Campbell Junior College, where he starred on the baseball teams. Signed by the Chicago Cubs, he entered the big leagues at twenty-one. On August 2, 1967, the Mets picked him up on waivers. He was 6–4 in 1968 and 6–3 in the championship season, went to Boston in 1970, and quit after the 1971 season at thirty.

"I was only two courses away from a B.S. degree. I could have gone to the minors and hoped to work my way back. I had traveled enough. I didn't want to uproot the family again—we have four children now—so I stayed home."

Koonce taught social studies and coached baseball in his hometown. He accepted a coaching position at Campbell College in 1979, and left there in 1986 to return to baseball as the general manager of the Detroit farm club, the Fayetteville Generals.

"The children are grown now and Peggy and I could move back into baseball," he said. "I wouldn't mind getting back in the big leagues. I'm also in local politics as the mayor pro tem of Hope. I have a couple of options open with my future."

Koonce was 6–3 with 7 saves in the championship season, doing what was asked, never bitching, never complaining when he wasn't used.

"I had so much respect for Gil. I was in awe of him. I knew of his record as one of the heroes of those old Brooklyn Dodger teams. He was a quiet leader, the dominant personality. I always had every confidence in Gil. I think everyone did. I never questioned any move of his. I'd like to think I'd be like Gil if I managed. I see many of his qualities in myself."

Hodges influenced the Mets even without talking. "We were playing the Cubs. Bill Hands hit Tommie Agee. Gil said nothing. Koosman went out to the mound. Ron Santo was the first hitter. Koosman hit him with a fastball right in the chest. Gil never blinked."

Koonce lived in a rented home in Roslyn Heights, drove to Shea with buddies Al Weis, J. C. Martin, and Don Cardwell, prepared for the game, and did a professional job when he was called on.

As a soft-spoken white Southerner, Koonce found questions around him in those emotional days of race riots and street demonstrations. He answered all of them with dignity. The blacks on the team, Ed Charles, Donn Clendenon, Tommie Agee, Cleon Jones, were comfortable with him.

"We were just one group," Koonce said. "I kidded with all the guys. We sat together on the team bus. We talked easily. I felt as much a part of the club as anybody."

Two decades later Koonce still credits Hodges with much of the success of the 1969 Mets.

"We just had so much confidence in him that when he asked us to do something we did it without question. We knew it was right. When somebody else was called from the bullpen I agreed with the decision. I was tickled with the other guy's success."

His championship ring does more than just impress the kids on the Fayetteville Generals. "I flash that thing every chance I get. I was up to Winston-Salem the other day trying to sell some tickets for our games. We talked about the championship ring. It helps sales."

Hodges was the battlefield commander. Koonce was one of his good soldiers. Every man is needed in a baseball war.

\* \* \*

It may well be that the starters on the Mets in 1969, Seaver, Koosman, Gentry, Ryan, Cardwell, McAndrew, were the finest group assembled in modern times.

McGraw, Taylor, and Koonce helped immeasureably. No Met starter ever pitched with fear of the seventh, eighth, or ninth inning.

# 4

## *If at First*

February 18, 1969: Gunmen in Zurich, Switzerland, shot at an Israeli airliner as it was taxiing toward takeoff. Airport sources said the attackers were Arabs. One terrorist was shot dead. The incident was seen as an escalation of the conflict between Israel and the Arab states. Less than two months earlier, on December 26, 1968, Arab guerrillas hit an Israeli plane leaving the airport in Athens, Greece. One Israeli was killed and several wounded. Israel retaliated several days later with a heavy bombing of the airport at Beirut, Lebanon. In the United States, Defense Secretary Melvin Laird proposed a draft lottery to fill the needs for military manpower. In Southeast Asia, American B-52's staged a massive attack on enemy forces near Saigon. Latest casualty figures included the names of Sp4 James Vincent Cavanaugh, nineteen, of Pawtucket, Rhode Island, killed in a small-arms fire fight, Sgt. Patrick Joseph Ronan, twenty, of Philadelphia, killed in an aircraft crash, and Cpl. William O'Shea II, nineteen, of Newark, New Jersey, killed by small-arms fire.

In South Farmingdale, Long Island, New York, Edward Emil Kranepool III, twenty-four years old, prepared to drive south with his pregnant wife, Carole, for his eighth Met season.

A small, low-slung factory building is located in the heart of the industrial area of Jamaica, Queens, one of the shabbier neighborhoods in this blue-collar section of New York City. The outside factory walls are pale, in need of some work, with chipped paint and a cracked sidewalk. A young black girl sits behind a small receptionist counter inside the office. She announces my arrival and I wait as the company president finishes a phone call.

Workers stream in and out of the office, and I can see the activity on the floor. The company manufactures point-of-purchase displays from design. Cartons sit stacked around the edges of the factory floor, awaiting shipment. The phone is constantly humming.

Soon, Kranepool arrives from a back office. He smiles easily and offers a large hand. I follow him into his office. The simply decorated office has a large desk, two telephones, some note pads, an overstuffed metal in-and-out container, and some letters scattered on his desk. Forty-three years old, he seemed to have been around forever. I could only think of that poignant banner that was unfurled at Shea early in 1964 after Kranepool had struck out in a big spot. The banner asked, "Is Ed Kranepool Over the Hill?" He was nineteen years old that summer.

Kranepool has not played since 1979, but he remains in New York, attends many sports banquets, is deeply involved in several charities, appears often as a guest on radio and television, and serves as a visible reminder of the early days of the Mets. He stands six feet, three inches tall and weighed over two hundred pounds most of his career. He always appeared fleshy and slightly out of condition as a player, with a little pouch in front. Heavy-legged and a poor runner, he was incredibly quick with his glove and bat, extremely well coordinated, and looked graceful at first base, in the outfield, at bat, or on a golf course, basketball or tennis court in his recreational time. He seems less fleshy now. His face shows some signs of aging, his hair is thinning, but he is still a handsome, tall, impressive figure. Only a paperweight on his desk from the 1986 Equitable Series at Cincinnati's Riverfront Stadium and that glowing, heavy World Series ring from 1969 indicate this is anything but a busy, successful businessman. Even as a youngster, Kranepool was a commanding figure, self-confident, intelligent, and nervy. When Kranepool was in a batting slump as an eighteen-year-old Met, future Hall of Famer Duke Snider, a teammate, suggested he change his batting style. Replied Kranepool to the suggestion, "Duke, you're not going so good yourself."

"I was cocky, maybe a little outspoken, I know that. I had some early success. It's hard for things like being in the big leagues at the age of seventeen and facing future Hall of Famers not to affect you. Sure I should have gone out earlier, but the club decided to keep me. I remember once they asked Casey why I was with the big club at the age of eighteen. 'Because he's my best hitter, for crissakes.' The old man knew I could hit."

Circumstances forced Kranepool to mature at an early age. He was born November 8, 1944. His father, Edward Emil II, had been killed three months earlier while serving in the U.S. Army in France. He finds it difficult to speak of his father, a man he never knew. He was close to his mother, who died two years ago. His older, married sister lives in Houston.

"I grew up in the Castle Hill section of the Bronx. My mother, Ethel, raised my sister and me on a widow's pension from the government. She did odd jobs—secretary, book-keeping, office work, things like that—for extra money. We lived in a nice house. We got by. I didn't feel any less privileged than the other kids in my neighborhood."

At fifteen he was a high school basketball and baseball star at James Monroe High in the Bronx. He broke many of the batting records at James Monroe set more than thirty years earlier by Hall of Famer Hank Greenberg. Kranepool was actually more renowned in school as a basketball player—a big, tough rebounder, a good shooter and a very competitive all-around athlete. By 1961 the Yankees had sent scouts to see him, and in 1962 the newly formed New York Mets became interested in the local kid. They invited him to the Polo Grounds for the opening game of the Mets local history. He sat in the stands as a guest of team owner Joan Payson. He remained a favorite of Mrs. Payson and Donald Grant throughout his Met career, a fact that caused him some grief as players whispered about favoritism. He signed with the team on June 27, 1962, upon graduation from high school. The Mets gave him an eighty-thousand-dollar bonus.

"I bought my mom a house in White Plains and lived there until I was married five years later."

The marriage to Carole, a stunning brunette he had met while working one winter in a Wall Street stock exchange office, caused some friction. His mother was strong-willed and quite possessive. She knew Carole was a fine young woman, but she thought her son was rushing things; he was only twenty-three. Kranepool's mother caused tensions in his marriage. They eased somewhat when she moved to Houston to be near her daughter. Carole and Ed have one son, Keith, a student at Ithaca College.

"After I got out of baseball there were some very rough times between us. It was an adjustment I couldn't quite handle. I had played baseball since I was seven years old. Now I was finished. It was not easy to deal with it. I had some health problems. I discovered that I was a diabetic. The pressures of the marriage dissolving contributed to that diabetes. I realized then why I was so tired so many times. I craved sweets. The marriage ended in 1981."

Both Carole and Ed remarried. Kranepool married a divorced woman with three children. Carole married Art Kass, owner of a successful record company. Carole and Ed remain friendly and share the joys and turmoil of raising a headstrong college-age son. Ed spends as much time as he can with his son, though he may not be as careful about important events—

birthdays, graduation, significant family dates as Carole would like. Their son, Keith, is more interested in music and business than he is in sports.

"I never pushed him. He used to hang around the clubhouse when he was little, but it was more to be with the kids of the other players than it was to play the game. He likes tennis and golf. He's even bigger than I am, maybe six four, six five by now, but he won't make his living as an athlete. That's for sure."

Kranepool played 153 games in 1965. His playing time decreased each year through 1969, when he played only 112 games, with 353 at bats and a .238 average. Donn Clendenon joined the Mets that June 15. Kranepool would never again have a chance to play every day.

"I wasn't upset when we made the trade for Clendenon. I wasn't playing every day anyway. Gil always seemed to find somebody else when we faced a left-hander. Clendenon added a lot to the team. He was very productive and a very professional player. He knew the game. He also had a good attitude. He was cocky and knew we could win. He also kidded around a lot, needled guys, black and white, and took a lot of the pressure off the younger players."

The Mets seemed comfortable that year with each other. There seemed no obvious divisions between black and white players. They would locker near each other, eat together on the road, share picnics and summer parties with their families at home.

"I was friendly with everybody but closer to some. That's the way it is on any team. I was very close to Swoboda and McGraw. We were really good friends. I always enjoyed going out with Koosman. He was a good old boy, one of those country farm boys who took everything in stride. He enjoyed the big leagues. Koosman enjoyed pitching and enjoyed partying. He treated every night like it was New Year's Eve. I wasn't terribly friendly with Seaver. I appreciated his talents but he was a little aloof, a little selfish. He was concerned with his own career. Maybe we all are, but he seemed to make it a little more obvious. Harrelson's relationship with Seaver made me a little uncomfortable. I thought it was one-sided. I think Buddy was a little insecure, and he liked being Seaver's pal."

Kranepool admits that he did not have the warmest relationship on the team with Gil Hodges. These were two stubborn men. Hodges was a bit of a martinet, demanding obedience, tolerating no disagreements, hard-and-fast in his operation of the team. Some players, Seaver, Harrelson, Grote, McGraw, responded magnificently to that teacher-student relationship. Some, notably Kranepool, Swoboda, Jones, and Shamsky, found it more difficult to accept. Kranepool had been in the big leagues since he was seventeen, was in his eighth season as a Met, was frustrated by the team's lack of progress and his own inability to maximize his talent. He was one of the brightest players on the team, with a marvelous understanding of the subtle beauty of the game. He could also be sharp-tongued with teammates and impatient. Some suggested he was spoiled, a mama's boy for delicate reasons concerning the loss of a father. He did not shower Hodges with love and respect.

"I guess whatever relationship we had ended late in 1968. I was in a bad slump. I had gone 0–27 and was really struggling. Then we faced the Phillies. Chris Short, a very tough left-hander, was pitching for them. I didn't expect to start. Gil put me in the lineup. I went 0–4 and now I was 0–31. The next day a right-hander starts and I don't play. Then in the seventh inning Gil calls me to pinch-hit. I yelled on the bench that he was trying to show me up. I went out and when I came back to the bench I screamed, "If you're so smart why didn't I get four chances against this guy?" Gil was silent. He could cut you dead with his silence.

"After the game it was awful quiet in the clubhouse. Gil was shaving. I walked in the bathroom and we started arguing again. Then he says, 'You won't play for this club again,' and my roomie, Swoboda, moves towards him and says, 'Gil, he didn't mean it.' Now Rocky and Gil are going at it. He got real excited. I could see his face getting flushed.

"We took off from Philadelphia and flew to Atlanta. The next night he had his heart attack. I felt very bad about that. I don't know if I contributed to that, but I didn't make it any easier for him."

Kranepool and Hodges never had a warm word after that incident in Philadelphia, not even during the joyous 1969 season, the pennant run, the exciting playoff or the World Series. Kranepool homered in the third game of the Series.

"The next year he got back at me. I had played on a World Championship team, I had homered in the Series, and he sent me out to the minors. Bob Scheffing was the general manager then after John Murphy died, and he called me in and told me. I was very upset. I hit .310 down there and they brought me back. I only hit .170 for the Mets that year but played in only a few [43] games.

"The next year I hit very well [.280] and things seemed to get a little better between us, Gil and me. I think we were beginning to understand each other. I had matured and was becoming a more productive player. Then he got his fatal heart attack in West Palm Beach that next spring of 1972 and Yogi took over. Maybe I never appreciated Gil. I don't know. He was a hard man to get to know. He was very tough, very strong. But he was smart. I think he was the first to know in 1969 just how good we were. I think Gil knew a lot sooner than anybody else that this team was good enough to win the pennant."

By mid-season even the newest of Mets understood this team was a legitimate contender. The papers pointed out daily how many games over .500 the club was and how strange it seemed for the Mets players and fans to actually be following the standings with strict attention.

"The most significant thing about the mid-season games,

especially those games against the first-place Cubs, was that they mattered," Kranepool said. "We took July and August games seriously, something that had never happened before when we were already fifteen or twenty games out by then. At last we had shaken the clown image. This team had a chance to win any game."

Kranepool would rise late each summer day at his large, red-brick Farmingdale, Long Island, home. He would often sit in his sauna or take a swim in his pool. He would eat a light lunch, fool with his dog, run a few errands in the neighborhood for Carole, talk on the phone, and leave for the ball park around three o'clock.

"There was really no pressure on us. We were too young as a team to understand the tensions of a pennant race. Each day was an adventure. We weren't expected to win; hell, we had finished ninth the year before under Gil. But we kept winning, winning, winning. We looked up, it was September, we beat the Cubs head-to-head again, and all of a sudden we were in the World Series and the governor, the mayor, the president, everybody wanted to throw a party for us. To me it seemed to happen overnight. One day we were the laughingstock of baseball, and the next day we were champions. I can't tell you when it happened. It was there before I thought about it. I think late in September, we were five or six games ahead already, and McGraw and Swoboda and I were out to dinner and somebody said that we were going to win the pennant and we just started giggling."

When the Mets clinched the division on September 24 with Gary Gentry beating Steve Carlton of the Cards, Kranepool was one of the wilder celebrants in the clubhouse. Swoboda and McGraw joined him in a shaving cream and champagne fight with their faces covered with shaving cream and the bubbly running down their necks. The satisfaction had been a long time in coming.

Hodges stayed with his platoon play at first, and Kranepool

started all three games in the NLCS against Atlanta right-handers. Then he started only one game of the Series against Baltimore's Jim Palmer. He hit a homer in that third Series game against relief pitcher Dave Leonhard. The ball traveled high and far over the right-field wall. Kranepool watched for an instant and then started out in that slightly tilted running style of his. He rounded first base, got a pat from Yogi Berra, and broke into a smile, and with his head down and his face erupting in glee, he bounded all the way around the bases. It was a moment he remembers well twenty years later.

"I just couldn't stop grinning. It was very satisfying to think that after all those cold years, I had hit a World Series home run. It didn't change the past, all that losing, all that ridicule. But it meant I could laugh now. I had that home run."

The joys of the postseason were wondrous, with parties, a Las Vegas appearance in an act put together by comedian Phil Foster, several lucrative appearances, a long vacation, and cries of recognition everywhere he went in town.

Trouble was evident from the first day of spring training in 1970. Hodges didn't want to forgive and forget. He played Kranepool sparingly. The first baseman was pressing. He didn't hit. Finally he got a call from GM Bob Scheffing, the new front-office boss after Johnny Murphy died, on January 14, 1970. Hodges wanted to send him back to the minors.

"I was very hurt," said Kranepool. "I had been the first baseman on a World Series team and now after a one-month slump I was being sent out. I went to see Don Grant. He told me to take it like a man, play hard down there and I would come back. They brought me back, but 1970 was a lost season. Maybe it helped. In 1971 I was a much better hitter."

Kranepool batted a strong .280 and at twenty-seven seemed set for another good year in 1972. Then Hodges died.

"I felt very unhappy. We would never have been great friends, but I think I was changing and he was changing towards me. I was maturing and now I was able to understand him and the way he operated a lot better than I had. Gil was a great manager, a very smart baseball man. I'm sure I would have learned a lot more about the game if he had lived."

Yogi Berra took over that season, and the Mets won again in 1973. Kranepool slumped to .239 but rebounded to his first .300 year in 1974. Berra was fired in 1975, and Kranepool was a part-time first baseman and pinch hitter most of the rest of his career, under managers Joe Frazier and his teammate and pal, Joe Torre. He had a distinguished late career as a pinch hitter and the cries of "Eddie, Eddie, Eddie," filled Shea Stadium in any pinch-hitting appearance or possible appearance. He finished with a .210 mark in 1978 and .232 in 1979. His career mark was .261.

Free agency was exploding on the baseball scene in the 1970s, and Kranepool opted to play out his option after the last season. Joe McDonald, who had taken over the operation of the club for the new owner, Mrs. Payson's daughter, Lorinda De Roulet, decided not to offer Kranepool a contract. After eighteen seasons with the club and at the age of thirty-four he was finished. It was a bitter experience.

"I told McDonald he was incompetent. We never got along. He had been a ticket taker and a farm director. He had no qualifications for general manager. When I saw the way he was ruining the club I got upset. I probably said some things I shouldn't have if I wanted to continue working for the Mets."

As the months passed, Mrs. De Roulet announced that she would sell the club. She could not run it anymore. She had been helped by her two inexperienced daughters, Whitney and Bebe, and the jokes around the team abounded about these young ladies becoming general manager. Several groups became involved in a possible sale for the club, including Earl Smith, former ambassador to Cuba; Herman Franks, the former Giants manager grown wealthy in real estate; and Robert Abplanalp, a close friend of former president Richard Nixon.

Abplanalp had made contact with the De Roulet family and also with Kranepool.

"I had several people interested in buying the club," Kranepool said. "I knew Bob Abplanalp, and he told me if he got the team I would be the operating head. At the last minute we lost the club to the Doubleday group."

Kranepool tried to find a baseball job in 1980. For some strange reason—maybe the baseball establishment had labeled him a clubhouse lawyer—there were no takers. The kid who sat in the Polo Grounds on the Opening Day of the 1962 season at the age of seventeen was out in the cold at thirty-four.

"I loved the game, I loved playing it and being part of it when I was in it. But unlike a lot of guys it wasn't my whole life. I wasn't going to be like Buddy Harrelson and sit around Shea until they let me throw batting practice and beg for a job. I worked every winter that I was in baseball, in Wall Street, in a restaurant I owned with Swoboda, in a lot of other business interests. I didn't expect to play all my life. It just happened sooner than I expected. I wasn't going to be a batting coach or a minor-league instructor. I wanted an administrative job in baseball around New York. None developed so I went into my own business."

Kranepool is busy on the phone each day, makes appointments, sees customers, flashes the World Series ring if he feels that will help a deal.

"I had ups and downs in baseball. I handled that all right. I have ups and downs in business. Once in a while I watch a game and something flashes back and it seems like yesterday and I'm hitting a big home run off Ferguson Jenkins or getting my first big-league hit off Don Elston or making a big fielding play. I had some tough times after I got out of the game with my marriage breaking up and my health not what it should be. There were tensions and unhappy times. I enjoy what I'm doing now. I'm making a good living, I enjoy playing golf and tennis. I get out to the park once in a while."

Kranepool leaned back in his office chair. He stared out of a window. He rubbed that ring on his finger as if he expected a genie to emerge and make him young again, give him back the reflexes, make him more mature in those early years so he could realize that enormous potential and enjoy the successes.

"I'm proud of my career. I could have done better, sure. But I have the ring, the World Series homer, and I can still remember that feeling of floating after hitting it. Whenever I'm down I think of that and I get a smile on my face. That was then. This is now. I enjoy a successful business deal almost as much. I have no regrets."

The air is cold outside Kranepool's drab-looking factory. Until 1980 he had been part of the Mets franchise every year. Business is business. There is no spring training in the packaging of displays. It could have been different.


One of the least likely places to find an old ballplayer would seem to be at the headquarters of one of the largest firms in Sioux Falls, South Dakota. In the law offices of Anderson, Carlson, Carter and Hoyo, a tall, handsome, well-dressed black man sits behind a desk. Fifty-three years old, he wears glasses, speaks with a deep baritone, and chooses his words carefully.

"I've always been a country guy," said Donn Clendenon. "This is just a wonderful place to live."

Clendenon was born in Neosho, a small town in the southwest corner of Missouri, near its intersection with Arkansas and Oklahoma. When his parents split up, he moved in with grandparents in Atlanta, Georgia, attended Booker T. Washington High School there, made all-state in basketball, football, and baseball, and won a scholarship to all-black

Morehouse College. At Morehouse he earned a degree in mathematics and physical education and was offered professional contracts in basketball by the New York Knickerbockers and the Harlem Globetrotters, in football by the Cleveland Browns, and in baseball by the Pittsburgh Pirates. He chose the Pittsburgh offer, signed in 1957 at the age of twenty-two and made it to the Pirates for a while in 1961 before sticking with the big club in 1962. A slugging first baseman with enormous power and a propensity for striking out, Clendenon had his best year as a Pirate in 1965 with a .301 average. He hit .299 the next season but then slumped to .249 in 1967 and .257 in 1968.

With the baseball expansion to twelve teams in 1969, Pittsburgh left Clendenon unprotected. He was selected by the new Montreal Expos. After being traded to the Houston Astros he decided to retire.

"I didn't want to play south of the border. I had some personal problems at the time. My father was ill and soon passed. I had entered law school at Duquesne in Pittsburgh and didn't want to leave there. When they traded me to Houston—this was before a player had any say in a trade—I said some terrible things about Houston. I was going into law and that was it. Then Bowie Kuhn got in the middle of it."

The commissioner of baseball decided it would not be good for the game if a player selected in the expansion draft just upped and left. Clendenon was adamant about not reporting to Houston. A deal was worked out after Clendenon's contract was sweetened so that substitute players would go to Houston and Clendenon would report to the Expos. Still unhappy in Canada, Clendenon was traded to the Mets on June 15. He was the second-oldest player on the team. Ed Charles was three months older.

"Baseball was always an avocation to me. I knew I was using it to establish myself in the law later on. That's what I really wanted to do. I came there with enthusiasm. It was a young team and I knew I could help guide them. I was comfortable right away."

Clendenon became the fourth black player on the team, along with Ed Charles, Cleon Jones and Tommie Agee. At six feet, four inches tall, weighing 215 pounds, graceful and quick, Clendenon was an immediate hit. He platooned with Ed Kranepool at first and seemed always to be driving in big runs. He hit a dozen home runs for the Mets, finished the season with 16 (including 4 for the Expos), had 51 RBIs and batted .248. He did not play in the playoff against Atlanta as Gil Hodges stayed with Kranepool against the Braves right-handers but he started four of the five World Series games and hit 3 home runs. He won the coveted World Series Most Valuable Player award.

"The Mets needed somebody to pound the ball. That was my job. I also kept the team loose. I got on everybody, black and white. I kept the guys free of pressure. No matter what happened that day there was always the next day. I learned that with some good Pittsburgh teams. There were no racial problems. I wouldn't allow it. When I saw something going wrong I got the guy in front of my locker and we talked."

Clendenon, a big man with a commanding presence, was an enforcer. When a player didn't hustle, Clendenon let him have it, suggesting the player would answer to him for stealing his money. When a player griped about conditions, Clendenon reminded him of how sorry conditions were in the outside world. He was an unelected captain of the team.

"I lived in a Manhattan brownstone that summer and enjoyed the city. I would drive to the park or take the subway. People weren't accustomed to seeing me out of uniform so I was never recognized. I wore glasses to read and carried a briefcase with my studying. Nobody bothered me.

"I would get to the clubhouse early and kid around with the guys. The coaches were important on that team, Yogi, Eddie Yost, Rube Walker, Joe Pignatano, and they were always there early. One of the reasons there were no racial problems was because they wouldn't allow it. Rube was a Southerner, but you could see he treated everybody the same. The pitchers all loved him and would get on him about that silly middle name, Bluford. Gus Mauch, the trainer, was always in early. I would get a rubdown from him and while he was working on me I would say, 'Are these the hands that rubbed Mantle and Ford and DiMaggio? Now they are rubbing this beautiful, black body.' Everybody would laugh."

It must be noted that in 1947 the trainer of the Brooklyn Dodgers refused to rub the body of Jackie Robinson, the game's first black. He actually told friends he was concerned that some of the blackness would rub off on his own hands.

"There were guys I had to get on. Swoboda was one. He would lose his concentration and you had to keep his head in the game. That's why they called him Rocky. Remember that great catch he made in the World Series off Brooks Robinson, diving full out? I chewed him out right after that because he was all gushy about it coming into the dugout. I told him he never should have left his feet. If the ball goes by him it might have been a home run. I had to remind him a few times during the year that if he ran his mouth he had to produce."

Clendenon hit a two-run homer in the fifth game of the Series with the Mets trailing, 3–0. It got them started. Al Weis homered to tie it, the Mets scored a couple of more runs, and the Series was over. He hit .357 in the Series. He played two more years with the Mets, was traded to St. Louis, and retired after the 1972 season.

"I wanted to be a general manager. I thought the Mets would hire me. They never did. I can't tell you why. You'll have to ask them. Was it because I was black? You'll have to ask them."

Clendenon was the highest-paid Met in 1969 with a salary of a hundred and twenty thousand dollars. Hank Aaron was making a hundred and forty thousand that year, highest in the league.

"I used to kid Aaron a lot. One time I was getting on him

from first base and I told him what was coming. He thought I wouldn't do such a ridiculous thing. I said a fastball was coming over the middle of the plate, and when it was a fastball he just stood there frozen."

Clendenon's marriage broke up after his playing days ended. He went back to law school, earned his degree, practiced law in Pittsburgh, got into real estate, moved to Columbus, Ohio, tried working as a sports agent, entered into a few more business deals, and finally moved to a law firm in Sioux Falls in 1987.

"I've had a few business failures and that hurts," he said. "I was always so successful in my baseball career. I figured if you worked hard and played hard you would make out all right. It doesn't work that way in business. Sometimes you need more than hard work and good fortune. Now I do some tax law, sports law, banking work. It is fine. I enjoy it out here. It is very serene, very pleasant, and I'm surrounded with a lot of bright, young people."

Clendenon has been to Shea Stadium only once since he retired from baseball.

"That was in 1979 when they brought back the '69 team for a tenth-anniversary reunion. I was in the midst of some personal problems then with my marriage and my career. I had gained a lot of weight. I was well over 240 pounds and I felt sloppy. I'm losing the weight now. I'm going to be slim and trim and beautiful again for the 1989 reunion, when we come back for the twentieth anniversary."

Clendenon doesn't see any big-league baseball games now except for an occasional look on television. He is not happy with what he sees.

"I think there is too much individualism. With the big bucks all they care about are their own numbers. That's not the way to win. You have to learn how to play as a team, to push the ball to the right side to advance a guy, to make a good play in the field at the expense of your body when you need it, to be part of the team even when you are sitting on the bench. That was one of Gil Hodges's strengths. Every guy on that team knew his job. That makes things so much easier. I think the other thing the players don't do today is concern themselves with their lives off the field. All they think about is what goes on between the white lines. A team has to be a team off the field, too."

It was now time for the big guy to resume his legal work as he prepared for a trial. He would deal with that with as much enthusiasm and effort as he dealt with hitting those Baltimore pitchers some two decades earlier.

"You know what I enjoyed most about baseball? I enjoyed hitting under pressure. That was the most fun, to get up there against Ferguson Jenkins or Bob Gibson or one of those really great pitchers and getting a big base hit against them. That was satisfying. I don't think I'll ever do anything as satisfying as that again."

The 1969 Mets were a collection of twenty-five talented baseball players, each with his own job, each with his own role on this most memorable of teams. Clendenon's role was as the right-handed–hitting first baseman, making the Mets a slugging presence against left-handed pitchers, intimidating the opposition as they had never been intimidated in all the years before. After Clendenon's arrival, it was a team that no pitcher could consider lightly. After Clendenon's arrival, it was a team that would not lack for leadership.

They were so different, these Met first basemen, so unique in their approach to the game. Kranepool may have underachieved in his career. Clendenon clearly overachieved. The Mets could not have won without both.

Clendenon's image as a championship player of 1969 was severely damaged in 1988. He pleaded guilty in Sioux Falls to a charge of cocaine possession.

He was sentenced to seven days in the Minnehaha County jail, was put on probation for two years and was ordered to perform two hundred hours of community service work.

The felony will be wiped off Clendenon's record if he successfully completes probation.

"What I did was kind of stupid on my part," he told a local wire service reporter. "No one ever said I was brilliant. I'm drug free now. I have been in treatment."

His life was clearly a struggle twenty years after the miracle.

# 5

# *Inner Strength*

March 18, 1969: Mayor John V. Lindsay of New York formally announced he would run for reelection. "I cannot abandon the fight to make this a decent, safe, livable city," said Lindsay. In Albany, New York, a group of militant Negroes took over a student demonstration at the State Capitol. In Saigon, American forces numbering well over ten thousand men moved out into the field for the express purpose of clearing the area of Viet Cong. Latest casualties included S. Sgt. Thomas Mitchell Dietz, twenty-one, of Baltimore, killed in a small-arms fire fight, Sp4 Robert Lee Mitchell, nineteen, of Lockport, Pennsylvania, killed in a small-arms fire fight, and Cpl. Jerry Ernest Samson, eighteen, of Flint, Michigan, killed by rocket fire. In St. Petersburg, Florida, Joe Torre, a player long coveted by the Mets, was traded to the St. Louis Cardinals for Orlando Cepeda. On the other side of St. Petersburg, at the New York Mets camp, outfielder Ron Swoboda pulled a muscle running after a fly ball. Shortstop Bud Harrelson, trying to recover from surgery to remove a torn cartilage from his right knee and from a .219 batting average in 1968, excelled in an exhibition game against the Pittsburgh Pirates.

\* \* \*

The bony face, the long chin, the deep-blue eyes, the thin arms seem to give the lie to the excellence of Derrel McKinley Harrelson's career.

"I remember the first day of spring training in 1969 as if it was yesterday," said Harrelson. "We had to weigh in, and Gil Hodges walked by just as I tipped the scale at 147 pounds, and he said, 'God, you are probably the strongest guy I ever saw at one forty-seven.' A few years later I was weighing in again when Yogi Berra was the manager. He looked at the scale, saw that memorable 147 pounds, made a Yogi face, and said, 'When it gets hot, you'll die at one forty-seven.'"

Buddy Harrelson is a burly 170-pound coach for the New York Mets. He is forty-four years old, still relatively lean and boyish-looking with a wide smile and straight teeth. He is sitting in the author's home after a long day of lunch with Met outfielder Lee Mazzilli near his Greenwich, Connecticut, home, eighteen holes of golf, and a draggy speaking engagement. He had driven more than two hours from his Long Island home.

He talked long and honestly about some tough days and nights with the Mets, some frustrations, some disappointments, so much success, respect and admiration from his teammates, one busted marriage and, finally, a sweet second marriage with a young lady who once baby-sat for his first two children.

Harrelson's first marriage, to Yvonne Harrelson, a striking brunette, ended in 1975 amidst some ugly stories around the club about infidelity on his wife's part, a sometimes occupational disease of ballplayers.

"It is a wonder that any ballplayer ever stays married," said Harrelson. "It does seem like there was an exceptional amount of broken marriages. I guess there was more pressure on us than we thought."

When the marriage erupted, Harrelson began dating Kim

Battaglia. She had sat for his children a half dozen years earlier.

"I knew her father from Long Island. We had been in some business deals together. Through the years we had been together, at parties, at other social events in the area. When I decided I wanted to take her out, I asked her father if it was all right. He said if it was all right with Kim it was all right with him."

Bud and Kim Harrelson, a doe-eyed, dark-haired beauty, now have three children of their own, Alexandra, six, Kassandra, three, and baby Troy Joseph, born July 8, 1987. His two older children with wife Yvonne are Kimberly, twenty-one, married and living back in California, and Timmy, eighteen, a shoe salesman born in that exalted summer of '69.

"Imagine me with five kids," he laughed. "And you first saw me eating bananas to fatten up."

He had flown overnight from his California home in February of 1964 to participate in a Mets early camp, called an instructional camp, for the organization's prime prospects. He arrived wearing Army khakis directly from his military-reserve-unit training. Clubhouse attendant Herb Norman refused him admission to the clubhouse since he could not believe the man struggling to keep his uniform pants from falling below his knees could possibly be a player. Casey Stengel, usually the first to arrive, rescued Harrelson from this embarrassment.

"I was pretty tired and pretty skinny then. I guess I didn't look much like a ballplayer," he said.

He would soon be on the field taking ground balls. No one would ever deny his credentials again. His movements were fluid and sure, his grace and style were unique, his range was remarkable, and his contributions to the team were immeasurable.

"We simply don't win two pennants without him," says Tom Seaver, his friend and roommate.

Harrelson and Seaver would be as close as ballplayers ever get. There were suggestions that Harrelson extended himself further for Seaver than for any other pitcher, a malicious canard. It was just that they knew each other so well, read each other's movements, played together with an impeccable rhythm. Ground balls always found Harrelson's glove when Seaver was pitching.

"We roomed together for eight years. When he left the Mets I knew I would never room with anybody else again. It's just that we enjoyed being together. I remember when he first joined the organization from college in Homestead, Florida, in 1966. The press was all over him. He went out to pitch batting practice, and every eye was on him. I hadn't met him but I had heard of him. I said, 'Oh, oh, this guy throws hard and he'll probably try and blow it by me to impress the reporters.' He threw nice and easy, got his work in, and I got my good swings.

"We got to know each other, understand our moods, never pushed one on the other. He didn't like me smoking cigarettes and I hated his cigars. He would be a cutup for three days and then quiet on the day he pitched. I would leave him alone. If he lost, he needed space. If he won, we could go out after the game, have a beer, have a few laughs. He'd get over losses quickly, but sometimes he would do it by himself or with friends outside baseball."

Seaver, Jerry Koosman, and Harrelson shared many beers and many tears the night before Seaver was traded by the Mets in 1977. It was not an evening any would soon forget.

"Sure we were friends, but we went our own way. We weren't married," said Harrelson.


Derrell McKinley Harrelson was born June 6, 1944, D-Day, in Niles, California. His father sold automobiles. The family nicknamed him Buddy, and many fans have no idea of his given name. Despite his small size he was a tremendous high school athlete in Hayward, California, captaining the school baseball, football, and basketball teams his senior year. He won a basketball scholarship to San Francisco State despite weighing 137 pounds and standing five foot, ten inches tall. The Mets signed him on June 7, 1963, after he had completed his freshman year.

In 1963 and 1964 he hit only .221 and .231 in Class A ball. He moved to Triple A in Buffalo in 1965 and batted .251. He played nineteen games with the Mets at the end of that 1965 season, played at Jacksonville in 1966, and again with the Mets at the end of that year.

"I had two big breaks. Eddie Bressoud was the shortstop when I first came up and the Mets moved him. Roy McMillan was the next shortstop and he was wonderful with me, helping me, teaching me tricks, rapidly advancing my career. Then his arm blew out. The Mets looked up and I was the only shortstop they had."

The Mets had no questions about his glove. They were confident the skinny shortstop from California would anchor their inner defense for years. Would he hit? To guarantee that he would hit more than originally forecast, he was ordered to work as a switch-hitter in the spring of 1967. Hitting lefty would give him a slight edge against hard-throwing right-handers and also take advantage of his exceptional speed. If he could hit grounders the opposite way and bunt effectively, he would improve his average enough to hold the job steadily. It worked just that way. He hit .254 in his first full season of 1967. Although he slumped to .219 in an injury-filled 1968, Gil Hodges stayed with him. Ironically, Harrelson would undergo knee surgery on the exact date, September 24, 1968, that Hodges would suffer his heart attack in Atlanta.

"Gil saw what I could do in 1968. He helped my confidence. He was a man you had to respect. We all knew his reputation for strength and dignity. The man had been a legend in New

York sports. No one would challenge him. God and family even came before the team. One time my kids were sick. He saw that I was upset. He never hesitated. 'Go home and stay there until they are better.' "

Through the laborious 1969 spring training, Hodges brought Harrelson along slowly. He played him only occasionally, and kept him away from long trips. (Hodges had damaged his own knee as a Met in 1962 by sitting in a cramped position on a team bus ride across Florida. His knee had stiffened when the journey ended.) Hodges played Harrelson in only nine of the team's twenty-four spring games. Harrelson hit only .200, but by late March he was running reasonably well and fielding normally. He was in the Opening Day lineup against Montreal at Shea on April 8.

"I don't care what he hits," Hodges said that first day of the 1969 season. "I want him in our lineup."

Harrelson was soon playing brilliantly. His sure-handed style, his remarkable poise, and his durability astonished many observers. After long, tough games he would sometimes appear emotionally and physically drained, but he continued to play full-time. The only time he was absent was on those rare occasions when Hodges chose to rest him in the second game of a doubleheader or when he was forced to attend Army reserve meetings. He was on military leave from the Mets in the early part of July. After he finished his duties as a driver on July 9 at Fort Drum, in Watertown, New York, he went to a local Italian restaurant with his Army buddies.

"This outfit was made up of all kinds of guys from around New York, doctors, lawyers, truck drivers, garment-center workers, every kind of businessman. They knew who I was but we got along great. On that night of July 9 we were eating pizza, drinking beer and watching the Mets against the Cubs on television. Seaver was pitching. They kept saying he had a no-hitter and a perfect game. I didn't think much about it because he often had overwhelming stuff.

"This time it got into the sixth, seventh, and eighth inning. Guys kept asking me, 'Don't you wish you were there?' There wasn't much I could do about it. A lot of guys in the Army were in worse places than Fort Drum. Then Jimmy Qualls got that hit and I saw the look on Tom's face. It was so sad. I really wished I could have been there. I don't know what I would have said but maybe it would have been something that helped. It was his greatest game but certainly one of his most disappointing."

Harrelson returned to the lineup on July 12. He was as good a shortstop as there was in baseball over the last six weeks of the 1969 season when the Mets drove from 9½ games back to the 8-game pennant-winning margin.

On September 23, against future Hall of Famer Bob Gibson, Harrelson lashed a single to right field to give the Mets a 4–3 win over the Cards in eleven innings. It clinched a tie for the division title.

He batted only .182 and .176 in the playoffs and Series but his fielding was impeccable.

"On a team like ours that year when you knew there were a lot of 1–0, 2–1 games you had to win," says Seaver, "Buddy was clearly the most irreplaceable player we had."

Said Harrelson, "There were a lot of pressures as a result of winning. I was making thirty-five thousand dollars and I guess I was living in the fast lane. People were always coming to you with deals and wanting favors. It was always hard for me to turn them down. There were so many parties, so many activities as a team and for each of us. It sometimes got over-whelming. I would leave Shea after a game and stand outside the gate signing autographs for half an hour. I just couldn't turn the kids down.

"Grote was a good friend of mine and we used to ride together. He would push past the kids and just sit in the car waiting for me. He just wouldn't sign, and we would argue about it sometimes. But I got along with Grote real well. We even had some business dealings together, and our families were close. There were other guys I didn't get along with as well. Kranepool could be blunt. He often rubbed me the wrong way. I don't think Seaver liked him very much. We were friends with everybody, but my closest friends were Seaver, Koosman, Grote, Boswell, and Al Weis."

Harrelson remained the shortstop of the Mets through 1977. His best offensive year was 1973 when he batted .258 and the Mets won the pennant. All observers agreed it was Harrelson's steady play during the last weeks of that tumultuous season that was the keynote to the pennant. His fight with burly Pete Rose at second base in the playoff against the Cincinnati Reds so angered Mets fans that a fan revolt and possible violence seemed certain until several players, including Willie Mays, Rusty Staub, and Seaver, begged for calm after a walk to the outfield. When Seaver was traded to the Reds on June 15, 1977, after a bitter contract dispute, much of Harrelson's heart drifted away with him. The Mets were in disarray then, and it was not long before Harrelson, another member of the aging Met old guard, was disposed of in a deal with the Phillies. He was a backup shortstop with Philadelphia and Texas before being released in 1981 nine days before the season opener.

"I was lost. I felt like I was in a boat without a paddle," he said. "I knew the end was coming, but I didn't think it would come that soon. I wasn't emotionally prepared."

Harrelson tried several businesses in 1981. None satisfied him. Some days he would appear at Shea late in the afternoon, suit up, and throw batting practice. Forlorn, he was caught staring at coaches and managers. He seemed slow about taking his uniform off each day, going upstairs to the press box, tearing those bonds away.

"I had been involved in some cable work. Early in 1982 Frank Cashen (the new Mets GM) called me at home. He asked if I would come in and see him. I told him I would. I had no idea what he wanted. We talked for a while, and he said he had a broadcasting position and a minor-league coaching position open. He asked if I would be interested. I couldn't restrain myself. I told him I would consider either. He finally offered the coaching job. I was back in the game."

His son by his first marriage, having trouble at home in California, came to live with Bud and Kim that summer. It helped the boy, and it helped Harrelson get to know his son better after several years away from him. Harrelson felt better about things all around.

The next season he began in the broadcasting booth for the Mets, and then managed in the Mets organization, first at Little Falls and then at Columbia, South Carolina. He piloted Columbia to the title in 1984. On May 17, 1985, he was managing Columbia when he got a call from New York. Third-base coach Bobby Valentine had signed to manage Texas, and Harrelson returned to New York as the Mets third-base coach. He was there in 1986 when the team won its second world championship. He is now a bench coach, and could be among the candidates for skipper after Davey Johnson.

"My first consideration is to do a good job in whatever I do in baseball. I have a family to support so I have to make a living at this. I don't have to make a killing. I've never had grand ideas. I live modestly now, within my means. I could stay in baseball the rest of my working life as a manager, if that works out, or as a coach if that is the way it goes. If I got another managerial offer out of New York it would be difficult to leave."

Harrelson has always been able to exceed expectations. He seemed too slight to be an everyday big-league shortstop, but fielded brilliantly day after day. He seemed too weak to be a player capable of a long career, but lasted sixteen years. He seemed too friendly, too gentle to be a successful manager, but he won in the only full shot he had. Bet big that he will manage a big-league club someday.

"If it happens," he laughs, "I will train my team on bananas."

Harrelson never was officially named the captain of the
Mets. It was an honor he deserved. The team won two pennants because of his play. Nineteen sixty-nine remains the
sweetest memory.

"I remember when we got our rings. I couldn't stop looking
at it. Then I flew out to California after that season and gave
it to my father. I didn't need it to prove anything anymore."

There was that Texas twang, those overgrown sideburns,
thick eyebrows, and lean, athletic body. Ken Boswell chose
1969 to have his career year. Mets fans loved him for it. He
was a handsome devil and enjoyed living in the jungle of
Manhattan night life, running with Art Shamsky, parading
through city streets wearing genuine Texas leather boots, needling teammates and lining clutch singles to right field.

"God, we were so young that year and it was all so wonderful. Lord knows, I'd still like to be playing but when you
had a part in that season you already had a lot more than most
players ever have. I can't have any regrets."

It is early winter and the deer season is about to open around
Austin, Texas. Kenneth George Boswell is the new truck manager of a Chevrolet dealership outside Austin. He arranges
his schedule in such a way that he can escape the early shift
during deer season. He will return with his quota because he
knows how to handle a rifle as well as he knew how to handle
a baseball bat.

"I remember living in my Manhattan apartment that summer. Sometimes I would come in by subway train and sometimes I would get a ride from Arthur Richman, the traveling
secretary. Once in a while I would get picked up by Donald
Grant and driven in his limousine to the ball park. One time
we pulled into Shea Stadium and he was driving his own car.

We get to the park and Grant says, 'I'll put on my chauffeur's cap now,' and he picks that thing up from the seat and puts it on. I couldn't stop laughing. Grant had a stuffy image with the press but he was really a pretty good guy."

Boswell, born in Austin on February 23, 1946, grew up in the wide open central Texas country. He spent a lot of time tramping through the fields, shooting rabbits, riding horses, learning how to hunt with his father and playing sports.

"We weren't very far from where Lyndon Johnson had his ranch, and we would see him every so often. In the 1960s when he was president we would see him driving by in a big car or catch his Secret Service men doing some shopping in town. When the river would get a little dirty we figured Lyndon had one of his big barbecues and all the garbage wound up floating our way."

At six feet and 170 pounds, Boswell developed a sweet swing. An outstanding baseball and basketball player at W. B. Travis High in Austin, he captained both teams in his senior year, set batting records in baseball, and led the basketball team in scoring. Upon his graduation from high school at nineteen, he was signed by Mets scout Red Murff.

Boswell hit .285 at Auburn in his first pro season, and .299 the next year at Williamsport. A little awkward at second base, he showed marked improvement at Jacksonville in 1966 and again in 1967 when he returned to Triple A. He got into 11 games with the Mets in 1967 and played 75 games in 1968 under Hodges, mostly platooning with Al Weis at second base against right-handed pitchers. He was a sharp line-drive hitter without much power. Hodges got him to cut down on his swing and make better contact.

"Gil was the smartest man I ever met in baseball. He was really the creator of that team. He wasn't the friendliest guy around the club. He often seemed distracted. He was just a quiet, strong leader. He could get mad and yell at umpires or scream at any of us when things went badly. But mostly he seemed to be leaning forward on the bench all the time thinking ahead to moves. He also knew the rule book better than the umpires. I remember when he came to the plate after Cleon Jones got hit on the foot with a pitch in the World Series. He actually had a rule book in his back pocket and he might have pulled it out if he thought he needed it for evidence. Once he showed them the scuff marks on the ball, that was it. They gave Cleon the base."

Boswell had a ready wit and was an important contributor to the team with a needle for any player who might need it. He also played another vital role on the team in being as comfortable with Ed Charles, Tommie Agee, Cleon Jones and later, Donn Clendenon, when he joined the club, as he was with any white player. In the tensions of the 1960s that was as vital to the success of the team as the line drives he hit and the ground balls he fielded.

"That team just had a collection of very unselfish players. We all got along very well. Me, Sham, Cleon, and Tommie often hung out together, went to dinner together, played golf on the road, just had a good time. I never thought anything about any differences. We were teammates."

At the age of twenty-two, Boswell was the Mets' hope for a solid second baseman. He got off hot in his rookie year, was batting well over .300 into June, and was being talked about as a candidate for 1968 Rookie of the Year, an award later won by a young Cincinnati catcher, Johnny Bench, over Mets rookie left-hander Jerry Koosman by a single vote. Then he suffered a broken ring finger when a throw from second baseman Tommy Helms of the Reds glanced off his hand. He missed nearly two months of the season and finished the year with a .261 average.

In 1969 he batted .286 in spring training, won the starting job opening day, batted third, the spot usually reserved for a team's best hitter, and played well early despite military obligations.

"There were times when I would get on a plane at midnight after military meetings in Texas, fly all night and arrive at Shea in time for a nap on the trainer's table and then the game. I really didn't mind it though. I was so young and so excited about being in the big leagues that it didn't matter. I often played without any sleep."

There were a lot of nights without sleep for that team. It seemed the Mets had a favorite location for a party in every town.

"Sometimes we would go out to the homes of one of the players' families. In Texas it would be at my home or Grote's. In California it might be at Harrelson's. In St. Louis it was always at Sham's."

Shamsky and Boswell seemed an odd couple. Shamsky was a tall, sharp Jewish outfielder from St. Louis. Boz was a skinny, drawling Texan from Austin. They just hit it off. They are in contact to this day, rare among baseball teammates separated by so much geography between Austin and New York, where Shamsky now makes his home.

"I want to say one thing about Art Shamsky for the record," said Boswell. "Sham was the greatest player I ever saw."

There may be a little partisanship in that, but the emotion is clear. These two Mets were and still are sincere friends.

After Boswell returned from military duty for the last time in 1969, he got very hot with the bat. He had 37 hits in 91 at bats for a .407 mark from August 23 to the end of the season. He moved his average up from .236 to .279. He singled in the twelfth inning on September 10 in the first game of a Shea doubleheader against Montreal to put the Mets in first place for the first time in their history. They did not drop from the top spot for the remainder of the season.

Boswell, in Hodges's left-handed playoff lineup, had 4 hits in 12 times against Atlanta and then played only one game against Baltimore in the Series. He had a single.

"I started against Jim Palmer. Baltimore's other starters

were left-handers. I understood the system. I just rooted as hard as I could for the other guys."

When the Series ended in a Mets triumph and the rings were delivered, Boswell presented it to his father.

He played behind Felix Millan on the 1973 National League champions, played some third base, pinch-hit in 42 games, and ended his Met career after the 1974 season. He was an extra man for three seasons with Houston before retiring after the 1977 season at thirty-one.

"I could have hung on with some other clubs but I was finished. I had some business dealings with a couple of guys from the champion Jets, Curly Johnson and Jim Hudson. I was doing all right. I enjoyed baseball while it lasted. It wasn't my life. It was too much of a hassle a good part of the time."

He and his wife, Toney, live in a large lakefront house outside Austin with their two teenage daughters. Boz said he is doing well in the truck business. He is happy at home. His daughters enjoy school. He stays active with golf, hunts a lot, talks to Sham once in a while on the phone and enjoys seeing his teammates on special occasions.

"Actually I don't look forward to going back to New York now. It's too much trouble. I'd just as soon stay around here. I think about those days once in a while, especially when I read of the big salaries today. I still think they pay a price. I've heard of so many of my teammates having broken marriages. I often wonder why. I don't know. I was married when I left home for work this morning. Maybe I'd better check before I go back."

Boz wasn't much over his playing weight at the age of forty-one, and he looked like he could still stroke a line single to right field. Most likely, it would occur at an important time in the game.

There were twenty-five of them that summer of '69, each contributing in his own way. Gil Hodges seemed always to have the perfect touch for the correct man at the correct time. Hodges had decided to stay with a guy in 1969 who had batted only .172 the season before after coming over in a big trade. The Mets got Tommie Agee in that deal and sent Jack Fisher and Tommy Davis to Chicago. Al Weis was a must for the Mets to make the deal.

"We needed a professional utility infielder with so many of our infielders having military obligations," GM John Murphy said.

Albert John Weis wore a crew cut in the style that was popular two decades earlier. As hair grew longer that summer of '69, his grew shorter. He spoke only when spoken to, had a soft voice, and seemed separated from the hijinks of the clubhouse. He was a serious man who looked on baseball as an earnest profession. He worked hard at his job and maximized his limited talents.

The two series that made the Mets contenders occurred in July against Leo Durocher's Cubs, the first at Shea, the second at Chicago's Wrigley Field. Al Weis had hit four big-league homers in 650 at bats before he hit two in two days at Wrigley Field, a three-run game-winner off Dick Selma on July 15 and another off Ferguson Jenkins the next day to send the Cubs big right-hander on his way to a 9–5 defeat.

The hair is crew-cut again now after a few years of flirting with the 1980s. He is a bit fleshier than he was in his playing days at New York when he carried one hundred and sixty-five pounds on a six foot frame.

"Gil gave me a lot of confidence. I knew I wouldn't be playing every day with that team. I also knew I would make important contributions, especially since Boz and Harrelson were away so much in service. I had never gotten much of a chance with the White Sox because I was behind Luis Aparicio and Nelson Fox all those years. Then in 1967, when Eddie Stanky was the manager, I learned a lot about the game. He used to walk up and down the dugout and quiz the players, 'What's the count, what inning is it, what does this guy throw, who's the next hitter?" He really taught me to concentrate. When I came to the Mets I knew I wouldn't get into the game until late. I concentrated all game. I knew the situation and was ready to play when Gil called for me."

Weis was born in Franklin Square, Long Island, New York, and grew up in Farmingdale. He excelled on the baseball and basketball teams, entered the Navy after high school, starred at the Norfolk Naval Base and was signed by the White Sox in 1959. He remained with the White Sox through 1967. That year he had been battered by a hard slide by MVP Frank Robinson. Weis had to undergo knee surgery. Robinson had headaches for weeks. The White Sox thought Weis would never have adequate range again and sent him to the Mets.

"I was very disappointed going over to the Mets. They had a bad team, and I knew I wouldn't play much. I was pretty discouraged in 1968 and had a terrible year. Then the team started winning in 1969, and I realized how important my contributions were. It is impossible to sit on the bench for a losing team. It's a lot easier for a winner."

He played in 103 games for the 1969 Mets. There was never a dropoff in the inner defense when Boswell or Harrelson, or even both, were away in the military. Weis was a tremendous plus for the team.

His biggest moments came in the World Series.

"I had a sleepless night before the opener. They had a left-hander going (Mike Cuellar), and I knew I was starting. I was exhausted coming to the park. I had sweaty palms when I took the field. I blew the first ball hit to me. Then I relaxed. After that it seemed easy."

Weis knocked in the only Met run in the opener with a sacrifice fly and had two walks. He got a base hit to win the second game for Jerry Koosman in the ninth. He hit the home run—his eighth in professional baseball—to tie the fifth and deciding game of the Series. He won the New York Baseball Writers award as World Series Most Valuable Player. The honor is called the Babe Ruth award. Teammates called him Babe often the next year.

He lasted two more years with the Mets and was released before the 1972 season.

"They had Wayne Garrett needing more playing time and Teddy Martinez as a backup. There was just no room for me. I wanted to stay in baseball a little while longer. I was only thirty-two. I made some phone calls. The Reds said I could come to spring training and try to win a job as a backup to Dave Concepcion. I went there for a few weeks, and they decided to go with younger players. They gave me a plane ticket home. That was the end of my baseball career."

At the age of thirty-two, with no skills outside the game, married and the father of two children, Weis studied the help-wanted ads in the Chicago papers. He got a job in the shipping department of a large Chicago furniture company. He never mentioned that he was the guy who beat the Cubs a few summers earlier and beat the Orioles in the World Series.

"I've been there more than fifteen years, and I work nine to five. My son is in college as a finance major, and my daughter is working in the banking business. Barbara and I have a lot of time to ourselves now."

He has returned to Shea a couple of times for old-timers' events and also has attended a few dream camps in Florida, where he suits up and quietly tells some early-middle-aged businessmen, who have paid three thousand dollars for the privilege, how to turn a double play. As his fiftieth birthday approaches, he lives comfortably in the Chicago suburb of Elmhurst, does not torture himself about what might have been, and measures successes in small ways.

"I read about those big salaries players make today and I am asked about it when I go to a baseball card show or do an infrequent appearance. That seems to be on the mind of people a lot. I think about it. I have to admit it, I never made more than thirty-two thousand dollars. Then I realize that I'm happy doing what I'm doing. I look at the few trophies I have, the ball and bat I used in the Series, and I'm proud of that. I'm not so sure those big salaries make you any happier. Actually, when you read some of these things, you have to think maybe you are better off when you don't make salaries like that."

There is some gray in the crew cut now and a few extra pounds around the middle. Al Weis still talks softly when he does talk. He still makes a lot of sense.

# 6

# At the Front Office

April 8, 1969: Doctors at St. Luke's Episcopal Hospital in Houston today started an operation to remove the heart of Haskell Karp, forty-seven, and replace it with a mechanical heart. The medical team was led by Dr. Denton Cooley. In Hollywood, CBS announced the firing of Tom and Dick Smothers. Network spokesman did not detail reasons for the firing, but it was learned that CBS received numerous phone calls about a political skit on the show performed by the Smothers Brothers and written by David Steinberg. In Beirut, King Hussein of Jordan forecast "peace with Israel" provided it was based on justice. Hussein also announced he had requested President Nixon lead the fight to obtain Big Four aid for the underdeveloped Arab nations. In Saigon, the American military command announced that fourteen GIs were listed killed in action in the latest casualty count, with twenty-eight wounded. Fighting was reportedly tapering off. Among the latest casualties were W. O. Francis Dominick Alivento, twenty-two, of New York, killed in an aircraft crash; Cpl. James Melvin Truelove, twenty, of Sulligent, Alabama, dead of multiple fragmentation wounds, and Cpl. Leon Wilson, nineteen, of Jeffersonville, Georgia, dead of wounds suffered after stepping on a land mine.

At Shea Stadium in New York, the Mets lost their eighth straight season opener, this time to a team playing its first game ever. The new expansion franchise, the Montreal Expos, beat the Mets 11–10 in ten innings. Rookie Duffy Dyer hit a two-out, two-on pinch-hit three-run homer in the ninth inning to tie it at 9–9. Cal Koonce gave up a run in the tenth and ex-Met Don Shaw was the winner when rookie Rod Gaspar struck out against reliever Carroll Sembera.

In his private suite on the third floor of Shea Stadium, Chairman of the Board M. Donald Grant entertained friends long after the game ended. Grant's Opening Day guest list included friends from Wall Street, other executives of the Mets, and some baseball officials.

M. Donald Grant. Even the name reeks of stuffiness. A tall man, always impeccably dressed, wearing starched shirts and finely tailored suits, rarely seen without a jacket, with a resonant speaking voice and a commanding presence. Tall and debonair, he seems to the manor born. He wasn't.

Michael Donald Grant (he began using M. Donald as a Wall Street executive) was born in Montreal, Quebec, Canada, of modest circumstances. He worked as a hotel clerk in Montreal at the Windsor Hotel (the Mets would stay there on their first 1969 visit to Montreal for nostalgic reasons), left home in the late 1920s, just before the crash, and worked his way up from a Wall Street clerk to one of the directors of a huge investment firm.

One of his clients was Joan Whitney Payson. He was soon so successful managing Mrs. Payson's stock portfolio that she put him completely in charge of all of her investment millions. She owned a piece of the New York Giants and it was Grant, technically, who voted against the Giants' move from New York to San Francisco. He was voting Mrs. Payson's shares. He advised her later that a prudent investment would be made in the new Continental League. This soon developed into the New York Mets of the National League. When the franchise was awarded to Mrs. Payson, Grant was put in charge. He was quick to hire the best baseball man he could find, George Weiss, and let him build his team his own way, including the hiring of Casey Stengel, a man Grant first found uncomfortable to deal with but later grew to admire. Grant even took to driving Stengel back to Manhattan after each home game. "I learned to appreciate his knowledge and wisdom," he says. Grant spoke warmly in Stengel's eulogy at St. Patrick's Cathedral in 1975.

Grant was seen around the club often. He attended most every home game, appeared at Florida exhibition games, especially on the East Coast of Florida, where he maintained a home at Hobe Sound, and always at the St. Petersburg opener in a box he shared with Mrs. Payson, the Mother Dumpling of the Mets. There was a Mr. Payson. There was a Mrs. Grant. They made rare public appearances at Shea. Grant ran the club for a short while after Mrs. Payson died in 1975 but soon was forced out by Mrs. Payson's daughter, Lorinda De Roulet. All connection with the team ended in 1980 when the Payson heirs sold the team to the Doubleday group.


It is early winter, and Grant is sitting in the sunlit living room of his beautiful Florida home on the Gold Coast. He appears a bit drawn after some illness, but his voice is as vigorous as ever.

"What I enjoyed most, what I miss most is walking down the street and having people stop me and say, 'You're Don Grant, the man who runs the Mets. You brought Willie Mays back to New York.' Those were things I liked."

Grant would put in a full day at the offices of Fahnestock and Company, call for his driver, and make the journey to Shea for most night games.

"My driver, Charlie, was very good about weaving through traffic. He would get us there in record time. I would sit in the back and shave with the electric razor. Then I would get to the park in time to entertain in the Director's Room with some of my friends. That was always a wonderful experience," he said.

In the early days of the Mets, Grant would have conversations about the team with George Weiss. He was never quite as comfortable with Bing Devine, Weiss's successor, who lasted barely two years, but he enjoyed talking with Johnny Murphy, a very solid, honest, direct baseball man.

"George was right on the mark eighty-five to ninety-five percent of the time in things he did. He wasn't so sure about Gil Hodges. When Washington called us in 1963 and said they wanted him for their manager, I asked George 'Don't you think he'll manage our ball club?' George said it would never happen. Then Gil did a wonderful job with Washington. We talked about making him our manager two or three years before it happened. We almost got Agee a year before we did. George didn't want to give up good, young players. He was right about that."

When the discussion turned to the season of 1969, Grant paused. He appeared to be deep in thought. The memories were oh, so sweet.

"We won the pennant in the spring when I refused to make the deal for Joe Torre. The Braves wanted three of our best young players, Jerry Grote, Nolan Ryan, and Amos Otis. We told them we wouldn't trade Otis and Grote and Ryan. They were our hope for the future, our untouchables. The newspapermen picked up on that and started riding us. I didn't like that. There are a lot of them I still wouldn't shake hands with today."

Grant developed a close relationship with Dick Young of the *News*. Grant fed him information, while my paper, the *New York Post*, depended on other sources. Grant would later hire Young's son-in-law with the Mets. This would lead to charges of conflict of interest, much tension around the team, and the final explosion in 1977 when Grant traded Tom Seaver away after Young attacked Seaver as an ingrate. Grant refuses to discuss that episode of his life.

"I don't want to deal in controversy or unpleasantness," he says.

The Braves came back to the Mets and said that they would take Ed Kranepool, Ryan and Otis. Grant again refused.

"Kranepool was one of our favorites. We also thought Torre had seen better days as a catcher. We thought we could win with our young players, if not in 1969, then in 1970 or 1971."

Torre was traded to the Cards on March 17 in a deal involving Orlando Cepeda. Kranepool, Grote, and Ryan contributed heavily to the Mets. Otis, refusing to learn how to play third base, was soon shipped out. He was traded in December of 1969 to Kansas City for Joe Foy, one of the worst Met deals ever. Otis became a star with KC, and Foy was a complete bust with the Mets. It would rival the trade of Ryan to California in December of 1971 for Jim Fregosi, who had seen better days. Ryan became a Hall of Fame pitcher.

"Who knows if Ryan would have done that with us?" says Grant.

The Mets won with their own players. Donn Clendenon was the only player obtained during the 1969 season from outside the organization.

The season began and the Mets quickly showed they had a solid club. On May 28 they beat San Diego and began an 11-game winning streak, longest in their history, combining wins against the Padres and, happily for Mets fans, against the now-hated Giants and Dodgers. On June 25 they were only 4½ games out of first place, a serious pennant contender. Where have you gone, Marv Throneberry? That night, Bud Harrelson, who had been playing marvelously well at shortstop, left for two weeks of military service.

"George Weiss came up to me that night and began talking about how much Harrelson meant to the team. We were bringing up a youngster from Tidewater (Bobby Pfeil, who would help win a couple of games), but he was no Harrelson. 'Donald, could you get Harrelson out of the military? You know a lot of people in this town.' I was really upset about that idea. I told him I couldn't and more importantly I wouldn't even if I could," Grant said.

The Mets had to have strong defense if they were going to win. They hit only .242 that year as a team. Their ERA was 2.99. The pitching would win it, but the defense would help.

"The next night," Grant said, "I went to Al Weis in the clubhouse. I knew he had been around but he was a nervous young man. I told him we had an opportunity to grab this thing. We had lost Harrelson for a couple of weeks, but I was sure he could do the job. I told him so. 'Let's take this opportunity and grab it.' He was encouraged and he did a beautiful job for us."

When the Mets won the pennant, Grant followed the team to Atlanta for the National League Championship Series and led a party of his pals to Baltimore for the World Series. He was quick to enter the clubhouse and shake Hodges's hand and the hand of every coach after the stirring triumph.

"Those were wonderful days. You know I never took a salary for running the club. It was just for fun, and we all enjoyed it so much." Of course, he made many millions as an investor and part owner of the club.

When the Mets won again in 1973, on the flight west to Oakland, Grant urged Yogi Berra, the new manager, to skip the turn of left-hander George Stone, a soft thrower but a winner that year (12–3) and lock up the Series with his aces, Seaver and Jon Matlack. Berra went along, lost with Seaver, and lost the Series with Matlack in the seventh game. It was an area of contention between them that would last through the next two seasons until Berra was fired by Grant in 1975.

After that season, free agency would explode on the baseball market. Grant was adamant. He would not pay for expensive free agents. It was at the heart of the bitter dispute with Seaver and would make Grant a hated man in New York, especially after I conducted a public poll in the *Post* asking for his head.

Grant had little influence on Lorinda De Roulet and was happy to leave when conditions changed. He continues working daily in his office and watches games on television, but has not been back to Shea since 1980.

"I think I was right. You don't see the new people (the Doubleday group) spending money on free agents, either. The owners have let this salary thing get out of hand, but you can't run a ball club unless you do it on a businesslike basis."

As he nears his eighty-fifth birthday, Grant is having some difficulty with his health. He suffered serious problems early in 1988 but recovered. He is made happy by talking about that glorious 1969.

"There were some very fine people associated with that team," he said. "I enjoyed every moment of it. I don't have the World Series ring, though. It was stolen from my home some years ago. I do have the memories. Nobody can steal that."

It was time to bid farewell to M. Donald Grant. It was clear that historians would treat him more fairly than journalists did.

"Goodbye, Don."

"Goodbye. Be kind to me."


Arthur's gallery is a lot more interesting than rogues' gallery. At Shea Stadium on the office wall of Arthur Richman, the team's director of travel and assistant to GM Frank Cashen, are pictures of Georgie Brett, Tom Seaver, President Nixon, President Reagan, Joe DiMaggio, and Ted Williams . . . and isn't that a young Johnny Bench or President Carter over there or Governor Rockefeller and Mayor Koch and Mayor Lindsay and Mayor Wagner or General Westmoreland? When Arthur fell and injured his knees in Pittsburgh in 1987 the cards, letters and phone calls started with President Nixon and Commissioner Peter Ueberroth and continued with Willie Mays and George Steinbrenner, and on and on and on. You get the idea. He knows everybody.

A round-faced, bald man with more stories about more people than Georgie Jessel ever had, Arthur Richman has been around the Mets almost from the beginning. Brother of the well-known late sports journalist, Milton Richman, columnist for United Press International, Arthur was a newspaper reporter for the *Daily Mirror*, but after the *Mirror* folded in 1963 and he took a whirl at advertising, he joined the Mets on February 22, 1965, as director of promotions. He would serve as publicity director, traveling secretary, assistant to the GM, and all-around idea and contact man ever since. He and his statuesque wife, Martha, would be seen often at baseball functions or at dinner at Rusty Staub's restaurant. A baseball affair or a charity event involving sports can hardly be run in New York without Richman.

"I joined the club in 1965, and the first thing that happened was that I slipped on the ice getting out of my apartment to go to work for the first day. I fractured my elbow in twelve places and when I came in with my arm in a cast everybody said, 'You look like you belong here.' I was a true Met from the beginning. Actually when the paper folded I got letters from both Casey and Weiss. Then George invited me to dinner and offered me a job."

Richman got along well with the laconic Weiss and was sorry to see him replaced by Bing Devine. Devine brought Hodges in at the end of the 1967 season.

"Hodges wasn't one of my favorite guys. It was hard to get to know Gil. We never had any disagreements I can remember. It was just that we weren't terribly comfortable with each other."

The big event of Opening Day in 1969 was the entrance of

the new Montreal Expos into the league. Montreal and San Diego had joined the National League. The Expos opened at Shea.

"I arranged for Montreal mayor Jean Drapeau to throw out the first ball. I thought that would be a nice touch in their first game. I wanted to entertain the fans with something special and pay tribute to our friends from Canada. Nothing more identifies the Canadians for Americans than the Royal Canadian Mounted Police. We've all seen them in the movies if we haven't seen them in person.

"We had, I don't know, thirty or forty, of these big, handsome Mounted Police with their horses ready to parade into Shea for the first ball ceremonies and the raising of the flags and the singing of our national anthems, something that has become a tradition at Shea when the Expos come in. The horses are outside the gates ready to come in, and the Mounties are dressing under the stands. All of a sudden I get a call from one of the Canadian guys. The Mounties have left their red coats back in the hotel. I had to dispatch somebody to race to the hotel, load the truck with the uniform trunk, and race back to Shea. They got here just in time."

So much of the 1969 season was colored by the activities in Southeast Asia. Richman often arranged for wounded vets to come to Shea as guests of the Mets. He even had the club set up a section at the Series in deep left field reserved for them.

"One of the most thrilling days at Shea was when we got Captain Gerald Coffee out to the park. He had been a prisoner of the North Vietnamese for many years. He had been in the notorious camp they nicknamed the Hanoi Hilton and now he was freed. He came to the game, was introduced, saluted the crowd, and walked off the field. He got a huge ovation, and I don't think there was a dry eye in the place.

"I used to bring the wounded out here from the hospitals. They would come in ambulances, and you would see everything. There would be kids with their arms blown off or their eyes gone or their legs missing. It was horrible. But they all loved baseball, and they always had a good time. I remember when that season ended and some of the guys were going to Las Vegas to be in an act put together by Phil Foster. They were getting ten thousand dollars for the appearance. One of the guys they wanted was Ed Charles. I had asked him months before to go to Vietnam with me at the end of the year. He agreed. Then we won and he got that offer and I thought he would back out. 'Arthur, we're going.' I told him he could back out, get his ten grand, I understood. He said, 'I gave you my word.' That was it. He went and we saw everything. It was a very moving trip."

The most memorable game of the year for Arthur had to be the Seaver game in July when he lost his perfect game with one out in the ninth to the Cubs when Jimmy Qualls got that little single.

"That was some game. I'm usually downstairs until the fifth or sixth inning but I got upstairs early to watch that. I think we had the biggest crowd we ever had for a game that night, fifty-seven, fifty-nine thousand, something like that. People were everywhere. The aisles were jammed. Jim Thomson (the club's business manager) hated that night. None of the vendors could get through the aisles with the beer, and everybody lost money. I don't think we ever allowed that many people in the park after that."

There were several political demonstrations that year, many opposing the war. A good percentage of Mets fans were Army-age young men.

"It was building all year, and finally after we won there was a moritorium day calling for a halt to the war during the fourth game of the Series. I had a band from the Kings Point Merchant Marine Academy, and I had some wounded coming over in buses from area hospitals. Kids held up the buses, and when the wounded saw the demonstrators they never got out of their bus. They just turned around and went home. Who could blame them?"

Seaver was pitching that game, and demonstrators were at his car as he arrived at the park. They handed him brochures, and he said he would support their cause. He did tell the press after his win that day that he opposed the war and would do what he could. There is no record that he did more than express his feelings.

"I got along with Seaver, I got along with everybody, but Tom is an independent guy. He also had his favorites among the press corps. His big buddy was Red Smith. Tom was always sitting in the clubhouse doing the *Times* crossword puzzle. Things like that annoyed people. Koosman was terrific. He would do anything I asked. Grote was a little rough around the edges. A real personality. I liked Harrelson a lot and used to get him many speaking engagements. In those days a speaking engagement for a hundred bucks for a guy making fifteen thousand dollars was a big deal. Tug McGraw hung around all winter after that '69 season, and when I got him a Little League dinner for twenty-five bucks he was thrilled. One day Nolan Ryan came up to me. 'Arthur, how come you never ask me to do a speaking date?' I told him it was because I never heard him speak. He was a real quiet kid in those days."

Richman did some little jobs around the club that never got much attention but helped keep things moving smoothly.

"I remember once on picture day. We were all assembled on the field. I suddenly noticed Cleon Jones wasn't there. I knew Gil would be upset. I ran into the clubhouse and dragged him out. Gil just stared but he didn't say anything. I think I saved Gil some aggravation, and I know I saved Cleon some money."

Richman was especially close with the Mets coaches, Rube Walker, Eddie Yost, Joe Pignatano, and Yogi Berra. "I was close to Yogi as much as anyone can get close to Yogi."

The Mets won the World Series and a few months later Richman was sitting in the Bickford's cafeteria in Manhattan.

"Actually I wasn't sitting there. I was sitting in my car. I had been at a dinner, stayed late, was real tired and fell asleep at the wheel. I jumped the curb and went through the window into Bickford's. I wasn't hurt. A guy came up to me, noticed my ring, and asked where I got it. I told him I was with the Mets and he asked to see the ring. Here I was, all shook up, covered with glass, a little bruised and bloody, and this guy wants to see my ring."

The following spring Mets GM Johnny Murphy sent Richman to Florida to arrange for the rental of cars for the team officials during spring training.

"I was very close to Johnny Murphy. When he pitched for the Yankees in the 1930s he lived in the Bronx on Grand Avenue. We lived on Fremont Avenue, right around the corner. I followed his career and we became good friends. He had been with the Mets since the beginning. I went to Florida that day for the cars and got a call that Johnny Murphy had suddenly died. It was one of the saddest days of my life."

After Harold Weissman retired, Richman became the club's publicity director. The hardest job any PR director in sports probably ever had was Richman's chore on June 15, 1977. He had to inform the press in a steamy clubhouse in Atlanta that Tom Seaver had been traded to the Cincinnati Reds. An hour later, with the Mets flying home from Atlanta on a plane at thirty-five thousand feet, he also announced that slugger Dave Kingman, a moody bore, was also traded to San Diego. I moved to the front of the plane to ask Kingman to comment on his trade. "Get the hell out of here," he bellowed. With no place to go at that height, I sulked away. Richman walked up and whispered, "The guy's crazy. Leave him alone. I'll get you quotes."

Richman has remained with the Mets through the years. He is now easing off his work load a bit.

"It's been fun but it has also been a lot of long hours and hard work. How can I leave? Who will help me take down my pictures?"

He was soft on them, fatherly and always a sort of comic relief. They called him Bluford. Albert Bluford Walker of Lenior, North Carolina, was the mother hen of the great Mets pitching staff of 1969. He chaperoned a staff of three probable Hall of Famers—Tom Seaver, Tug McGraw, and Nolan Ryan—and three more quality pitchers in Jerry Koosman, Gary Gentry, and Jim McAndrew. More significantly, in an era when pitchers are used up by teams and discarded, Seaver, Koosman, Ryan, and McGraw each had careers that lasted a good two decades.

Rube Walker, a Falstaffian character at six feet, one inch and 220 pounds plus, was a fine receiver and solid left-handed hitter on the old Brooklyn Dodgers. He backed up Roy Campanella and was behind the plate October 3, 1951, when Ralph Branca threw an inside fastball that Bobby Thomson pulled into the seats for the pennant-winning home run. "It was a good pitch because it was going to set up the curve outside on the next pitch. Ralph just got it out over the plate a little too much," says Walker.

Walker coached later for the Dodgers, managed in the minors, and went to Washington under Gil Hodges in 1965. He moved to Shea with Hodges in 1968.

Rube Walker is a scout for the St. Louis Cardinals. His boss is Dal Maxvill, his former coaching mate on the Mets under Joe Torre. He smiles when he is asked about the 1969 Mets. "The greatest collection of young arms I ever saw," he says. "We were just fortunate."

When he is reminded that at least four of them lasted twenty years more or less, he shakes his head. "We took care of all of them the same way. It was just a lucky thing. We took care of Gentry, and he blew out his arm in two or three years. It happens."

Hodges made all the decisions on pitching with the Mets. Walker, sitting next to him on the bench, supplied the information.

"Our philosophy was simple. We had a lot of good hard throwers. We had them establish their fastballs, use their breaking pitches carefully, and throw an occasional change. Good stuff, good luck, and a few runs made that staff."

Walker is the father of two grown daughters. In 1969 he added about ten sons to his family.

Eddie Yost was a local product, a guy from Queens who graduated from New York University right into the big leagues with Washington. A fine fielding third baseman and a lifetime .254 hitter with good power, he had a good eye at the plate and drew 1,614 walks to earn the nickname the Walking Man. He coached for Hodges in Washington and then moved with him to Shea. He was the Mets third-base coach and a talented giver of team signals. Now retired, he lives outside Boston, where he ended his coaching career four years ago.

"I never played on a winning team all those years with the Washington and Detroit clubs. I did have a chance at Detroit in 1960, but they caught us in September and beat us out of the pennant.

"When I got to work for Gil I was thrilled. He was one of the finest men I ever met in the game. Winning that year was just wonderful. How can I describe it? I had been in the game twenty-five years, and I knew what it took to win. It was a shame we didn't win a couple of more before Gil died. The real shame is that he went so early. I was there, on that golf course in West Palm Beach. One minute I was talking to him, and the next minute he was dead. It's a lot of years later but I still think about that a lot."

\*   \*   \*

For an older generation the baseball nickname the Babe means most. For a generation that became interested in baseball after World War II, it has to be Yogi. Hall of Famer Lawrence Peter Berra was a catcher with the Yankees for twenty years. He was signed by the Yankees off the sandlots in St. Louis in 1943, played a year for Norfolk, spent the next two years in the Navy, returned to baseball with Newark in 1946 and joined the Bronx Bombers that September. Short and stumpy-looking, he was a figure of derision in his Navy uniform when he first reported to Yankee Stadium before his assignment to Newark. He won three Most Valuable Player titles, played in more World Series (14) than any player in baseball history, became one of the most beloved baseball figures of all time and was often called by Casey Stengel, "My assistant manager."

He was a player-coach for the Yankees in 1963 and named the manager of the team in 1964. He won a pennant in his first try and lost the World Series to St. Louis in seven games. He was fired by the Yankees the day after the Series ended. Two weeks later he received a call from Stengel, now managing the Mets, asking if Yogi wanted to join his team as a player-coach.

"I knew I couldn't play much but I wanted to stay in baseball. Casey wanted me to come over so I went to the Mets," he said.

Berra played in only four games in 1965, coached first base the rest of the time and stayed on as a coach with the Mets into the 1972 season. He was named the team's manager after Gil Hodges suffered a fatal heart attack. He won a pennant in 1973 with the Mets, was fired in August of 1975 and returned to the Yankees as a coach under old buddy Billy Martin in 1976. He coached there through 1983. He was the manager of the team in 1984, was fired after 16 games and was named a coach of the Houston Astros in 1986. Born May 12, 1925, Berra has been in baseball 45 years as he sits in the dugout at Shea Stadium early in 1988. He looks cute in his orange and gold Houston uniform.

"You had to say 1969 was a great year. Everything went right. Sometimes it don't happen even when you have great arms. It was tough to lose too many games with Seaver and Koosman and Ryan and them other guys and Cardwell and McGraw and Taylor in the bullpen. We won with pitching and enough hitting and great defense. That's the way you win. I liked it over there a lot. I was home most of the time. I live in Montclair (N.J.) so it was easy. Why wouldn't you like it if you are home and you win?"

Berra went to Houston in 1986 because his good friend and golfing buddy, Dr. John J. McMullen, a Montclair neighbor and the owner of the Astros, asked him to join the team and help the rookie manager, Hal Lanier.

"Yogi knows an awful lot about baseball and the players all enjoy being around him and talking baseball with him," said Lanier.

"In that 1969 season I'll say we had the closest coaching staff I've ever been involved with. We used to have dinner together on the road almost every night. We did everything together, went to the park early, played cards, talked to Gil about the game, stayed together a lot after the game, played golf together on off days, sat in the bus together. These were great guys, Rube and Piggy and Yostie and I enjoyed that season a lot. Spring training was fun when Carmen (Berra's beautiful wife of 40 years) would be down in Florida and all the coaches and the wives would get together. We'd have barbecues in somebody's back yard and sit around and talk and enjoy the closeness."

Berra had been an incredibly popular player with the Yankees. Hodges had been almost as popular with Brooklyn Dodger fans.

"Gil was the boss. I didn't have any trouble with Gil. It was his ball club. That's the way it should be with any team. You can have five or six coaches on a team but you can only have one manager. Gil was the manager."

Pignatano and Walker were former Brooklyn teammates of Hodges but they never seemed any closer to Gil than Yost or Yogi did.

"We were a team, just the way the players were a team. I kept the same coaches when they made me the manager, didn't I?"

Yogi seems to enjoy his secondary role with the Astros. He is still a very popular figure on the winter baseball banquet circuit and an immediately recognizable face. His popularity led to a successful new career in 1988 as a television movie reviewer. At the age of 63, he seems to have lost none of his enthusiasm for the game.

"I'm happy doing this with Houston. I don't know if I'd manage again. Let's see if somebody asks. I know I won't work for George (Steinbrenner) again. He won't have another chance to fire me. Sure I enjoyed the 1969 season. It was a great team and we won. I got the ring and I got some World Series money. If it's baseball, I know I'll like it."


Perhaps he was the closest coach to Gil Hodges. Some suggested he was a flunky for the manager. They were rarely apart that year of 1969. Joe Pignatano walked in the sunlight given off by Hodges. Pignatano was a journeyman catcher from Brooklyn, New York, who wound up playing for the hometown Dodgers. He played until 1964, and then coached for Hodges in Washington and with the Mets. He coached for Joe Torre at Atlanta and returned to baseball, after a four-year absence in 1988, as a pitching coach for the Atlanta organization in Raleigh-Durham, North Carolina. "I was playing golf every chance I got, but I missed baseball. I'm thrilled to be back."


He is wearing the Mets uniform again at a dream camp in Florida for middle-aged men who can afford three thousand for a week of fantasy play at being ballplayers.

"People think I was related to Hodges or my wife was. That wasn't so. We were just good friends. I remember the first day I met him. It was the spring of 1955 and I was training with Brooklyn at Vero Beach," said Piggy. "I was in the shower and he came up to me and patted me on the leg and said, 'Good to have you. Good luck.' That was some thrill to me."

"We had a bad ball club in Washington but Gil improved it. Then we came to the Mets in 1968. We coasted through that first year as Gil studied his players. Then we opened camp in 1969 and Gil said, 'Losing is not funny. It's a sickness.' He had seen enough. Now he was ready to win. The team was talented with all that pitching, but nobody knew how good it was. Gil predicted in the spring with the press that we would finish better than .500. That seemed a wild idea with that team."

Pignatano said that Hodges was a very intense man, very hardworking, very organized.

"He carried a pad and he would write things down. When he wanted to talk to a guy, he just kept his office door open and called him in when the player walked by. As the season went on, the games got more tense for him. He would sneak under the dugout for a smoke back in that ramp. Sometimes he would sit on the bench with a cigarette cupped in his hand. You weren't supposed to smoke on the field so he had to hide it from the umpires. I could always tell when he was real nervous. He had this habit of taking off his cap and running those huge hands through his hair. He would do that over and over again before he put that cap back on."

Every player who played under Hodges learned from him. "A couple of years ago I was at a banquet, and Cleon Jones was there. We know how Cleon didn't work as hard as he could. Gil was frustrated by him. Cleon came up to me that night and said, 'I should have listened more. I would have been a better player.' It took some guys longer to realize."

Hodges could also be tough and stubborn.

"We had this game against the Braves in the spring at West Palm Beach. Johnny Murphy rushed into the clubhouse after he saw the lineup card. McAndrew was starting. He started yelling that the Lady (Mrs. Payson) was there with Grant and they wanted to see Seaver or Koosman pitch. They didn't want any fourth or fifth pitcher. 'The Lady wants Seaver.' Gil was red-faced as he yelled back at Murphy, 'I don't care who the Lady wants. It's McAndrew's turn. If he can't pitch in front of the Lady, he can't pitch in the big leagues.' He pitched down there, and Gil got some big ball games out of him during the year."

Pignatano worked out of the bullpen. Out there, he babysat a lot of crazy people that season.

"Taylor could be very funny. Just a lot of one-liners for the moment, getting on some guy about something. I can't remember now what they were, but I know I laughed a lot. The day McGraw got that waiter in a white suit to bring trays of ribs and chicken and hamburgers to the bullpen and started heating everything over a sterno can really was something. It wasn't the food that annoyed me. It was that the guy said I had to pay the bill."

Pignatano thinks the Mets won the pennant when Jerry Koosman hit Ron Santo of the Cubs.

"After that nobody would intimidate us. I think Koosman was a better big-game pitcher for us that year than Seaver. Santo had that heel-clicking crap after a win. The fans in Chicago loved that act but it wasn't professional. You don't show up the other team. They beat us one day and Santo

clicked his heels, and I ran into him in the ramp leading to
the clubhouse and I told him that was bush. He said, 'I'm
just doing it for the fans. I think it's funny.' I said, 'I thought
you were a pro.' Then Koosman hit him after Bill Hands hit
Tommie Agee. I don't think Santo clicked his heels after that."

Pignatano remembers one other pitch from the 1969 season
with much fondness. It was the third game of the playoff after
the Mets beat the Braves twice in Atlanta. The next game
was at Shea with Atlanta leading, 2–0, and Gary Gentry pitching for the Mets. Atlanta had a man on second base.

"Rico Carty, one of the best hitters in the game, was up.
Gentry got a strike on him with a long foul. Then he hit the
next pitch into the upper deck. It went foul at the last instant.
Gil came out to the mound with the count oh and two and
brought in Ryan. Now Ryan had a hundred-mile-an-hour fastball, and Carty was a great fastball hitter. The whole ball park
expected Ryan to challenge Carty with that fastball. Instead
Gil told him to throw a curve, and Ryan let go one of the
sweetest curve balls you ever saw. Carty just stood there—I
mean he was frozen. He just watched that thing cut across
the plate as pretty as could be. It was the best pitch I saw all
year. We went on to win the game and then win the Series
easily."

"Before it [the World Series opener in Baltimore] started
they had this meeting with Earl Weaver and Gil and the
commissioner's people to go over the Series rules. Weaver
kept coming up with all sorts of little, picky things about taking
the field and where the pitchers could stand during batting
practice and how many guys could be around the cage at one
time and things like that. Gil just kept nodding his head. After
all this crap, somebody asked Gil if he had any questions or
suggestions. 'No, everything's fine with me. I thought we just
came down here to play ball.' Gil didn't worry about unimportant things."

The conversation finally got around to that emotional day,

April 2, 1972. Baseball players were on strike. The Mets were in West Palm Beach for a scheduled spring game. With all games canceled, Hodges and his coaches went out to play golf alongside the team hotel on the Ramada Inn course. With Yogi Berra visiting friends in Miami, Hodges was joined by Eddie Yost, Rube Walker, and Pignatano.

"We finished playing on a real fine day. Then we sat down with Jack Sanford, the old Giants pitcher, who was the club pro, and had a couple of beers at the nineteenth hole. We began walking back to the hotel, maybe fifty yards away. We were talking about the golf as we walked across the grass to the concrete path leading to the hotel rooms. Yost and Rube were off to the left, and Gil and I had rooms to the right. Just as we reached the walk where the paths split, I turned slightly to Gil and asked, 'What time do you want to meet for dinner?' He never answered. He just fell over backwards on that path and landed on his head. You could hear the crack as his head hit the sidewalk."

Hodges had died instantly of a massive heart attack two days before his forty-eighth birthday.

More than an hour later I arrived at the hotel from Fort Lauderdale, some sixty miles away, after speeding there upon hearing the news. The concrete walk was still covered with the manager's blood.

Pignatano got up from his chair in that Florida dream-camp clubhouse. He shook his head. There were tears in his eyes. The interview was over.

# 7

# *Catch as Catch Can*

---

May 25, 1969: James Earl Ray, admitted killer of civil rights leader Martin Luther King, today was denied a new trial. Ray had pleaded guilty to the 1968 assassination of the spokesman for nonviolence on a motel balcony in Memphis. In Toronto, John Lennon, wearing a beard and with his hair more scraggly than ever, arrived from London with wife, Yoko Ono, and her daughter, Kyoko, five, for an announced "bed-in for peace" in hopes of bringing the Vietnam War closer to an end. More involved in antiwar causes than in his music, the most militant Beatle held an airport press conference. He also said he was hopeful of being allowed back into the United States. He had been barred as an undesirable because of a marijuana conviction in England. Latest casualties in the Southeast Asia conflict included Sfc. Ronnie Ellis Hogbin, twenty-nine, of Miami Beach, dead of undisclosed causes, Cpl. Michael Anthony Powell, nineteen, of Atlanta, killed in an artillery-rocket explosion and Cpl. John Winters, eighteen, of Clark, New Jersey, killed by artillery-rocket fragments. In space developments, *Apollo 10* landed safely near Pago-Pago after a seven-thousand-mile test trip.

The Apollo trip was made with less incident than the Mets trip. The struggling team finished a road trip with a 3–4 record after losing one game in Atlanta and being swept in all three at Houston. They would not win a game in Texas all year.

Gary Gentry, Jerry Koosman, and Tom Seaver were beaten in Houston. All three were hit hard. The team record fell to 18–22, fourth place, 9 games out of first. In a postgame interview with the press, Gil Hodges attacked his hitters for being "a bunch of wooden soldiers" for scoring four runs in three games and striking out twenty-four times, twelve of them on called third strikes. The flight home from Houston to New York after the Sunday game was delayed on takeoff and then forced to stop with engine problems in Memphis. A sour bunch of Mets arrived at Shea Stadium shortly before daybreak. They would have one short day off before playing the San Diego Padres at Shea Tuesday night.

When sportswriter Joe Valerio wrote in the *New York Post* that "Will Rogers never met Jerry Grote," the funny line drew nods of approval from other sportswriters, some teammates, and many fans. Grote was hard to like. He was combative, quick to anger, and ice cold with strangers. He viewed sportswriters and fans with disdain. His job did not involve amenities. He was there to catch and hit and saw no need for common courtesy, socializing, or artificial friendships.

Unliked by most of the press, he was, at the same time, greatly admired for his total dedication to the game, his intensity, and his excellence. He took charge of a game the way a skilled captain takes charge of a sailing ship. He called games aggressively. His arm was better than any catcher in the league's, and he often threw the ball back to his own pitchers as hard as he threw to first base on pickoff attempts. Jerry Koosman once threatened to deck Grote during a tense game if one more throw from home stung his hand.

He brazenly planted himself as close to a batter at the plate as humanly possible. He gave his pitchers a magnificent target and bounced around with the grace of a tiger for any ball that needed attention. He never engaged opposing hitters in conversation, and he would often intimidate them by throwing pitched balls back with a whizzing sound near their earlobes. He tolerated no lack of intensity among his teammates. Grote quickly earned the respect of his peers. "If I was on that team," said future Hall of Famer Johnny Bench, the catcher by which all others in the 1960s and 1970s were measured, "I would be moved to third base." Lou Brock, the all-time base-stealing leader, called Grote the "toughest catcher to steal on" in all of baseball.

Gerald Wayne Grote was born October 6, 1942, in San Antonio, Texas. He was arrogantly Texan, wearing cowboy boots, talking with a deep Texas twang, associating most comfortably with other Texans on the team (Ken Boswell and Nolan Ryan), playing country music on his radio, and forever talking about the joys of Texas. He lived on a ranch as a youngster and worked as a cowboy in his time off from school. He was an outstanding athlete in high school as a catcher and pitcher on the baseball team, won a state cross-country title and honors in the mile run. He accepted a scholarship to Trinity College in Austin and was signed in 1962 by the Houston Astros. He broke into organized baseball in his hometown of San Antonio, where he hit .268. He made it to Houston late in 1963 and became the expansion team's regular catcher in 1964 at the age of twenty-one. He hit only .181, and the Astros sent him back to the minor leagues with Oklahoma City in 1965, where he batted .265.

Still struggling to find a catcher ever since Casey Stengel's era, the team traded for Grote on November 29, 1965. Houston was happy to let him go. They thought he would be a fine receiver but were convinced he would never hit. Hard to discipline, he took criticism poorly and was determined to control the game, sometimes in opposition to his manager and pitcher. Grote reported to manager Wes Westrum the following spring in St. Petersburg, and it was not long before he was discovered by the New York media and his teammates to be, in baseball vernacular, a red-ass, hair-triggered, short-tempered, and volatile. But he could catch. There were no doubts about that. "He was about the finest young receiver I had ever seen," says Westrum.

He hit only .237 in 1966 as a Met and slipped to .195 the next season. In 1968, under Hodges, his Met future was clearly in doubt. Pressures were building on Grote off the field as well as on. He had married early and was the father of three small children. His wife, Sharon, a tall, willowy blonde, had become his bride at the age of sixteen, a small-town girl suddenly thrust into the vibrations of New York with three babies. Grote could sometimes be uncommunicative at home, and Sharon Grote often took solace in sharing simple pleasures with other young wives when the team was on the road. She was especially close to Cecilia Swoboda, Carole Kranepool, and Yvonne Harrelson.

Grote stood five feet, ten inches tall, weighed a strong 190 pounds, and thought of himself as a long-ball hitter. Gil Hodges changed all that in 1968. Hodges shortened his swing, moved his hands up on the bat, changed his concepts of hitting, and made him an effective line-drive contact hitter. Grote listened because a .195 average will do that to a player. In 1968 he hit .282, and in 1969 .252, strong considering his magnificent defense.

Grote's ruggedly handsome good looks, marred slightly by a skin rash on the right side of his face, seemed diminished by his constant scowl. It would soften somewhat in later years as he finished out his career with the Los Angeles Dodgers, Kansas City, and the Dodgers again.

Grote left baseball in 1981, dabbled in the real estate business, tried selling cattle, got into trouble with the law on a livestock deal that went sour, wrote many clubs for coaching and managerial jobs, and finally landed a spot with the Detroit organization at their Lakeland, Florida, club. In mid-season he moved up to Birmingham. He was not offered a position the next season. He is now involved in the real estate business in San Antonio, has been divorced by Sharon, lives with his youngest son in a tasteful condominium, and speaks fondly of those days gone by. As was once said by sportswriter Frank Graham of Yankee outfielder Bob Meusel, "He learned how to say hello when it was time to say goodbye." Despite his marvelous play and his inordinate value to the World Champion 1969 Mets, Grote clearly did not get his earned public praise.

It is late evening on a pleasant fall day in San Antonio. Gerald Wayne Grote, sales manager for development of a large San Antonio firm, is relaxed as he talks about his team.

"When I first came to the Mets in 1966 I got along with the sportswriters well enough. I didn't think it was part of my job to talk with them. I was interested in baseball, interested in getting better as a player and winning."

Hodges joined the club, and in mid-season Grote was benched for a small slump. He said something about the benching to a reporter, and it came out stronger than intended. It almost sounded as if Grote, whose sinking career was being resurrected by Hodges, was criticizing the manager.

"I vowed then and there I wouldn't have anything to do with sportswriters. I could play the game as well without them. Hodges had really gotten on me after he read what I supposedly said, and I didn't want to go through that again. I was determined I would never be misquoted again."

Once in a while he would break down and violate his own rule, discussing a game, a play, or a particular pitcher. He was always bright and articulate about the game, clearly one of the most knowledgeable individuals about the sweet subtlety of baseball. He knew the mechanics, he understood the strange minds of pitchers, and he could generally outthink a hitter at the plate.

His personality never changed through his Mets time despite eleven years with the team, his own success, and two pennants. When the Mets won in 1973, clinching in Chicago, Grote celebrated the National East title by dumping ice water on some unsuspecting sportswriters. It was a war he could not win.

"I was glad to come over to the Mets from Houston. I knew that team would never win. They had too many old players, and they had no defense. It was different with the Mets. You could see the young talent. We had strong pitching and strong defense, and in 1969 I thought we were a lot like the 1965 Dodgers. We had something else no other club had and that was Buddy Harrelson. I would tell our pitchers that all they had to do was get the batter to hit the ball to Harrelson. He was the most sure-handed shortstop I ever saw."

Grote credits Hodges fully for salvaging his career.

"Gil changed me completely as a hitter. I used to be way down on the bat and swung hard on every pitch. That was the way I was taught to hit. Gil got me up on the bat and told me all I had to do was make contact, keep the ball in play, use the whole field. I started doing it that way and it worked. After that I gave up trying to pull everything. I would hit an occasional long ball (39 homers in 16 seasons), but I was most often just trying to punch the ball through the middle."

The Mets started driving for the pennant in the middle of August. Grote chose that time to have his hottest streak of the year. He was hitting .218 on August 1 and finished with 43 for 140 in the last two months, .307, to finish at the respectable .252 mark.

There were two other catchers on the Mets, rookie Duffy Dyer and veteran J. C. Martin, but Grote did almost all of the catching in the final two months. He also caught every inning of both the National League Championship series against the Braves and the World Series against the Baltimore Orioles. He was clearly the most significant player defensively the Mets had in 1969.

"I think the game that convinced me we were serious contenders was the Dodger game in June at Shea. The Dodgers
had always been very tough on us. We had them in a scoreless
game in the fifteenth inning. It was the kind of game we always
lost. This time Agee got on first, Garrett hit a single, and
Willie Davis, the Dodger center fielder, let the ball go
through him for an error. I was certain things were going to
be different now. This time we were making the big play and
the other team was making the mistakes."

The Mets felt from that time on they were in every game
because their pitching and defense, especially Grote, Harrelson, and Agee, were so strong.

"What gave me so much confidence was that I stopped
worrying about what I did at bat. I wanted to work with the
pitchers. Anything I contributed offensively was extra. We
just got to the point where we knew if we could squeeze out
a run in any game we had a chance to win."

Each of the pitchers on that staff was talented in his own
way. Some threw exceptionally hard. Some had nasty sinkers
or sliders. All of them had a distinct understanding of the
strike zone. Few games were lost on bad judgment. The Mets
were a thinking man's team. They made the most of their
talents.

"Actually the most amazing pitcher on the team was
McGraw. Nobody, not Seaver, not Koosman, not Ryan even,
not any of them, had the kind of stuff McGraw had. He had
a great fastball, a great curve, a screwball, and a change that
he could control and pinpoint when he was on. He was a
catcher's dream. It was just impossible to get a good swing
against Tug."

Grote roomed with fellow-Texan Ryan, then a struggling
young hard thrower, and they would talk baseball all night
long.

"Nolan still wasn't sure of himself and sure of his abilities.
He wasn't a regular starter because of the military obligations,

and he never got into a good rhythm all year. But when he was healthy, when he was throwing well, he was as hard to hit as any pitcher I've ever seen. I told him all he needed was regular work and I was sure he would get it. How could anybody ignore that arm very long?"

The Mets pitching jelled in mid-season, and the team rushed to the pennant. Grote knew the roller-coaster ride would not stop until after the Mets had gone through the NL playoffs and the World Series.

"We could shut any team out any day so there was no more concern about the playoffs and Series than there was about any regular season game."

Grote caught every inning of every game with great skill and poise. The Mets, surprisingly, didn't have much pitching in the playoffs but they won easily. They had overwhelming pitching in the Series, and they allowed the Orioles all of six runs in the five Series games. Grote hit .167 in the playoffs and .211 in the Series. He still drew raves from opposing manager Earl Weaver.

"That tough guy behind the plate," Weaver said, "really controls the game for them."

Grote took a pounding behind the plate in the next few years. He caught as few as 59 games in 1972 and 81 in 1973. Although hurt, he played a good part of the time, almost always keeping the injuries secret from the press, sometimes even from his teammates.

On August 31, 1977, the Mets traded Grote to the Dodgers for a couple of minor-leaguers. It hardly made a fuss in the local papers. This was a little more than two and a half months after Seaver had been traded, and the fans were still shell-shocked. Grote did a good job as a backup for the Dodgers and wound up playing in the 1977 and 1978 World Series for Los Angeles against the Yankees. Some of his old newspaper "buddies" found him downright accommodating in those Series interviews.

Grote's life seemed measured by baseball. There was not much success in business for him after he quit, and his stabilizer, Sharon Grote, ended their marriage. He tried several things but what he wanted, really wanted, was to wear that uniform again, squat down behind a hitter, or even make contact with a pitched ball. He began writing letters and calling ball clubs. His reputation had preceded him, and most clubs even refused to show him the courtesy of a return letter or call. They thought he was too hot to handle. He finally landed a baseball job with the Tigers.

"I really enjoyed working with the kids in Lakeland. Around Memorial Day, Lee Walls, who was managing at Birmingham, became quite ill. They called me from Detroit to take over that club. I drove all night to get there and took over for the next game. We finished strong. The next year I was not offered a contract."

The Tigers just say they decided to look elsewhere. There were suggestions in the Detroit press that the Tigers' young farmhands found Grote's abrasive personality a little too hard to take.

Maybe Grote came along a generation too late. He played the game with such animal vigor that it seemed he might have been more comfortable, more appreciated, a lot better off emotionally as a teammate of Ty Cobb's than of Ron Swoboda's. He clearly was not a well-liked personality on that championship team, but those who took the time to get to know him, such as Harrelson, Koosman, Ryan, Boswell, and the occasional sportswriters he exchanged baseball karma with, speak highly of his intelligence, his devotion, his loyalty, and his incredible wisdom about the sport.

"You know," Grote said, "I used to miss it a lot more than I do now. I enjoy being home with my son and I enjoy playing golf and I still enjoy putting a cold beer in my mouth. Maybe being away from it a little longer has given me a better perspective. It was a very special time for me, for all of us. Hell, we were young, winning and having a hell of a time. I have no regrets about any of those days, anything we did with the Mets. It was a wonderful experience."

At forty-six, with some bad times behind him, Grote is looking ahead. It took some time to get that uniform off his back, truly, but he seems finally to have done it.

As Stengel said of Landrith, "If you don't have a catcher you have a lot of passed balls." The Mets of 1969 had one terrific catcher. Grote's only problem was not allowing the world in on that secret.

There was a storybook beginning to the big-league career of Duffy Dyer. He came jogging in from the bullpen on Opening Day of that championship season, picked up a bat, strolled to home plate, took a couple of pitches, and then hit a three-run home run the first time he swung.

If it had been fiction, the three-run shot would have won the game and Dyer would have been carried off the field at Shea by his delirious teammates as Caesar was carried in his chariot by his followers. Dyer got a few handshakes and a pat on the back, but the blow only tied the game. The Montreal Expos, playing the first game in their history, rallied for a run in the tenth inning, and Dyer was all but forgotten in the postgame disappointment. Dyer would hit 30 homers in 14 big-league seasons, none of them quite as memorable as his Opening Day blow in 1969.

Don Robert Dyer ("Duffy" is a family nickname) was born August 15, 1945, in Dayton, Ohio. His father was an accountant who, when struck ill with arthritis, was forced to move his family to a warmer climate. He chose Phoenix, Arizona, where he took up truck driving since he no longer had the coordination for doing the delicate work of an accountant. Dyer, an outstanding athlete at Cortez High School, captained and quarterbacked the football team, made all-state honors, and starred as a catcher on the baseball team. He won a scholarship to Arizona State, where he led the team to the 1965 national championship. Although drafted by the Atlanta Braves that year, he decided to spend another year in college. He was drafted and signed by the Mets after he completed the 1966 college season.

He struggled at Williamsport that first professional season with a .173 average, improved to .246 the next year at Greenville, had another poor season (.194) at Williamsport in 1967, and hit .230 at Jacksonville in 1968. He made the Mets in spring training of 1969.

A soft-spoken young man, who stood six feet tall and weighed a stocky 195 pounds in his playing days, Duffy and his wife, Lynn, a demure-looking blonde, lived in a rented home in Queens. There are three children, two boys and a girl, and the second Dyer son, Kevin, was born in Manhattan while Duffy was on the road with the Mets.

Dyer stayed with the Mets from 1969 through 1974, mostly as a bullpen catcher. He never complained. He made one appearance as a pinch hitter in the 1969 Series and failed to get into a game during the 1973 World Series against Oakland. Dyer was traded for Pittsburgh outfielder Gene Clines after the 1974 season, moved on to Montreal, and finished up as a player with Detroit in 1981. He coached in the Milwaukee Brewers organization in 1981, went into real estate in 1982, missed baseball too much, came back in 1983 as a bullpen coach with the Cubs, managed in the minors for the Twins, and took over the Milwaukee Brewers Double A team in El Paso, Texas. He managed the Milwaukee Triple A club at Denver in 1988, the heir apparent to the big-league job at the age of forty-three. Unfortunately for Dyer, the Milwaukee manager is Tom Trebelhorn, forty years old in January of 1988.

\* \* \*

He seems hardly older than he did a couple of decades ago, that first day at Shea. There is a handsome brush mustache and some lines around the edges of his mouth, and he is actually lighter than he was as a player. He holds a catcher's mitt in his strong hands as he watches the giddy old campers go through their straining exercises. Duffy Dyer is sitting in the sun at a training complex of the Cincinnati Reds in Tampa, Florida. He is wearing his Mets uniform as an instructor in the Mets dream camp being conducted shortly before Dyer has to report to his team's training site at Chandler, Arizona, a short drive from his home outside Phoenix. He chooses his words carefully and smiles when he reminisces about that first day at Shea.

"I was out in the bullpen warming somebody up when the phone rang. Piggy answered it and then he turned to me and said, 'Go on in. They want you to hit.' I wasn't aware of the situation in the game because I was concentrating on getting the pitcher ready. I just grabbed my jacket and started racing in. By the time I got to the dugout and got a bat, I was shaking. I was scared to death. Don Shaw was the pitcher and he had been in the Mets organization and I knew him. I settled down after I got to the plate, took a pitch and caught my breath. Then he threw a high slider and I hit it hard. I saw it was going out as I started running. I guess I was jogging around second base when I realized what I had done. 'My God, I've hit a homer my first time up.' That was really exciting. My knees felt weak."

Dyer would get into only 29 games that first season with 74 at bats. When the roster got jammed up in early July with returnees from military reserve duty, Gil Hodges sent him to Tidewater. He remained there until August 9.

"I guess I made the ball club in spring training. I had been doing well but wasn't sure what the situation was. I knew Grote was the number-one catcher and J.C. Martin would be there because he was a left-handed hitter. The only question seemed to be whether or not they would carry three catchers. With about a week to go, Hodges called me into his office. 'We're going to carry three catchers. You're going north with us.' That was all he said. I just felt thrilled."

At twenty-three, Dyer got his first look at Shea Stadium on that first day of the 1969 season.

"I was just in awe of the surroundings. The park seemed so huge after playing in the minors, and when I went to the bullpen as the game started I looked up and saw the place almost filled. It was an incredible experience."

After that first big day, things settled into a quiet routine for Dyer. He would most often warm up the starting pitcher. Some twenty minutes before the game he would march to the bullpen, get the pitcher ready, pick out his spot on the bullpen bench, and remain there all game. There would be an occasional pinch-hitting spot, even a start here and there when Hodges decided Grote needed a rest, but mostly it was a summer spent behind the bullpen fence in right field.

"I really learned a lot being out there. Don Cardwell and Cal Koonce were there a good part of the time, and they were two very knowledgeable guys. I never felt that the team was separated by older guys and younger guys as sometimes happens. There were no cliques on that team. I was close to everybody. Garrett was my roommate, but we would go out with all the guys on the road, Seaver, Koosman, Ryan, Garrett, Gentry. It was just a good bunch of guys."

Some of the wives were even closer to each other than the players were to their teammates. Lynn Dyer and Janet Gentry were almost always together, two young baseball wives from the Phoenix area, bound by their youth, their insecurities about New York, and the pressures of being baseball wives, never an easy job.

"They still talk on the phone and visit once in a while. Actually our closest friends in New York were the people whose home we rented. They lived next door and were very friendly older people. They were like grandparents to the kids, and we would often leave the children with them and go out on an occasional day off. We enjoyed our relationship with them very much."

Despite not getting much playing time, Dyer always felt he was a significant part of the team.

"We had great pitching and I was a part of that, working with them, warming them up, helping in any way I could. I always felt good when we had a strong pitched game as if I had contributed in some small way. There was a lot of pitching talk around that team, with all the pitchers, the catchers, and Rube and Piggy, who had been catchers and were now coaches. It was just a wonderful situation every way you looked at it."

Dyer said he enjoys seeing the guys from the 1969 Mets at an occasional reunion but has no close friends today among any of his former mates.

"People's lives move in different directions. I'm still in baseball so I run across some guys who are in the game. The others all live too far away. I don't have much time to think of that season. I'm trying to concentrate on winning with my own ball club."

Once in a while, when he wants to motivate his players and they spot that World Series ring on his finger and they ask about it, he shyly admits he played on a world championship team.

"If somebody is my age or older, they probably know I was on that team. Kids can't know that. I just remind them the ring is what it is all about and if they work hard it is possible for them."

Dyer is hopeful a big-league job will open up for him. For now, he enjoys working with young players, playing an occasional round of golf, and relaxing with his family.

"You know what I think about most involving that team? That we were all so young and it seemed to happen so fast and maybe we didn't pause long enough to enjoy it as much as we should have. You go through something like that, you have fun, but you don't feel the impact until it is too late. Sometimes I wish I could have stopped time for just a little bit in 1969."

Duffy Dyer was a solid citizen of the 1969 Mets, not spectacular, not covered with stardust, not an emotional, gabby player. He was a team player in a team sport. You would feel comfortable sharing a foxhole with Duffy Dyer in any battle.

He was one of the senior citizens of the Mets that summer, a farm boy from Virginia who had helped pick corn and hay as a kid and now, at thirty-two in his eleventh big-league season, finally had a chance to win.

Joseph Clifton Martin was born December 13, 1936, in Axton, Virginia. Called J.C. as a youngster, he was signed by the Chicago White Sox out of high school in 1956. He spent five years in the minors before making it to Chicago. A tall, handsome first baseman with dimpled cheeks and a broad smile, standing six feet, two inches and weighing 188 pounds, Martin was converted into a catcher by manager Al Lopez in 1962. He came to the Mets after the 1967 season in a deal involving third baseman Ken Boyer. He backed up Grote in 1968 and got into 66 games in 1969 as a part-time receiver and pinch hitter with a .209 average. He won one game with a hit in a 1–0 victory for Gentry in June, and won another with a two-run homer against the Reds in July. His most memorable play came in the fourth game of the World Series when Baltimore left-handed pitcher Pete Richert fielded his pinch bunt, whirled, and threw to first. The ball hit Martin on the left wrist and bounced away, which allowed Rod Gaspar to score from second base with the winning run in the only World Series game Tom Seaver ever won.

Controversy swirled around the play. Press-box observers

clearly believed Martin was out of the base line when the throw hit him. Later photos indicated conclusively that was the case. When asked after the game how the throw managed to hit him, Martin smiled and said, "I swelled up."

Martin finished his career with the Cubs after the 1972 season, coached and managed in the minors for a while, worked for a rubber company, started his own construction business only to see it fail, worked in excavation, and ran an electric utilities business. Two or three years ago he went to work for a local nursery in the Chicago area where he lives with his wife, Barbara. They have three grown children and one grandchild. He is involved in landscaping, works with trees, drives a truck for the nursery, and puts in long hours.

"I'm still in baseball," he drawls, as he sits in the living room of his home in Wheaton, Illinois. "I'm involved with Koosman in this program for youngsters called America's Best. We recruit kids to work with us in improving their skills. These are mostly high school boys, and we are trying to get them college scholarships. Maybe a few of them will get signed, but that's not the point of the program."

Martin still would like to get back into baseball. He didn't like the way he left it a few years back.

"I called Bobby Winkles, who was running the White Sox minor-league department. He hired me to manage a rookie team. Then management changed. Hawk Harrelson took over, and he fired me without even talking to me. I felt upset about that."

Martin was always a low-key, soft-spoken man, slow to anger, but he remembers when he did get most angry in 1969.

"We were sitting in the bullpen one night during a game with the Cards. Harry Caray was the announcer, and we had a radio out there. He started talking about our ball club, and all of a sudden he starts putting the whole club down. 'There isn't one guy on this Mets roster who could make the Cards lineup.' Well, we felt that was a cheap shot. We talked about it and told the other guys after the game, and we decided we would show them we could play. I never did like the Cards. Then we go and win the division, and we clinched it against the Cards at Shea. I felt like going up to the radio booth and asking Harry if he thought any of us could make the Cards."

Martin also remembered Koosman hitting Ron Santo in Chicago in the big series against the Cubs.

"That delivered a message and I think there was never any question about our team after that."

Martin said he knew his role on that team and played about as much as he had expected. He got some big hits in his occasional appearances but is still asked most of the time about the World Series play when he shows up at a baseball-card show or convention.

"I kid around with the fans and show them how I swelled up. I just stick my arms out. I don't care what some people say about the play or what I did. The umpire said I was safe so I must have been safe."

Teammate Al Weis lives in the Chicago area, but Martin said he has seen him only at a Mets reunion at Shea.

"I think that everybody goes in their own direction after they get out of baseball. It was different with us; we didn't make a million dollars. My top salary was something like thirty thousand dollars so I had to go to work right away when I got out of the game. I didn't make a million bucks the way these guys do today. I would have liked that. I wouldn't have minded getting fat."

Martin says he is too busy now to spend much time watching baseball on television or going to the ball park in Chicago.

"I'll tell you when I did get interested again. That was during the 1986 World Series. The Mets were in it against Boston and I guess I'm still a little bit of a Met fan and I like to see how they are doing. I was watching it and all of a sudden they started playing some old film from the Mets' other World Series in 1973 and 1969. They played my old play again at first base and I could see that ball bouncing off my wrist. It didn't hurt a bit then and it doesn't hurt now. I just get a kick out of seeing that ball roll away and old Rodney [Gaspar] running around those bases and getting in for that winning run. That's a satisfying scene, yes sir, it certainly is."

Martin is working hard these days, but he seems content. He is close to his family and doesn't mind working hard for a living. Catchers always work hard.

"Maybe when you have grown up on a farm you are used to hard work. I don't know. I don't mind it. It's like catching. You work with your hands and you are in the dirt all day. I've been in the dirt before. It doesn't bother me one single bit."

Casey Stengel used to say third-string catchers might cause more trouble on a ball club than moody stars. They don't play much and they almost always let the manager hear about it. On the 1969 Mets, Jerry Grote was the main man. Both Duffy Dyer and J. C. Martin understood that. More importantly, they went along with the program. It may well be that Dyer and Martin, with their willingness to accept secondary roles, had as much to do with the team success as anybody. No one felt left out on that team. A championship ring was earned by all.

# 8

# *Safe at Third*

June 2, 1969: President Richard Nixon, in an angry talk at General Beadle College in Madison, South Dakota, today assailed what he called "attempts at insurrection" in cities and colleges across the country. Demonstrations against the war in Vietnam and against racism at home continued unabated. While Nixon attacked students for opposing the war in the United States, President Thieu announced in Saigon that he expected his government to crush the Viet Cong. "There will be no compromise with the Viet Cong, no coalition government," he said in an outright rejection of proposals for shared power. Included in the latest casualty list from Southeast Asia were the names of Sgt. George Robert Palermo, twenty-five, of Boston, killed in a small-arms fire fight, Sgt. Dennis Glenn Prince, twenty, of Westland, Michigan, dead of multiple fragmentation wounds, and Cpl. Preston Taylor, Jr., eighteen, of Sumter, South Carolina, killed by small-arms fire. In Washington, the Senate Judiciary Committee unanimously approved Nixon's nomination of Warren E. Burger as the next chief justice of the United States Supreme Court after a committee hearing lasting one hour and forty-five minutes.

Jerry Koosman beat Los Angeles Dodgers left-hander Claude Osteen, 2–1, at Shea Stadium. It put the Mets at .500 with a 23–23 record. They had achieved that goal for the first time only eleven days earlier when Tom Seaver beat Phil

Niekro for an 18–18 mark. One of the big Mets hits came from third baseman Ed Charles. "Never throw a slider to the Glider," said Koosman in a happy Mets clubhouse.

He was the father figure of the 1969 Mets, the oldest player on the team that season, thirty-six years old that April, a gentle, sensitive, wounded man. Edwin Douglas Charles was the spiritual leader of the Mets. He had spent eleven years in the minor leagues, a victim of racism as well as his own stubborn pride. He had wasted so many seasons of his talent, seemingly always out of sync with the teams he joined. He had flecks of gray in his hair and constantly fought the fleshiness he so easily acquired around his face and under his belt.

He had made the team the season before as an invited nonroster player from the Mets minor-league team at Jacksonville. He had forced Gil Hodges to keep him with his spirited play and responded with a sparkling .276 season, a club-leading 15 home runs and a league-leading 3 pinch home runs. He had joined the Mets originally in 1967 after being purchased from Kansas City. His career appeared over when he was placed on the Jacksonville roster that winter but was taken north by Hodges after spring training in 1968 as a backup third baseman. His experience as well as his sunny disposition, despite so many hurts, convinced Hodges he could help his young team.

In 1969 he could speak softly to the two emotional black players, Tommie Agee and Cleon Jones, soothing their anger, weaning them away from hate, integrating them finally into the oneness of the team.

Charles was a deeply caring man, always available for hospital visits and charity causes. He wrote sweet stanzas of poetry, some touching on the hurt in his heart over the frustrations of his life, on and off the baseball field. He had been shunted aside for others so many times in baseball. In his own life, he had been scarred by the birth of a son with cerebral palsy. He and his wife, Betty, struggled to deal with this crushing blow. By mid-season of 1969, no longer ashamed, he began bringing the five-year-old boy to the ball park, dressing him in a Mets uniform, watching him perform as best he could during the adventures of Family Day.

Ed Charles was born in Daytona Beach, Florida, on April 29, 1933, the fifth child of a father who worked as baker-bartender and a mother who was a domestic. Damaged by the depths of Florida's racism, he escaped into the world of sports, starring in baseball, basketball, and football at his all-black high school. In 1947, at thirteen, his life was changed forever by the arrival of the Brooklyn Dodgers for an exhibition game in his hometown. Jackie Robinson was on that team, soon to be elevated to the big leagues. Charles watched the game that day in the black, segregated section of the old park, along with some very old black people, some very young, and even some crippled citizens who dragged their damaged bodies to the game for this historic event. When it was over, Charles and his friends followed the Dodgers on foot to the railroad station and watched as these famous players boarded their train north. Charles had eyes only for one man, that big, black first baseman, Jackie Robinson. "We followed the train after it left as far as we could. We figured we could stay close to Jackie by holding on to the track after it. We ran as far as we could and then we put our heads down on the track to feel the vibrations, to stay with Jackie Robinson as long as possible."

There was a breakup of his parents' marriage, some violence in his home, many pressures from the anguish of poverty. He dropped out of school after the eighth grade, crossed the state to St. Petersburg and moved in with his grandfather, a Baptist minister. He played at Gibbs High School in St. Petersburg but left school again after the tenth grade, unhappy with his environment, uncertain of his future. He drifted back to Daytona Beach and joined up with some friends in forming a semiprofessional black team, the Daytona Beach Dodgers.

"We were all Dodger fans by then because of Jackie, but we didn't believe there would be a place for us in white baseball. There were only one or two Negro players then, and it all seemed like too much of a dream. My hope was to make the Negro League teams."

At seventeen he was playing for a Negro team in St. Petersburg in early March of 1951 when the phone rang in his grandfather's home. A man said he wanted to talk to an Edwin Charles. "I got on the phone and this fellow said he had seen me play at Gibbs High and around St. Petersburg and he wondered if I would come to a tryout camp the Boston Braves were having at Al Lang Field in St. Petersburg the next day. I went, but it was the same runaround. They looked at me for a few minutes and then said they would contact me. I heard nothing and soon signed with the Indianapolis Clowns in the Negro League for two hundred dollars a month. I thought it was a fortune. I figured that was where I would spend my career."

The following spring, 1952, Charles received another call from the same scout, Hugh Wise, who had seen him the year before. This time he wanted Charles to show up at another camp the Braves were running, in Myrtle Beach, South Carolina. The Braves would pay his expenses.

"I showed up there and I'm shaking like a leaf. This was a real opportunity. If they had called me back I knew they had to be interested. I didn't do very well, but after it was over Hugh Wise comes up to me. 'Are you the same kid I saw last spring? You don't even look like the same kid.' I had grown and matured. They said they were interested and would let me know. I figured it was the same story. I left Myrtle Beach and went up to Harlem in New York, where I had an aunt. I thought I'd see the big city. They called me there and offered me a contract. I was dazed."

Charles reported to manager George McQuinn at their Class C team in Quebec City, Canada. Thus he would begin an odyssey of eight teams in eleven years with a season out for military service in Germany in 1954, where he was voted the outstanding player in the Army in Europe.

"Every time I talked to the Braves about moving to a big-league club, especially after I had good seasons in Triple A at Wichita (.284) and Louisville (.270) and Vancouver (.305), there would be another excuse. Let's face it. There was a quota system for black players. I didn't make the cut."

Finally, in December of 1961, his contract was traded by the Braves to the Kansas City A's. He hit .288 for Charlie Finley's Kansas City team and made the league's all-rookie team in 1962 at the advanced age of twenty-nine.

"I was making the minimum of seven thousand dollars, and in the middle of the season Finley tore up my contract and gave me a new one for ten thousand dollars. After the season, Charlie said he would give me a five-thousand-dollar raise. When I got my contract it called for a salary of twelve thousand. I expected fifteen thousand, five thousand over the ten I finished with. I called Charlie up. He said, 'I told Pat Friday (KC's general manager) to give you a five-thousand-dollar raise. Didn't he do it?' I told him it was only three thousand over the final figure of the year before. 'That's what you're getting. Take it or leave it.' Then Charlie hung up the phone. I never played with much enthusiasm in Kansas City after that. Maybe I hurt myself. I was just sour about the whole thing."

Charles hit .246 for KC in 1967. They thought he was finished and shipped him to New York for cash. He hit .238 in 1967, .276 in 1968, and .209 in spot duty with the 1969 Mets. His style and grace on the field was eye-catching, earning him the nickname of the Glider.

\* \* \*

It is a crisp fall afternoon on Manhattan's Upper West Side. Ed Charles lives in a small apartment in the shadow of Columbia University. A group of black girls are jumping rope in the street across from his home. One end of the rope is tied to a fence at the entrance of the Academy of Seventh Day Adventists. His building is neatly kept, but the structure is severely in need of repair and a coat of paint.

At fifty-five, he is heavier and his hair is almost all white around the edges. His voice is strong, and there is some of the old, familiar singsong lilt. The apartment is small but tastefully furnished. There are no signs of his baseball past anywhere. Divorced by Betty in 1983, he now lives alone. His handicapped son, Eric, now twenty-three, is in a care facility outside Kansas City.

"I see him occasionally. He is doing well. My other son, Eddie, was born in 1970, and he's a terrific kid. He comes to stay with me sometimes. He has played in high school."

Charles had worked for the Mets as a scout and minor-league instructor for several years. It ended in 1983.

"Eddie was coming down to see me in Florida. It was timed so as not to interfere with my regimen with the Mets. I was working with Ken Berry, and we reported to Steve Schryver, the Mets minor-league boss. I was there early and took off to see Eddie in St. Petersburg. Berry complained to Schryver, and Schryver called me up and yelled, 'You think you can take off anytime you want because you were a big-leaguer. It doesn't work that way around here.' I had worked for them for nine years. That was uncalled for. I left."

Charles feels the entire situation had racial overtones.

"I was making nineteen thousand dollars a year. They thought they were doing me a favor. They had talked of giving me Tommy Holmes' job the next year if Tommy retired. He was the director of community relations, and they said he was retiring. They told me that for three years, and I didn't believe them anymore. I just kept my head high and left."

In 1986, Charles took the civil service exam in New York City. He passed and was appointed to the city's Juvenile Justice Department. He works with kids on parole, kids needing guidance, kids hopeful of avoiding more trouble.

"I'm making about what I made with the Mets. I can stay here until I retire and make thirty thousand dollars. I enjoy the kids, I enjoy the job. I'm not bitter. I'm just disappointed in the Mets."

There is a glow in his face when he talks of the 1969 Mets. He was so important to that team, so much a part of their character, so valuable off the field as well as on.

"The guys poked fun at me for my age and the way I played, and I took it all in fun. 'Never throw a slider to the Glider.' Koosman said that all the time. Guys gravitated to me because I was older, both the black and the white players. Being in the minors so long was something a lot of them couldn't understand. They had made the bigs after a year or two. When I first got there in 1967, they would laugh after losing games. That changed with Hodges. I wanted to make sure the guys didn't slip back into that frame of mind after the 1968 season. I stayed on them all the time that next year. Nobody laughed when we lost. We were playing serious baseball."

Charles said there were some disagreements, some tensions, around that team as there were around any team.

"When I heard things I would go over and talk to the guy and squash it. If I saw something brewing I would get in the middle, act as a cooler head. I felt comfortable with all those guys, Koosman, Seaver, Swoboda, Kranepool, everybody. Some guys had trouble with Seaver. He was a perfectionist. A lot of guys took this as snobbishness. I don't think Kranepool and Swoboda really liked Seaver. He just demanded excellence. One problem, and you would hear it all the time, was the electronic media. They focused on Nancy Seaver, and some of the other wives didn't take too kindly to that. It wasn't her fault. They weren't deciding what to put on the air."

Charles said there were some remarks passed privately among the Mets about Cleon Jones.

"Guys said he didn't play hard, and I would get in the middle and tell them he was putting out even if it didn't look like it. Some guys don't look like they are hustling when they are. I know Hodges took him out that one time, but Cleon said he was hurt. I believed him. I think Cleon got a bad rap. The guy hit .340. What did they expect, .440?"

Charles did not think he would be around for the 1969 season. The way things worked out, he was a vital part of that machine.

"Mama Payson saw me after the 1968 season, and she said that the Mets would have to expose me to the draft. They were adding teams in Montreal and San Diego, and I knew I would be left off the roster. I asked her if I could come to spring training if I wasn't picked and win a job the way I had the year before. She said I could and as it turned out they had me on the expansion list, I wasn't picked, and I stayed on the roster."

One of the jobs Charles took upon himself in the spring of 1969 was working with a talented youngster named Amos Otis. Charles was going to help Otis learn how to play third base. If it worked out, Otis would probably take Charles's job.

"I wanted to help him and I didn't worry about my job. I thought they would keep me as a pinch hitter anyway. He just didn't want to learn that position. He just hated third base. He was afraid of the ball down there and he wasn't going to learn."

By the time the season started, Hodges had decided to platoon young Wayne Garrett, a left-handed hitter, with the right-handed–hitting Charles.

"After a while I had these vibes with Gil. I wouldn't say anything and he wouldn't say anything, but I always knew what he wanted. I think I acted as his emissary on the field."

By mid-season Hodges had that platoon working smoothly.

Charles played third against left-handers, and Garrett played against right-handers. Hodges used platoon situations at first, second, third and right field.

"It wasn't just going against left-handers and right-handers," said Charles. "It also helped rest our guys. One of the reasons we caught the Cubs was that we were stronger in July and August. They were older and more tired than us."

Charles became a fan favorite that season by exuding a rare warmth and charm. He deeply enjoyed being with people, and in his advanced baseball years, finally on a winner, it took away so much of the sting from his early frustrating seasons. Sportswriters hung around his locker after each game exchanging pleasantries. He was always open, warm, and intelligent.

"I have had my share of disappointments, but the Glider is tough. I always fought back. That year made it all worthwhile."

When Jerry Koosman got the final out of the World Series against Baltimore at Shea, the glowing smile of Ed Charles seemed to radiate through the Stadium. His photograph, leaping and laughing, was carried across the country as Jerry Grote jumped on the pitcher. Less than three weeks later it all turned sour.

The Mets decided to release Charles. He was not shocked though the press rallied to his side.

"It had been discussed in the spring. I was almost thirty-seven, and they had a lot of kids coming up. It just happened sooner than I thought. The Mets offered me a job in the promotion department. Johnny Murphy said I could start work right away. I was living in Kansas City, and we had to find the right school for Eric and my son, Eddie, was on the way and we had to organize a lot of things. The Mets said they would give me five thousand dollars for relocation expenses. I thought that was fair and I went home to Kansas City to work it all out with Betty and I called Johnny Murphy one day and asked him to send me the five thousand dollars. All of a sudden there was some stumbling and bumbling about that five thousand dollars. The long and short of it was that they didn't want to pay it to me because I had an apartment in Queens and they considered that my home. That just left a real sour taste in my mouth for the Mets. I stayed around New York, but I never did feel real comfortable about them for a long time."

He took a promotion job for Buddah records in New York, an outfit owned by Art Kass, later to marry Carole Kranepool, and he opened a short-lived novelty-item business.

"There were a lot of financial pressures in our marriage. We had a lot of bills because of Eric, and I wasn't making a great deal of money. Betty never could quite understand that it took time to work my way back up in business. I stayed with business for a few years, but I always wanted to get back into baseball. Then the Mets asked me to scout for them and work with their kids in 1978 and I accepted."

A few years back Ed Charles began drawing his baseball pension, some fifteen hundred dollars a month, a decent stipend when combined with his city job. He shows up at Shea Stadium for special events, brings some of his charges to the park, and appears yearly at the baseball dream camps in Florida, suiting up and instructing the overaged campers with the same enthusiasm he showed twenty years ago.

"I don't feel angry about the past. I enjoyed it. I played on a great championship team. That's something a lot of guys don't get. I've had some bumps but I don't let them get me down. You know my only regret? I didn't fulfill my ability. I should have been a better player and had a longer career. Eight years wasn't enough. It could have been different if I had gotten to the Mets earlier. The fans here appreciated me. They loved the Glider and I loved them."

It was late afternoon now, and the Glider walked back to his apartment, past some bustling Manhattan streets, past some rowdy teenagers, past some busy neighborhood stores. Nobody noticed him.

"Once in a while, when I am trying to reach the kids, I wear my World Series ring and talk to them about baseball. 'You played for the Mets?' They don't know. They weren't born then. I tell them I did, and they want to talk about Strawberry or Mookie or Hernandez. They don't have a sense of the time. How could they? It all rushes by so fast. It was sweet. I don't dwell on it. I do remember it. The way the team played, the excitement, the way everybody in the city got involved in it, well, it was just one big happening."

He was the youngest of them all that summer, just twenty-one, a Huckleberry Finn look-alike with flaming red hair, freckles, large teeth, and a contagious smile. Ronald Wayne Garrett, the third son of a baseball-playing family, was just a little more than three years out of Sarasota High School in Florida when he arrived at the Mets spring training camp. The Mets had drafted him out of the Atlanta Braves organization at the winter meetings the previous December, and he quickly impressed Gil Hodges that March with his bat speed and smooth glove. He was five feet, eleven inches tall, weighed 170 pounds, ran well, and threw accurately from third base. The Mets had spent eight years now searching for a third baseman to call their own ever since Don Zimmer, the original Opening Day third baseman, had failed miserably. Zimmer had gone hitless in 33 at bats that first season, collected a single, and was traded a day later. Explained Casey Stengel, "We had to trade him while he was still hot."

There would be a longing for Joe Torre of the Braves to play third base for them and an aborted attempt at converting spindly outfielder Amos Otis into a third baseman. Torre would be moved to the Cardinals, and Otis would refuse to make the attempt for the Mets. Ground balls off his chest were simply not a happy thought for a youngster soon to be christened Famous Amos, famous for refusing an offer to become a regular at third.

Shortly before spring training ended, Hodges would make the commitment to go north with Ed Charles and Wayne Garrett, the oldest and youngest players on the team, as his third-base platoon.

"He came to me with about a week to go," Garrett remembers, "and said I had made the ball club. It was just an offhand remark as he passed me in the clubhouse, but my heart was pounding the rest of the day."

Wayne Garrett was born December 3, 1947, in Brookville, Florida. His father, Henry, ran a small land-development business in Florida's west coast, operated his own crane, and worked long hours. All three of his sons, Adrian, Jim, and Wayne, played baseball, with Adrian Garrett spending eight years in the big leagues as a utility player. Wayne was an outstanding shortstop at Sarasota High and was drafted and signed by the Braves in 1965 at seventeen. At Sarasota, his first season, he batted .269 in 43 games. He moved up the ladder of the Braves organization quickly but never hit very much. The Braves left him unprotected after the 1968 season, and the Mets drafted him off the Shreveport roster for twenty-five thousand dollars.

Garrett hit only .218 that championship season in 124 games but fielded well and gave Hodges an extra left-handed bat for his platoon system. Garrett collected 5 hits in 13 at bats in the playoff against the Braves for a .385 mark. He batted only once in the Series, as Hodges used Charles against the Baltimore left-handers.

Garrett had his finest all-around season during the next pennant year of 1973 with a .256 average and suddenly found power resulting in 16 home runs. That fall he damaged his shoulder and could never throw well again.

"I had gotten to know the great jockey Eddie Arcaro

through a mutual friend. Arcaro owned some property in the Tennessee mountains near Gaithersburg. He had never actually seen the property, and he asked our mutual friend to take a look at it for him. We went down there together after the 1973 World Series and looked at the land. We were out riding horses through some of the back country. I had ridden before, so I was not concerned. We took this tame horse out and went through the property. It was huge.

"We came back to the stable and we were actually just sitting there quietly when for no reason the horse reared up and threw me. I was falling and reached out with my right arm to brace myself against the fall. I put a lot of weight on that arm and tore it up. It hurt all the time. The next spring I just couldn't throw. I never told the ball club but I was always in pain. It was probably a rotator tear, but in those days nobody knew what a rotator tear was."

Garrett played with the Mets through July of 1976 before being traded to Montreal. He injured his knee sliding in a game with the Expos in 1977, was traded to the Cardinals the next season, and finished his career in St. Louis. He was thirty years old.

"I just couldn't run anymore. The Cards could see that. I got an offer to go to Japan for two years and I accepted it. They paid me a hundred and twenty-five thousand dollars for the two seasons, about twice as much as I was making in the big leagues."

He went into the real estate business when he came back to Florida, worked as a site selector for an investment firm, saw the business dry up, tried selling on his own, struggled with that, explored a few other business opportunities to no avail. In the spring of 1988 he was driving a package-delivery truck.


He is wearing a Mets uniform as he sits in the locker room of the Cincinnati Reds old training complex in Tampa, Florida.

He is one of the instructors at a dream camp, and he is on vacation from his job. His hair is as thick and red as ever, but there are some deepening lines on his face and some small flab around his middle. He appears strong and agile and could probably get into big-league shape in a few days. He has recently celebrated his fortieth birthday.

"I thought I'd be all right after baseball. The outside world is more difficult than I expected. I really didn't want to stay in baseball after 1980. I was just sick of the traveling."

He is on his third marriage, and this time he thinks it will work.

"I was about twenty-two when I married Donna and she was twenty-seven. She had been married when she was seventeen and had two daughters, and I adopted them. The marriage just didn't work."

Donna Garrett was a busty brunette who loved to sit around the swimming pool wearing a tight bathing suit at the team hotel in Florida or on the road with the club. She had a marvelous figure, and sportswriters managed to interview Garrett more often when Donna was around than when she wasn't. Garrett laughed at the attention his wife received from onlookers. He never heard the snickers and the snide remarks. Baseball wives often drip with venom.

"Donna didn't know anything about baseball. She just enjoyed the attention. She wanted to be a star. When we won in 1973, she was thrilled at all the attention she got in the World Series. The next year we finished fifth and were out of it early. When it got towards October, Donna heard something on television about the World Series starting. 'When are we going?' She just didn't understand."

Garrett was single during the 1969 season. He met Donna two years later.

"That 1969 year I had a good time. I was just discovering everything, New York, night life, being a big-league ballplayer, having fun at all times. It was terrific. I did a little drinking. Gil was like a father to me and he would look at my eyes and say, 'You had too much to drink.' One time he said that and I hadn't been out. I told him he was falsely accusing me. In the three years I played for Gil, I never lied to him once."

By 1978, with his big-league career winding down, tensions increased between Garrett and Donna. They were soon divorced, and Donna remarried.

"I had adopted her daughters, and I didn't want to deal with that if I no longer was married to her. I gave up the children, and the new husband adopted them. I stayed friendly with the kids, and they would call me every so often. They called me once to tell me that Donna was sick. Then I heard she had cervical cancer. It wasn't long after that that I heard she had died. It all happened so fast."

Soon afterward, Garrett met an airline stewardess from Virginia. She also had two daughters. They soon married. It was a problem from the start.

"I was out of baseball now and I was struggling in the real estate business. We just didn't have any money. I was starving and she wanted fancy things. That marriage only lasted a couple of years."

Five years ago Garrett met and married his third wife, Connie. They have two children of their own.

"This one is going to work," he said. "It should. I have a lot of experience in marriage."

Garrett is a bouncy, friendly man but with an air of shyness about him.

"I never really liked the celebrity part of being in New York. I couldn't walk down a street then without somebody knowing me and yelling at me. I lived in Manhattan in 1969, and I used to ride the subway to the ball park. Kids were always recognizing me. Now nobody knows I ever played ball. People don't care about things like that in Florida. They just come down to Florida to die."

A couple of years back, Garrett was sitting in a restaurant in Panama City, Florida, with his family.

"This guy comes over almost as soon as he gets in there and he says, 'You look an awful lot like Wayne Garrett of the Mets.' What am I gonna do, lie? I admitted I was. He pulls out a pen and asks for my autograph and it was all very nice. Actually I was surprised that somebody in Florida, in an out-of-the-way place like that, would know me. Then he smiled at me and said, 'In 1969 I was living in New York and I must have gone to thirty Mets games that year.' Nobody in Florida who hasn't lived in New York knows who I am."

Since third base seemed to be the most significant Mets problem when they broke camp in 1969, the success of the platoon system there with Charles and Garrett relieved some pressure on the team.

"I think I could have played every day but Gil knew best. He got a lot out of both of us and it certainly kept the Glider going strong all year."

Ballplayers then still had roommates. Now they all make so much money they are willing to pay the difference between single and double rooms, if that is necessary, and almost all room alone. It may well be one of the reasons players today seem to get into more trouble, especially with drugs. They often spend more time with outsiders than with teammates.

"Duffy Dyer was my roommate and we got real close. He was very smart and I learned a lot of baseball rooming with him. He only let me down once. We were playing a day game in Chicago the year after the championship, and we had been out late the night before. We overslept and finally jumped up. I looked at the clock and saw what time it was. I knew we would be late and Gil would be all over us, and I was very upset at doing a dumb thing like that. I just swung my arm and gave myself a shot in the head. I forgot I was wearing my World Series ring. The ring caught me flush on the forehead and opened a huge gash.

"Duffy always got us up in time. He missed that day, and Gil fined both of us for being late. He also accused us of being out the night before because he saw the hole in my head. I told him how it really happened. I'm not sure to this day if he believed me."

Garrett enjoyed the game and enjoyed his teammates. He looks forward to the dream-camp activities each year and the old-timer games he attends.

"We used to spend a lot more time with each other than I think ballplayers do today. They make so much money they all seem tied up in ways to invest it. We didn't make enough to invest so it was no problem. I think my top salary with the Mets when I left there was a little over thirty thousand. Then I had my salary cut the next two years. I was single that season we won for the first time, and it was more important to enjoy myself than it was to make money. I used to look forward to road trips to places like Texas where we would have barbecues together at Grote's house or Boswell's or at Shamsky's in St. Louis or at home with Swoboda or Krane or Cleon. It sounds like a cliché but we really were one big, happy family. I think that had an awful lot to do with us winning. Guys really pulled for each other."

If there was one constant to the team, one indisputable force, it was Gil Hodges.

"He liked me from the start. I can't say why. I wasn't that great a player, but I guess I played as hard as I could and I knew the game. I had two older brothers who played, and I really picked things up from them. I may not have made the kind of rookie mistakes that other young players often make. Gil was very smart about baseball, very smart, and I think he appreciated players who understood the intricacies about the game."

Garrett said he looks back now and has to be disappointed that his career was cut short with severe injuries, especially the shoulder problem and the knee injury.

"Baseball isn't like golf. You can't just keep playing well until you are sixty years old. I was running out of steam when I quit. I had so many injuries, I was so discouraged, I was just burned out. I wished it had lasted a few more years, but I probably would have just been hanging on. If I could have played well, run and thrown normally, that would have been different. I went to Japan, took the money, and did as well as I could. I earned my salary there. It wasn't the same. It was just to make a few bucks. It wasn't a lot of fun."

In some few minutes now, Garrett would be on the mound throwing some batting practice to the dream-campers. The sun was hot and the sweat dripped off his forehead and darkened his shirt. He continued throwing for his alloted time until the next pitcher and the next group of chubby hitters took their turn in the batting cage. Ed Charles came in to relieve him as he had so many times in 1969. They kidded about the weak fastballs they were throwing up to these guys—"fifty-five-foot fastballs," they called them—and blamed it all on their lack of treatment from team trainer Tom McKenna. They said they wouldn't remind those dream-campers to tip unless they could get more of McKenna's magic rubdowns in the trainer's room. There was so much warmth in the byplay between the two old teammates, the black man from Florida, the oldest 1969 Met, and the redhead from Florida, the youngest.

Garrett walked off the field now, took off his cap, rubbed his hands through that red hair, and grimaced. Then he moved his right arm in a circular motion.

"I come down here every spring since they started these camps five years ago," he said, "and it still hurts."

There is a note in his voice which suggests Wayne Garrett is not only talking about his sore shoulder.

# 9

# *Armed and Dangerous*

---

July 9, 1969: At the Kennedy Space Center, Florida, all was in readiness today for the launching of *Apollo 11*. The craft was expected to send astronaut Neil Armstrong to his destiny as the first man on the moon. In Moscow, Soviet foreign minister Andrei Gromyko issued a statement condemning Red China for "hostile actions" and clearly making a bid for friendlier relations with the United States. In New York City, the Metropolitan Transportation Authority unveiled new subway cars. MTA chairman William J. Ronan proudly exhibited the cars and bragged about the state-of-the-art air conditioning. In Southeast Asia, heavy fighting continued in the highlands of South Vietnam despite torrential rains. Latest casualties included Sp5 Daniel Sullivan, twenty-one, of Liberty, Mississippi, killed by artillery rocket fire, Sp4 Juan Luis Terrazas, twenty-one, of Los Angeles, dead of multiple fragmentation wounds, and Maj. Thomas Henry Green, forty-three, of Columbus, Georgia, killed in an accident of undisclosed origins.

At Shea Stadium, a twenty-four-year-old Mets pitcher named George Thomas Seaver, who had served six months in the Marines, enthralled 50,709 fans by retiring twenty-five straight Chicago Cub hitters in order. The crowd became enraptured from the sixth inning on. Mets pitching coach Rube Walker had turned to Gil Hodges as early as the second inning and whispered, "He's got enough stuff to pitch a no-hitter."

The Associated Press, sensing a possible perfect game and having only an inexperienced stringer on hand at Shea, dispatched veteran sportswriter Ed Schyler to the Flushing ball park. He entered the stadium as Randy Hundley of the Cubs led off the ninth inning with a bunt. Tom Seaver fielded it for the twenty-fifth straight out. Schyler climbed the ramp to the press level in time to hear a gasping sound in the Stadium, then silence, and finally a huge ovation. Jimmy Qualls, a .234 hitter, had singled to left field to end Seaver's bid for a perfect game. Seaver retired the next two batters after a long, pregnant pause, the Mets won, 4–0, and the Cubs were now only three games ahead of them in the division standings. It was the closest to first place the Mets had ever been at this late stage of a season. A pennant race was on, and the Mets were in it.

After the game, asked by the press his opinion on everything from baseball and moon shots to the war in Vietnam and civil rights disturbances, Seaver said, "I drink beer, I swear, but I keep my hair short. I guess you could say I'm an all-American boy." After the interview Seaver greeted his tearful wife, Nancy, in the runway outside the clubhouse. "What are you crying for? We won, 4–0." She answered, "A one-hit shutout is better than nothing at all, I guess." The victory was the Mets' eighth in their last ten games. Seven pitchers had recorded wins in that period, two by Seaver and one each by Koosman, McGraw, Taylor, Gentry, McAndrew, and Cardwell.

This was in the spring of 1967 in a quiet, friendly little tavern along the beach at the Mets spring-training home of St. Petersburg, Florida. Don Cardwell, a tall, ruggedly handsome Mets pitcher recently acquired from the Pirates in the infamous deal involving Don Bosch, enjoyed a late afternoon cold beer. There was some discussion about the quality of the beer in St. Petersburg as compared to what he had known in Bradenton, the Pirates training base just up the road, and then a sneaky question about the opening-day starting pitcher for the Mets. With a week to go in camp, manager Wes Westrum had guarded that secret with the diligence of a CIA agent.

"Oh, it will be me," said the veteran right-hander, as he nervously rubbed his crew-cut hair after revealing the state secret. "But it shouldn't be."

Cardwell read the puzzled look on my face.

"The best pitcher in camp, the guy who deserves to start, is Seaver, the kid from USC," he said. "Only Wes is too frightened to open with a rookie. Too many questions and too much second-guessing from you guys in the press if he doesn't win."

"Yeah, I remember that," Cardwell was saying now as he sat in his office at Cloverdale Ford in Clemmons, North Carolina, where he is the fleet-truck manager. "I always had a big mouth."

Cardwell opened the 1967 season, but Seaver would open all the rest of them until he was traded away from the Mets in 1977.

"It didn't take a genius to see how good that kid was," said Cardwell.

It didn't take a genius to see how important Cardwell was to the success of the 1969 Mets. He won only 8 games against 10 losses, but he made 21 starts, relieved 9 times, pitched 152 innings, compiled an impressive 3.02 ERA and was always ready when one of the youngsters, Koosman, Gentry, or Ryan, would come down with arm trouble. He was a steadying influence on the team at the age of thirty-three with a long baseball history dating back to D ball in Pulaski, New York, in 1954.

Donald Eugene Cardwell was born in Winston-Salem, North Carolina, on December 7, 1935. He was an exceptional athlete at Winston-Salem High School as the leading scorer on the football and basketball teams, the star pitcher of the baseball team, and the school's best golfer. He was considered one of the finest golfers to ever wear a big-league baseball uniform with scores in the low 70s not unusual. He was nearly full-grown at six feet, four inches tall and 220 pounds when the Philadelphia Phillies signed him to a professional contract with a bonus of five hundred dollars. He reported to Pulaski at the age of eighteen. At twenty-one he was with the Phillies, and the next year, at twenty-two, was a regular starter.

Until being traded to Chicago in 1960 he enjoyed his time with the Phillies, starting and relieving, learning his pitching trade and honing his skills. He also spent a great deal of time with some fast-running Phillies, led by pitchers Dick Farrell and Jim Owens, soon to be immortalized in a *Sports Illustrated* article as "The Dalton Gang." Their escapades were legendary. Teammates tell of the time Farrell, later to be killed in an automobile accident in England, was discovered nude with a young lady on a public beach in Chicago. The cop ordered Farrell to dress, identify himself, and return to his squad car under arrest for indecent exposure. "I'm a married man," explained Farrell, "and as soon as I put these clothes on I'll start running. The only way you can stop me is by shooting me." No shots were fired and Farrell and The Dalton Gang swaggered on for years.

On May 15, 1960, the Phillies traded Cardwell to the Chicago Cubs. Two days later Cardwell made his first start for the Cubs, pitching a no-hitter against the St. Louis Cardinals, and thereby becoming the only pitcher in baseball history to make his first start with a new team after a trade so memorable.

The big, hard thrower was 9–16 that year and 15–14 the next season. He went to Pittsburgh in 1963 and moved over to the Mets in 1966. He was 6–6, 5–9, and 7–13 for bad Mets teams. He was 8–10 with a 3.02 ERA with the 1969 Mets. He also hit his fifteenth career homer that season, the only 1969 homer by a Met pitcher. Perhaps his biggest game was September 12 when he pitched the second game of a doubleheader against Pittsburgh. Jerry Koosman had beaten the Pirates, 1–0, in the first game and driven in the only Mets run. Cardwell repeated the performance with a 1–0 win in the second game and a base hit for the run.

"I hit Dock Ellis' best pitch for a rip single to center," laughs Cardwell. "If the truth be known, he hung a slider but I won't tell anybody."

Cardwell won five games in a row during the stretch drive from August 10—the last win before the Mets were swept in Houston by the Astros and fell a supposedly insurmountable 9½ games out of first place—until September 21. He pitched a scoreless inning against Atlanta in the NLCS but did not make it to the mound in the World Series. He was traded to Atlanta in 1970 and retired soon thereafter.

At fifty-three, Cardwell still wears that crew cut after flirting with long hair for a while. He works for the Ford dealership outside Winston-Salem, playing golf regularly, enjoying vacations with his wife, Sylvia, after three grown children all went out on their own. He weighs 235 pounds, carries it well, and speaks slowly and softly, the ring of North Carolina still coming from his words. There is no doubting the man was an athlete in his time, and he seems quite capable of squeezing off a good curve ball if need be.

"I started work here on January 3, 1971. It was an adjustment, a new life for me, getting up early in the morning, talking to customers. Actually I thought it would be more difficult than it was. I haven't found it a problem."

Cardwell laughed when asked about his strongest memory of the 1969 season.

"You know what I think about when somebody asks me about 1969? It's the strangest thing. All I think of is that Nolan Ryan is still pitching and making another million bucks. He always had that great arm, but he was a struggling kid pitcher in 1969, and now in 1988 he's still out there doing it. I've been retired almost twenty years, and one of my teammates is still pitching."

"I lived in Little Falls, New Jersey, near where Yogi Berra lives, and my children were small then and we really enjoyed the area. When I got over to the Mets in 1967 they weren't a real good ball club and I wasn't sure I would enjoy myself there. Then I started seeing those older, losing players replaced by younger players and I knew something was building. I remember the first time I saw Seaver pitch and I thought to myself, 'Wow, I wonder how many more of these kids they have in the system.' He was just so incredibly accomplished for a young pitcher. That first year he was a rookie, he pitched like he had been around for years. More importantly, he had a strong personality and wanted to win. He was a tremendous influence on that team."

Cardwell roomed with fellow North Carolinian Cal Koonce but was closest to Jerry Koosman despite an age difference of some eight years. "We just liked doing the same things, talking baseball, playing golf on our time off, having a couple of beers, enjoying ourselves. He was a terrific guy to be around."

Cardwell said one of the most satisfying things about the season was sharing it with the people of New York.

"I'd been around baseball a long time by then, Philadelphia, Pittsburgh, Chicago, but there was nothing like New York fans. When they got worked up, they could make an awful lot of noise. I think it helped us a lot, especially in those big games against the Cubs."

Chicago manager Leo Durocher was especially infuriated by Mets fans. He was once asked that season if he thought they contributed to the success of the Mets. He exploded in a vile tirade, something Durocher was well known for. Then he caught his breath and said slowly, "They are the same guys who used to get on me in Brooklyn." Durocher managed the Dodgers, and Brooklyn fans let him know verbally when they thought he wasn't doing a good job. Mets fans did it with banners. One read, during a Chicago series at Shea, "Where's Leo?" Another, close by, read, "Who's Leo?"

Cardwell said that he took his position on that team seriously. "The Mets had a good blend of young and older players. You can't win with just young players, and you certainly won't win with only older players. I think that's why the Cubs blew out that year. They had a lot of old players who got tired. I enjoyed my status on that team as an elder statesman."

Cardwell served another purpose. Big and strong, he was an enforcer, a guy who could use muscle against opponents or teammates if the mission was important. He also had a very soft side. It was in evidence that spring.

His wife, Sylvia, had visited a local doctor for a routine examination. The doctor discovered a swelling on her ankle, and immediate exploratory surgery revealed a malignancy. After the surgery, Sylvia Cardwell spent a long period of convalescence in bed. The obligations of the home and the care of their three small children that winter before the 1969 season fell on Cardwell.

"It was a very difficult time for us," Cardwell said that spring. "The players were on strike, but I had to sign my contract. We had enormous medical bills and expenses for housekeepers. I needed the money. I just had to take care of my family."

He did his work that spring, never complained, stayed in close touch with his family, and contributed heavily to the championship. His wife was able to attend the World Series in Baltimore.

"I still wear my World Series ring. Once in a while somebody sees that big thing and asks me what it is. I showed it to a guy in town recently when I was sitting in a cafeteria for lunch. He asked me if I really played baseball. It's been that long so some people don't know."

Cardwell has returned for a few old-timer events but doesn't have any association with baseball or any of his teammates now. He understands the rules of the game.

"Guys have their own lives to live. We go off in different directions. I used to get a Christmas card from some of the guys but that stops after a while. People move, you lose your addresses, things change—it was a different part of my life."

Without a lot of attention, without a great degree of recognition during those days or now, Cardwell was a mighty presence on the 1969 Mets. He offered advice freely, he led by example, he was a hard worker, he never caused problems, he never showed any jealousy toward his younger, more successful, more flamboyant teammates. He was a rock.

"I had a long career [fourteen years] but that was my most satisfying season. It had always been a dream of mine ever since I was a kid that I would play on a World Series team. It was very important to me that I finally made it."

He left baseball with his head held high, proud of his efforts and satisfied at the results. He has done enough in the automobile business to live a comfortable, unconcerned middle age.

"It was a lifetime dream and I got there. How could anybody complain after that? There are an awful lot of guys who play the game and don't have that kind of satisfaction."

There are a lot of golf courses for Don Cardwell to attack. He has a good time on all of them. The guy knew how to pitch, knew how to win, and knew how to smile.


He swaggered through that 1969 season. Gary Gentry, lean and hard and as rawhide tough as his native Arizona, won 13 games and lost 12 as a cocky rookie in his first big-league season. He started as many games, 35, as Tom Seaver and could have won another half dozen with better bullpen support.

"I always wanted to finish what I started, but Gil was rushing to get me out of there."

He often wore cowboy boots with gold buckles, blue jeans, and plaid shirts. His face was bony, his jaw thrust forward, his eyebrows thick, and his hair long. He had a high-pitched voice and he spoke in choppy sentences. Gentry, ignoring the rookie tradition, spoke up when he felt he was used or abused. He never liked it when Hodges would skip his pitching turn for Seaver or Jerry Koosman, and he often referred to a two-tier pitching staff—Seaver and the rest.

Gentry had been an exceptional college pitcher at Arizona State, leading the Sun Devils to the 1967 college championship. He had also pitched his junior-college team, Phoenix JC, to a national title two years earlier.

He was one of the brightest rookies to come along in years, with a quick mind, a good understanding of the game, and the ability to articulate his thoughts. Gentry made a major contribution to the success of the Mets that year and he won two of the most important games of 1969. He defeated the St. Louis Cardinals, 6–0, on September 24, 1969, at Shea Stadium to clinch the Eastern Division title and set off a wild demonstration by fans at Shea. They enveloped the field, tore up the turf, and stole the bases. More than two hours after the game ended at 9:07 P.M. on a double-play grounder by Joe Torre, long coveted by the Mets and later to be a player and manager for them, Gentry was standing at the mound with Seaver. They examined the destroyed turf as fans remained perched like so many small birds on the deepest part of the wooden center-field fence.

Gentry would have another memorable win in the World Series. After the Mets lost the first game to Baltimore and

1969 World Champion New York Mets

First manager Casey Stengel

Respected skipper Gil Hodges

Tommie Agee

Ken Boswell

Ed Charles

Donn Clendenon

Duffy Dyer

Wayne Garrett

Rod Gaspar

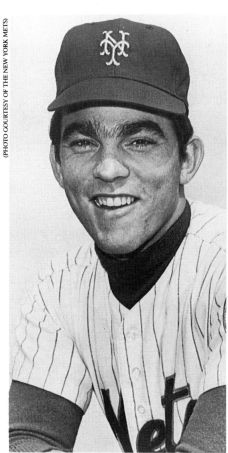

Gary Gentry

Jerry Grote

Bud Harrelson

Cleon Jones

Ed Kranepool

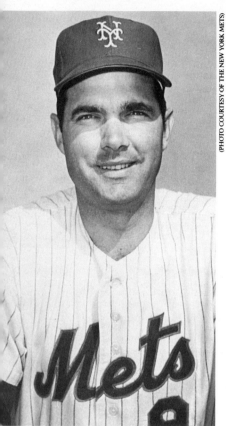

J. C. Martin

Jim McAndrew

Tug McGraw

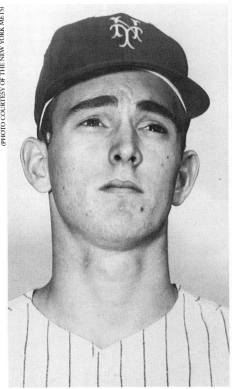

Nolan Ryan

Tom Seaver

Art Shamsky

Ron Swoboda

Ron Taylor

Marvelous Marv Throneberry

Al Weis

World Champion Mets at 1988 Baseball Dream Camp, from left, Bud
Harrelson, Duffy Dyer, Ed Charles, Wayne Garrett, coach Joe Pignatano

Ron Taylor and family

Ed Kranepool outside his Queens factory

Tom Seaver at home in Greenwich, Connecticut

Art Shamsky outside New York restaurant

won the second, Gentry was matched with Baltimore ace Jim Palmer. He outpitched Palmer, hit a two-run third-inning double, held the Orioles scoreless into the seventh inning, when he walked the bases loaded with two outs and turned the game over to Nolan Ryan. The young fastballer pitched two and a third scoreless innings to save the Mets win for Gentry.

"He was better than we thought," Baltimore manager Earl Weaver said of Gentry. "He threw harder and he had a better breaking ball. We expected to split the first two games with Seaver and Koosman and beat Gentry. It didn't work that way."

Baltimore general manager Frank Cashen, later to build the Mets championship team of 1986, would make a sour face whenever he heard Gentry's name.

Gentry was 9–9 in the next season and 12–11 in 1971. He struggled through a 7–10 season in 1972 under new manager Yogi Berra.

"Every time I started a game for Yogi he would start looking in the bullpen about the fifth inning, and I would be out of there in the sixth. I just couldn't pitch that way."

Gentry's arm also began bothering him that season. He was traded that November 1972 to Atlanta along with relief pitcher Danny Frisella for left-hander George Stone and second baseman Felix Millan. They would help the Mets win again in 1973.

Gentry underwent surgery to remove a bone chip in his elbow in 1973 and later underwent a more complicated procedure on his arm. The Braves waited for his arm to show new life, but it never happened. Gentry was released by the Braves after the 1975 season with a 46–49 career record in seven seasons. He went home to Phoenix. He was twenty-eight years old.

Gary Edward Gentry was born in Phoenix on October 6, 1946. He was an outstanding high school athlete, a second baseman, a football end, and a basketball guard at Camelback High. He received a scholarship to Phoenix JC, was converted into a pitcher, led his junior-college team to a national title, and repeated at Arizona State. He was 17–1 in 1967 with 229 strikeouts in 174 innings, a remarkable collegiate rate. He had been drafted by the Orioles, Astros, and Giants, his favorite team.

"The Giants trained in Phoenix and I wanted to play for them, but my father thought their offer [twenty-five thousand dollars] wasn't good enough to quit school for."

Mets scout Dee Fondy offered Gentry twice as much, and he signed with the team on June 22, 1967. He immediately reported to Williamsport, Pennsylvania, was 4–4 that season and 12–8 the next season with Jacksonville.

In 1969, at twenty-two, he was placed on the Mets forty-man roster and drove to St. Petersburg, Florida, with his wife, Janet, and their small son.

"It was quite a drive," he remembers. "Not only did we have the baby, we also had Zeke, my Saint Bernard. I weighed 165 pounds, and Zeke weighed 185 pounds. He ate more than I did."

While Gentry had to carry or buy food for Zeke along the way, he didn't bother with water.

"We just marched him into the garage men's room, pointed him to the toilet, and let him empty out the bowl."

Janet Gentry, a scrubbed-clean blonde and high school sweetheart, was an avid baseball fan and could be seen often at Shea with a baby in one hand and a scorecard in the other. Friction developed in the marriage soon after Gentry left the Mets. The tensions built for several years until the two finally parted. Janet Gentry told friends that Gary not only disappointed her in their marriage, he seemed unconcerned about his sons. Gentry and his second wife, Donna, live outside Phoenix in Cave Creek.

\* \* \*

There have been several businesses for Gary Gentry since that unhappy day in 1976 when he received his release from the Braves. He has stayed mostly in real estate, sometimes involved in land development, sometimes in home sales, and lately as a property manager for a large Phoenix firm.

"I've moved around a lot in business. It's just like baseball. You don't know where you might wind up."

He is only forty-one, but the wear and tear on his face seems to show him as several years older. His hair is still thick and graying. His body is still lean and hard, and he wears a brush mustache typical of the cowpokes. He had up and down years in the real estate business. His marriage ended. He searched for direction. His remarriage seems stable, and he says he is comfortable in his new business venture. There is no anger in his voice, no bitterness, only resignation.

"I wanted to play longer. Who the hell wouldn't? My arm just gave out. If I was pitching now and it happened, they could probably fix me up. In those days they weren't so good at that. The first operation was a fifteen-minute procedure. They told me I was fine; I wasn't. The second was a lot more complicated, and I just didn't come back fast enough. It was getting stronger at the end but it was too late. When the Braves released me I just went home. I had pain in my arm for so long I was just glad to get away from it."

Gentry felt he pitched better in his first big-league season than in any other year. "We were all so young and so loose. Nothing was expected of us. We just had a good time, enjoyed playing, and waited to see what would happen. There couldn't be any pressure on us. We certainly didn't come into that season with anybody expecting us to win anything."

Gentry said he never had any difficulty with Hodges or Berra in his time with the Mets. "I didn't fight with them. I just wanted to pitch. That was all. Those were the only disagreements I had."

He says he was not jealous of Seaver or Koosman or any other pitcher on the team. He just felt that he did not get the respect, the attention, the appreciation of his skills that he felt he deserved.

"I never had any doubts about my ability. I won thirteen games as a rookie and I know I could have won twenty. I didn't get too many breaks that year. After that I had some arm trouble, I had my turn skipped and I just couldn't pitch the way I wanted to."

Gentry said he is reminded often about his sparkling performance in the third game of the World Series.

"I've heard that Cashen was shocked by that game. I don't know why he should be. I was throwing well and the Orioles weren't that good. It's not that they had a down series. We were just a better team. Cashen runs the Mets now. Maybe that's why I don't get invited back there very often."

Gentry plays golf frequently, enjoys romping with his dogs, attends an occasional old-timer game, and appears at some dream camps. He is not terribly enthusiastic about amateurs.

"I just can't get worked up when I'm throwing batting practice to some middle-aged guys. The game meant too much to me. When I left, it was a tough adjustment. I couldn't just turn my back on it. A lot of years have gone by now. It's easier to look back. I don't miss it now. I like the business I'm in, I make my own schedule, I'm comfortable."

Gentry said he was not terribly interested in baseball today, didn't know the names of the players and was unconcerned about the big salaries.

"I was a participant. That's what I was. I'm not a guy who can get a kick out of watching it on television. Give me the ball and I'll get excited. From what I've seen lately, a lot of them don't know what to do with the ball when they get it."

As he approaches his middle years, Gentry seems not to have lost that crusty edge, that tough exterior, that athletic arrogance that was all too familiar a part of his personality twenty years ago.

"If they bring us all back for the twentieth anniversary in

1989, I'll enjoy it. It's always fun to see the guys. If they don't, I won't die. I've been away from it a lot longer now than I was in it."

Gary Gentry's star descended so rapidly. He was tough and he was good and he was smart. There should have been more to his career.

There are those who stand out on a baseball team because they are the tallest or the toughest or the most talented. Jim McAndrew stood out because he was the gentlest. He also came from a town in Iowa with the colorful name of Lost Nation. It would almost always get a plug when he pitched, with stories beginning, "Jim McAndrew of Lost Nation, Iowa." He had a soft, open face, smooth skin, a warm smile that seemed never to disappear despite some pitching bad luck. Six feet, two inches tall, weighing 175 pounds, he was stronger than he looked and could pitch mean with a fastball under the chin when necessary. McAndrew's sunny disposition, square life-style in the flamboyant 1960s, clean language, closeness to his family, and gentle manner earned him the derisive nickname Moms McAndrew. He never let on that he heard it.

James Clement McAndrew was born in Lost Nation on January 11, 1944, and raised on his parents' large farm.

"Dad raised cattle and grew corn and we worked some long, tough hours. We had between five hundred and seven hundred acres, and that is a large family farm. I got up early, helped out, went to school, played sports, and didn't have too much time for loafing," he says.

He was a basketball player of note at Lost Nation Community High as well as a baseball player. He won a scholarship to the University of Iowa and played both sports with some degree of success at the Big Ten school.

"I was not really an outstanding college pitcher. Actually I wasn't even the best pitcher on our team. I was never the number-one starter on any team I ever played for in amateur or professional baseball."

On June 17, 1965, he was signed by Mets scout Charley Frey and assigned to Marion, Virginia, in the rookie league. He pitched at Auburn, New York and Williamsport, Pennsylvania (where he beat Robin Roberts in the Hall of Fame pitcher's last professional start for Reading), moved to Jacksonville in 1968, and was called up for one game on July 19, losing to Bob Gibson and the Cards, 2–0. He was optioned back to Jacksonville and called back to the Mets July 30. He stayed until he was traded to San Diego in 1974.

McAndrew, a psychology major at Iowa, entered the energy field and spent nearly a dozen years selling alternative sources of energy. The business diminished in the early 1980s.

"I thought I would try getting back into baseball. I wrote every club in the big leagues. Only three clubs responded, the Mets and San Diego, clubs I had been with, and Milwaukee. Only Milwaukee offered a job as a pitching coach in Helena, Montana. They offered five thousand dollars for a three-month season. I could see the financial structure of the game, despite huge salaries being paid to players in the big leagues, hadn't changed very much. I tried it for a season, but I realized I would have to support my family in a more productive method."

Jim and Lyn McAndrew have four children. Two are in college, and the two younger ones are still at home. In 1987 McAndrew took a job as a salesman in the eastern-division office of a company that manufactures Astroturf for use in ball parks.

"We'll be living in New Jersey after we get settled. Funny the way things work. We were in Parker, Colorado, for a long time. Now we are just a drive away from Shea."

\* \* \*

He is forty-four years old now, still athletic-looking, with a thick, dark head of hair, looking incredibly fit as he sits on a baggage trunk in the clubhouse of the Mets dream camp in Tampa.

"I never looked at baseball as a vocation. It was an avocation. I knew I would be doing something else with my life. I returned last year to baseball because I wasn't quite sure what I wanted. I was convinced again baseball isn't a very good life if you aren't playing. I still will have some baseball connections in my new business," he said.

McAndrew thinks the success of the Mets was due to the closeness of the players as much as it was to the talent on the team.

"Many of us had grown up together, moved through the organization together, came to the Mets together. I was close to Garrett and Dyer and Gentry. Duffy and I had been roommates in the minors. I was pitching in Providence, Rhode Island, against the Pawtucket club for Williamsport in 1967. I was out of the room, and when I came back Duffy told me my in-laws had called and Lyn had given birth to our first child. A few hours later, after the game, Duffy had a glazed look on his face. He had gotten a call in the ball park. His wife, Lynn, had given birth to their first child."

McAndrew had some arm trouble at Jacksonville in 1967. He was 10–8 but didn't throw really well. Then his arm started coming back in 1968.

"I must have gained a foot on my fastball that season. I broke some adhesions or something and could really throw hard. I still wasn't pitching as much as I wanted to. The manager was Clyde McCullough and he just didn't like me. He skipped my turn every time he could. One day Whitey Herzog [then the Mets farm director] came down to Jacksonville. 'Are you OK?' I told Whitey I was. 'Why in hell aren't you pitching?' I explained that McCullough had skipped my turn. Whitey went to him and explained that the organization wanted to see me pitch. He would pitch me the next day. "Then Whitey left and when the next day came I didn't pitch again. Whitey came back down and he must have really jumped all over McCullough. I pitched in turn for six straight starts. Then I was in the big leagues. Lyn knew about it before I did. Whitey was in the park the last night I pitched in Jacksonville. He saw Lyn and said, 'You're going to New York.' When I found out after the game, she told me she had heard about it three hours earlier."

Whitey Herzog, the highly successful manager of the St. Louis Cardinals, was as vital a part of the 1969 Mets as Seaver, Koosman, Ryan, McGraw, or any of those other young pitchers. He found them all. "I've never been able to figure out why the Mets let Whitey go," McAndrew said.

Herzog had always wanted to manage the Mets. When Yogi Berra was named the team manager after the death of Gil Hodges in 1972, Herzog's dream of leading the Mets at Shea ended. He soon resigned and began his managerial career the following season at Texas. There were rumors his Mets future was damaged when he confronted board chairman M. Donald Grant with some cutting remarks after the Mets won in 1969. Neither man has ever addressed the matter publicly.

"I got up there in 1968 and had some tough games," McAndrew said. "I didn't win and my arm was still bothering me. I talked it over with my wife, and I told her I was quitting at the end of the year. She knew that expansion was coming in 1969 and if I didn't make the Mets staff I might make some other team. My arm started coming around in August, and I thought I'd try it another year. Then it was 1969 and all those wonderful things happened."

He didn't win a game until June 24—he was on the disabled list with a blistered finger from April 27 to May 24—but Hodges stayed with him. McAndrew was a hot pitcher in August when he pitched twenty-three successive scoreless innings and won four of the six 1969 victories he was able to post.

"Gil was very communicative with me. I got along very well with him. It really was a father-son relationship, and I felt comfortable with him. The year before I had been shut out more times in a month than any pitcher in baseball. I was very discouraged, and he kept me going. He was great, and so was Rube. I remember when I joined the team and Rube told me I was starting. 'Do your best. Pitch a shutout.' I didn't pitch a shutout, but I held the Cards to two runs. Unfortunately Bob Gibson held us to none."

McAndrew said that he learned a reality about the game that first season of 1968 with the Mets.

"Every team is two teams—the pitchers and the everyday players. There is simply no connection. It is hard to relate to a guy going oh for four or four for four when you know he'll be in there the next day. When I lost I had to wait five days, sometimes ten days, before I could pitch again."

McAndrew also offered another dimension of the Mets. Not only were pitchers and players different, a pitcher named Seaver and the other pitchers were different.

"Tom was a great pitcher. Nobody could deny that. He was a once-in-a-lifetime guy. As a result he got a lot of attention and so did his wife. I don't think he sought it out but it happened. Everybody else on the team was jealous. Every big-leaguer has a strong ego. That's what got him there. It was uncomfortable for some guys. If they don't admit they were jealous of all that, I think they're fibbing."

His career over, McAndrew went into the energy business. There were mountains to climb there as difficult and high as the ones he met in baseball.

"What I had to overcome was the dumb-jock syndrome. That's the way people perceived me. It didn't matter if I had as good an education as they did or would rank higher on an IQ. All they associated me with was baseball. The World

Series ring was an indication to some people that I wasn't very bright. It took a while to undo that."

McAndrew says he still retains some bitterness about baseball.

"I never liked the way they treated people. There is a plantation mentality, especially in the minors. They look at you as property. They do with you as they see fit, move you around, make up their minds about you for reasons having nothing to do with performance. It may be a little different now with the players union as strong as it is, but a lot of things are the same, especially in the minors. I enjoyed playing. I enjoyed winning. I'm proud of the ring. But there is a lot of pain in being a big-league player, a lot of anguish for your family."

Cardwell, Gentry, and McAndrew won twenty-seven of the 1969 Mets' one hundred victories. They each pitched when asked, to the best of their ability, with no excuses. They may not have received as many headlines as other members of the pitching staff, but their contributions to that baseball miracle were significant. They should not be taken lightly or forgotten easily, for without them, there would not have been a 1969 championship ring on any Met finger.

# 10

# *A Rocky Road*

August 13, 1969: Senator Edward Kennedy of Massachusetts lashed back today in a public statement against what he called "whispers, innuendos and falsehoods" about the automobile-accident death on July 18 of Mary Jo Kopechne. Kennedy said he had described the events leading to the drowning of Miss Kopechne at Chappaquidick Island fully to investigators. He would not discuss the matter publicly any further. In Washington, President Nixon moved closer to firing United States attorney Robert Morgenthau over "policy differences." In Los Angeles, as investigators combed the Hollywood hills for clues, there were no leads in the savage mass murder of actress Sharon Tate and several friends. In Southeast Asia, fighting seemed sporadic throughout the rain-drenched countryside north of Saigon. Latest casualty lists from Vietnam included the names of Pfc. Nelson Andino, eighteen, of New York City, killed in a grenade explosion, Pfc. Michael James Holloway, twenty, of Chicago, a drowning victim, and Sgt. John Lionel Fielder, twenty-seven, of Winston-Salem, North Carolina, an alleged suicide.

In baseball, a long deadlock was resolved between National League president Charles Feeney and New York Yankee owner Michael Burke with the compromise selection of Bowie K. Kuhn, the National League attorney and a Princeton graduate, as the new commissioner of baseball.

In Houston, the Mets were beaten, 8–2, by the Astros for the third straight time. It gave the Mets an unenviable Texas record for 1969 of 0–6. Gary Gentry was hit hard. The loss dropped the Mets to 9½ games behind the leading Chicago Cubs. It was the lowest point of the season. There were 49 games remaining. As the Mets left the field after the final out of the game, the organist played "Goodnight, Sweetheart." Gil Hodges was calm after the game. He was reminded that the Mets had a record of 49–87 in Houston over their eight seasons there. "Next year," he said, sounding very much like an old Brooklyn Dodger, "we'll turn the tide."

The discouraged Mets flew home quietly from Houston. I worked on my story about the trip on the plane and filed it when we arrived in New York. It was played with a back-page *New York Post* headline reading, "Nice try, guys." The consensus of all observers was that the Mets season was over.

As the players were met by their wives at the airport, Ron Swoboda turned to me and said, "The trip wasn't so bad. At least the plane didn't crash."

There was no more amusing, articulate, entertaining, interesting, analytical member of the 1969 Mets than strongboy Ron Swoboda. He was a handsome, bright, well-built young man from Baltimore, Maryland, with the body of a Li'l Abner, and some said, the head to match. He was strong and stubborn, sometimes a little slow in his acceptance and understanding of the pure beauty of the game. He had earned the nickname of Rocky as a minor-league player, a tag many of his teammates enjoyed hurling at him in moments of their own desperation. For many players, Swoboda was an easy target. He talked freely with the press and sometimes said embarrassing or silly things. He would get mad at himself with a hair-trigger temper and do embarrassing things. He once struck out and slammed his batting helmet on the dugout floor. When he stepped on it and then attempted to shake it free, it stuck on the bottom of his shoes like gum. "I'm fining him for that," said an angry manager Casey Stengel. "Do I go around breaking up his property?"

Swoboda could colorfully describe the most routine of events. When the Mets won a rare game with an opposition error on a fly ball lost in the sunlight, Swoboda said, "Sometimes you need Mother Nature in left field more than you need Cleon Jones." On another occasion he struck out swinging five times in a doubleheader. "It's a good thing we won one of the games or I'd be eating my heart out," he said. "As it is, I'm only eating out my right ventricle."

He arrived on the Mets scene in 1964 out of the University of Maryland. Stengel was running an instructional camp for younger players, and when he saw the two-hundred-pound husky from Maryland he bellowed, "This boy can hit balls over buildings." Stengel described his younger players as the "Youth of America," and he envisioned the day they would lead the Mets to a championship. Three of the graduates of that early camp—shortstop Bud Harrelson, first baseman Ed Kranepool, and Swoboda, honored grads of the 1964 class of the "Youth of America"—would play vital roles on the championship team. Swoboda—the name means Freedom in Ukrainian—played one year of minor-league ball before joining the Mets in 1965. He hit 19 home runs that season, a Met rookie record that would last until Darryl Strawberry broke it with 23 in 1983. Swoboda—Stengel called him Suh-boda—became a Shea favorite with his slugging and erratic fielding. There was no denying his power potential as his home-run total in his first season exceeded the rookie home-run marks of Mickey Mantle, Roger Maris, and Stan Musial. His second big-league at bat resulted in a pinch-hit home run off Dick Farrell of the Philadelphia Phillies.

It was Swoboda's surprising power, uncontrollable enthusiasm, and quick wit that endeared him to the press and, through them, to the fans, hungry as they were in 1965 for a homegrown, young star. Kranepool was more serious, a little intemperate, and often surly. Harrelson was moderately shy and introspective. It would be Swoboda, and a bit later, Tug McGraw, who would be cheered and loved most by Mets fans for their boyish joy at participating in this Shea adventure.

For many of the reasons that helped fans identify with Swoboda—his open personality, his raw power, his youthful excitement, his careless mistakes—players were often angry at him. They would deride his inability to make contact at bat or in the field, his garrulousness and his appearance. He dressed casually and was often the object of teammate taunts for a bad case of acne he fought unsuccessfully for years on his face and body. In times of team tension, he could manage to say the wrong thing in the wrong way and needled pitcher Don Cardwell once just enough to cause the big pitcher to explode. In 1969, after a losing game, the Mets' flight was quiet until Swoboda and Kranepool began arguing loudly, disturbing an important Cardwell nap. The pitcher jumped up, saw Swoboda, cursed at him and at the hippie beads he wore around his neck and hurled an ineffective punch. Something about a generation gap there.

Swoboda had several moments of glory in the 1969 season, none larger than his two home runs of September 15. He had hit his first career grand slam two days earlier to beat Pittsburgh, 5–2, for the Mets' tenth win in a row. They lost the next day, but as the Cubs also lost, the Mets retained a first-place lead of 3½ games. Then Steve Carlton of the Cards struck out a record nineteen Mets on September 15. Despite that, Swoboda hit two two-run homers off Carlton for a 4–2 Mets win. He was at his best from August 21 through September 24 that season when the Mets moved from 6½ games out of first to 6 games ahead in first and the division clinching. He was the Mets' best hitter in the World Series against Baltimore, with 6 hits in 15 at bats for a .400 average. The

World Series memory most retained by fans was of Swoboda, body stretched full out in flight to his right, catching with a backhanded lunge a line drive hit, with two runners on, by Brooks Robinson. It saved the game and allowed the Mets to win, 2–1, in the tenth for Tom Seaver's only Series victory.

There wasn't much more to his career after that, with a couple of more Mets seasons, a trade to Montreal after he popped off about not playing in 1971 under Gil Hodges, a short stay with the Yankees, and then a release. He was twenty-nine years old.

Ronald Alan Swoboda was born in Baltimore on June 30, 1944, the second son of a garage-mechanic father and clerical-worker mother. "Together they made thirteen thousand dollars the year I was signed by the Mets for a thirty-five-thousand-dollar bonus," he says. Learning to play ball with his older brother, later an Air Force career airman, Swoboda never was an outstanding high school or college baseball player. He played more basketball and soccer than baseball, but had a strong summer season on a Baltimore amateur-club team after his freshman year at Maryland. He was signed by Mets scout Pete Gebrian on September 5, 1963.

He made his presence felt at the rookie camp in St. Petersburg in 1964, even for a time being considered a candidate for the Mets roster. "Why shouldn't I bring him north?" Stengel asked one day. "He ain't failed yet." A couple of training camp home runs got attention. The press hounded him for personal details. He described his college career, his routine middle-class life, and his career hopes. Then he said, "I can't wait until my Chinese grandfather gets here to watch me." He then explained that his grandmother had recently married the owner of a Chinese restaurant back in Baltimore. It was good for several Swoboda stories and anecdotes. "Why is it when Swoboda hits a home run, half an hour later you want him to hit another?" a reporter would ask. "Because he has a Chinese grandfather," others would answer.

He played at Buffalo and Williamsport—he homered against the Mets in an exhibition there—before joining them in 1965. He hit .228 as a rookie with those 19 home runs, only .222 the following year when he was threatened with a return to the minors, and .281 in his best year of 1967. He began that season as the Mets first baseman, dislodging buddy Ed Kranepool when Wes Westrum decided to platoon the two youngsters. Soon he was back in right field as Kranepool responded with a strong season of his own. He hit .242 in 1968 and .235 in the championship season, mostly as a platoon right fielder with Art Shamsky. He finished seven years in the big leagues with a .242 mark and 73 home runs.

The one constant for Swoboda in all those years, and now, was his smart, pretty, ever-reliable wife, Cecilia. She kept the family—they have two sons—in order with patience and care. She organized his logistics, got him places on time, and saw that he performed his career chores with freedom of spirit. A lesser woman would not have been able to tolerate endless baseball career moves, a capricious television broadcasting career, and periods of frustration and disappointment. Cecilia Swoboda has also earned a master's degree in her specialty of working with hearing-impaired children.

Swoboda's television career has taken him from New York to Milwaukee to New Orleans to Phoenix and back again to New Orleans. He now works for WVUE in New Orleans, the ABC affiliate, with a solid job as sports director on the local news, as solid as television jobs can get.


He still seems incredibly youthful and strong at forty-four. He talks enthusiastically and laughs heartily at some of the old memories. His face is a bit fleshier than in his playing days but there is much muscle around his shoulders and back. His hair is dark with small specks of gray at the edges. His eyebrows are thick and bushy, and his huge hands are as strong as ever. Thick patches of black hair creep out from under the sleeves of his jacket. It is early in 1988 and he is finally slowing down after an incredibly hectic professional football season in New Orleans that saw the Saints make the playoffs for the first time. He had to soften the disappointment of local fans with some encouraging words when the team went out in the first round. He has known that feeling often as a professional athlete.

"I think the viewers believed me when I talked about what a downer losing was," he says. "They know I've been there. This isn't some guy off the street saying losing is a tough pill to swallow. I play off that Mets identification as a television guy. I've never worked anyplace where that wasn't a factor. It's been a long time but that's one of the amazing things about that 1969 team. The memories remain for those old enough to remember, and they are told and retold for those who weren't old enough. The Mets, that's my signature. I wear that label proudly."

Swoboda's television career has had its highs and lows. He was inexperienced when he first went on the air in New York.

"They put me on without training. That's how they do it. I could get by for a while on enthusiasm and some natural talent. Then things came up that I didn't handle well. I didn't shut my mouth. I tried to do things my own way. It doesn't work in television. Hell, it didn't work in baseball. I never did learn to just do it and get along. I'm always figuring there has to be a better way."

Sometimes it was not his own fault. Sometimes it was simply numbers.

"There are no guarantees in this business. You get your thirteen weeks and then you look around. That sometimes happens. I came back to New Orleans last year. The Phoenix situation went downhill after the station was sold. They wanted to bring in their own guys. I was welcomed back here. That was great. The big thing is Cecilia. She is a trooper. She moves and changes jobs when I move, no complaints, no guilt feelings laid on me. That makes it all work."

Swoboda says he finds it difficult to relate to baseball players of today when he interviews them for his show.

"Economically, with those million- and two-million-dollar salaries there is no connection. It's a different world. I don't use the baseball connection much against modern players. I use it for the viewers. When I tell a player that I was on the 1969 Mets, he often looks at me like I'm some outer-space guy. It's like I came from the 1918 Yankees and I batted against Babe Ruth of the Red Sox."

Swoboda probably understood the human chemistry of a baseball team better than most. He could see the differences in personalities, the conflicts, the lack of serious bonds.

"The game brought us together. That was it. It was an artificial bond. It wasn't like you signed up for this team like people sign up for a literary club, because you have this common interest in good books. We had a common interest in playing as well as we could, in having the best career we could, in winning. That isn't much of a personality bond."

Swoboda was exceptionally close to Kranepool and McGraw and Koosman—everybody seemed close to Koosman—and had warm feelings for Agee, Shamsky, Jones, Charles, Boswell, Harrelson, Grote, and the rest. He had that little scuffle with Cardwell, soon dismissed as childish tension, but had no lingering animosity.

"I guess the only guy on the team I never really developed any kind of relationship with was Seaver. It was my fault, not his. I kind of screwed it up. In all the years we were teammates I never once went out to dinner with him on the road. Why didn't I ask him? I don't know. There was one little incident. I look back now and it sounds so ridiculous. Seaver was taking up a collection for something or other, a gift for somebody's baby or something like that, maybe two dollars a man. I wasn't in the clubhouse when he started collecting, and when he came to my locker he just reached into my pants pocket and took out two dollars. I came into the clubhouse later and he told me about it. I just went crazy. Here we were all contributing to something as a team and he wanted me to be part of it and I went wild. I don't know why. It wasn't that big a deal.

"I thought about it for a long time, but I never apologized. Here's a guy, the best pitcher of his time, a guy who is going into the Hall of Fame, and I blew any chance of ever being close to him by something this small. We stayed away from each other after that. I look back at it now with a little more maturity. I can see the reason. I was jealous of him; that's all it was. I wanted to be the best in the game at my position; I wasn't. He just made it look so easy, was so good—and it just frustrated me so much. I wasn't blowing up because he went into my pants pocket. I was blowing up because I wasn't as good at my job as he was at his."

Swoboda said Seaver had a marvelous relationship with Gil Hodges, something he could never achieve. "Seaver had this ability to read Hodges, to know what he wanted, to perform as Hodges hoped he would. I don't mean as a pitcher. I mean as a guy around the team. Tom was always so damn mature about things, so poised, so correct in his actions. Me? I just rebelled against Hodges like some damn idiot. One time, Hodges had this meeting and he brought us together to discuss curfew. He said he wanted a consensus of the team as to how many hours after the game should be curfew. Nobody said a thing. Everybody knew curfew was always two or two and a half hours after we got back to the hotel. Finally I jumped up and said, 'Make it three hours.' Gil said, 'No, that's too much.' Then I said, 'Then you just pick the damn time and tell us like you want to.' Gil just stared at me. I somehow had this knack of saying the wrong thing at the wrong time.

"I got off badly with Gil from the beginning. It was 1968 and he was the new manager and I was working hard in the outfield during spring training. I had this ritual, I would take hard line drives for ten or fifteen minutes, practice catching balls from all positions, and then come up throwing. I was working on catching balls off the bat—maybe that helped me make that Series catch—and getting the ball in hard and true. This went on this day for fifteen minutes, maybe, and then I went inside to get my arm rubbed. All of a sudden one of the coaches comes in the trainer's room and says Gil wants all the outfielders out on the field to work on their throws. I had worked on my throws and my arm was sore. This was real early in the spring. I told Piggy or whoever it was that my arm was sore and my throwing was good enough. You can imagine how well that went over with the new manager."

Hodges was a very strong, very stubborn personality. Swoboda had much the same personality makeup. Those types often clash. On a baseball team, only one of them can win a battle. It is not smart for a player of this type to take on a manager of this type. It is no wonder his teammates referred to Swoboda as Rocky.

"Krane had this thing on the bench with Hodges about not being used in the game with a right-hander out there. It got heated and everybody just sat and listened. After the game I went into the clubhouse to shave. Gil was in there. He was the fastest shaver I ever saw, up this side, down the other— over. If I shaved like that I wouldn't have a face. Anyway Gil had just gone down one side and he was about to go down the other side and all of a sudden I'm getting on him about not using Krane. It was between Krane and Gil, and that's where it should have stayed. I butted into the damn thing, and Gil just froze. He didn't have to explain his moves to me. I don't know what the hell I was thinking. I could see his muscles tighten. He didn't say another word. The next thing I knew I was standing against the urinal and I couldn't pee. When Gil wanted to intimidate somebody he could make all your body come to a stop."

Despite these conflicts, Swoboda admits he never lost confidence in Hodges as the leader of that team. He agrees the manager was in charge because he knew more baseball than anybody else around. "Intellectually, he was the quickest man I had ever met in the game. His mind was sharp and fast and you could see how far ahead of everybody else he almost always was. He would be making moves in the second and third inning that would pay off in the eighth or ninth. I think I recognized that in him early and maybe I made a game of challenging him for intellectual exercise. It was a game I couldn't win."

Of Swoboda's two closest buddies on the team, Kranepool and McGraw, only the left-handed pitcher found Hodges a heroic, fatherly figure.

"Krane and I just never warmed up to him. McGraw was exactly the opposite. Somehow, Tug brought out that soft side in Hodges and they became very close. I think McGraw took personal problems to Hodges, and they would examine McGraw's life together. I just couldn't do that—I had my own father; Gil was just my baseball manager."

Though he was not quite as close to them as he was to Kranepool and McGraw, Swoboda admired Koosman and Grote as teammates.

"I was close to Grote. He was a great catcher. I know he had a short fuse but that intensity really helped him as a player. He had the best arm in the league, a real cannon, and he was never afraid to throw, never afraid to make a mistake. He was a tremendous handler of pitchers, a take-charge guy that won over the pitchers. We used to socialize a lot, Grote and Sharon, Cecilia and I, and it was always fun. Grote was much different around his wife and kids. I don't know what happened with them. Cecilia talks to her all the time. Sharon has remarried and I hear she's happy. Things happen with ballplayers, with anybody. People grow apart, I guess. I don't know if winning, if all that attention, had anything to do with it. It's upsetting, all those divorces, Krane, McGraw, Grote. Nobody likes to hear that. With all the garbage we all go through, it's a miracle any player stays married."

While no one on the 1969 Mets and no one in the National League would dare argue the brilliance of Tom Seaver in 1969, there is much support for Koosman as the emotional leader of the staff, the big-game pitcher.

"There was something few people knew that year about Koosman. People didn't realize the physical problems the guy had. He was a wreck. His arm hurt him all the time, and he pitched the entire season in pain. He had as much trouble with his feet as he did with his arm. He had terrible bone spurs and he would wear these cushions in his shoe and he would favor one leg and that leg would go bad and the next time out he would favor the other one. I would see all that and he never complained, and I just admired the hell out of him."

Despite hanging around with Koosman and McGraw, two pretty smart left-handed pitchers, Swoboda didn't learn as much about left-handed pitchers as he should have learned.

"I wasn't as scientific about the game as I should have been. I had some success early and I thought I could just muscle the ball. It doesn't work that way. I didn't get smarter as I got more experienced. That's my major disappointment about my career."

One of the intangible elements of the 1969 Mets was the lack of racial tension at most times. Swoboda said he felt as close to Cleon Jones and Tommie Agee and Ed Charles— Donn Clendenon came to the team later—as he did to almost anybody.

"I grew up in Baltimore in the late 1940s and 1950s and it was a Southern, segregated city. I went to segregated schools. We played against black schools, and I never had any trouble with them. Once in a while I would say something like 'nigger this or nigger that' and once I said it at home. My mother jumped all over me. She wouldn't allow us to talk like that. She reminded us we weren't so well off ourselves. We weren't Vanderbilts and we were struggling and who were we to think we were better than anybody else for any reasons, color or anything else. When I got to the Mets I just never thought about race. The black guys and white guys were just the same, just teammates. I liked Tommie and Glider and Jones as much as anybody. I think Jones got a bad rap on that team. One time Gil got all over Cleon for not being on the field when he should have been. He sent one of the coaches in the clubhouse to look for him and he found Cleon watching films of himself at bat. He had been in a little slump, and he was trying to do something about it, watching films, trying to work out the kinks in his swing. Gil wouldn't hear of it. He was just angry that Cleon wasn't out there where he should have been."

Jones had this way of talking rapidly, getting more and more difficult to understand, his drawl deeper, his voice more high-pitched, as he got deeper and deeper into a story. A lot of players found him very difficult to understand.

"A lot of people in the South, a lot of white people, get to talking like that when they are telling a story. I don't think it was any more difficult than understanding a lot of other guys, white guys, on that team. I thought Cleon was a terrific storyteller, a very funny guy, and he sure helped pass the time on those long bus rides or those rain delays or those airport waits. He was also a great hitter. He was very disciplined, very smart, and he really could wait for his pitch. He had incredibly quick hands, bat speed, and it was hard to get a pitch past him. He was our best hitter and he could have been better, maybe, certainly for a longer time if he was handled differently. He had some good days with the Mets, but he also had some tough times. He was very talented, could run and field and throw, as well as hit. What do people remember about him? They remember he was taken out of a game by Gil and he was disciplined by Yogi. I was gone then but I don't think that was all Cleon's doing."

Jones was well liked by his teammates, and his wife, Angela, was a special favorite of most of the Mets' wives. She was always included in the doings of the wives when the team was on the road. At home Cleon and Angela Jones were a big part of the frequent backyard barbecues the Swobodas held in their large Syosset, Long Island, home after day games or on those rare off days.

"We laughed a lot with Cleon. We enjoyed each other. He was a good guy, a funny guy. He also helped make me a lot of money."

The Mets had blown past the Cubs and were driving to the title in mid-September. There was so much talk of this amazing baseball miracle. One game seemed to crystallize it all. On September 15, left-hander Steve Carlton struck out nineteen Mets for a big-league record. It would stand until Roger Clemens of Boston struck out twenty Seattle Mariners in 1986. Carlton owned the nastiest slider in baseball in 1969 and could rocket a fastball under any hitter's chin.

"I had been struggling a bit and during batting practice that day," recalls Swoboda. "I talked to [Met broadcaster] Ralph Kiner. He had been a free-swinger, a great home-run hitter in his day, and I respected him very much. He gave me a couple of pointers. They must have helped."

Swoboda had trouble with breaking pitches. Carlton knew that but he also knew that Swoboda would be looking for breaking pitches. He tried to whip a fastball by him. Swoboda hit it for a two-run homer. Later in the game he went to his slider. Swoboda was ready again and hit another two-run homer. Carlton had his nineteen K's, Swoboda had his two homers, the Mets had their victory. Their lead was four and a half games over the Cubs. Amazing.

With his fast finish to the season, Swoboda had ended the year with a batting average of .235. He had 52 runs batted in and only 9 home runs. He could feel his career slipping away at the age of twenty-five. "I knew they had rushed me along. Maybe I would have been a better player if they had sent me out. They didn't have anyone better in 1965 and 1966 when I should have been learning my trade. I tried to do it on natural ability."

It was instinct, intuition, innate sense of the game that catapulted Swoboda into the hearts of Mets fans forever. No revisionist history can take that joy away. He had always been a beloved Met figure, as much for his human failures and brutal honesty as for his rare successes. If any player could be described as Everyman on the Mets, it had to be Swoboda. That is why The Catch so locked in his Met image for fans.

It was the fourth game of the 1969 World Series. The Mets led, 1–0, in the ninth. Tom Seaver was pitching. The Orioles had runners on first and third with one out. Brooks Robinson hit a low, sizzling line drive toward the hole in right center between Swoboda and Tommie Agee.

"This became the ultimate of my ability at the perfect time," says Swoboda. "I had no time for conscious thought or judgment. The ball was out there too fast. I took off with the crack of the bat and dove. My body was stretched full out, and I felt as if I was disappearing into another world. I can't remember thrusting my glove across my body—I must have; the ball was in it. Then I turned over, bounced up, and threw it in."

Frank Robinson scored from third after the catch to tie the game, but the Mets scored a run in the tenth inning for a 2–1 win, the only World Series game Tom Seaver would win.

"When I see it on film now I'm still amazed by it. When they slow it down it seems impossible that I could reach the ball. It was just hit too hard. Somehow it happened. Somehow I got it. A miracle? Wasn't the entire season a miracle?"

There would be another Swoboda moment of glory in the final game of the Series. He hit a double to help Jerry Koosman beat the Orioles in the fifth game for a Mets championship. There wasn't much, really, to Swoboda's career after that. He struggled through the next season with another .233 mark. Hodges soured on him even further. Swoboda began complaining publicly and privately about lack of playing time. Teammates took to needling him sarcastically about the amount of attention he received from the press despite his decreased playing time.

"Tell them about it, Rocky," became a clubhouse cry from many players as the press entered the locker room after a Mets win. Some of the press, closer to him than some teammates, felt embarrassed for him. One of the sub rosa emotions around a ball club revolves around what players call ink. Few players—Reggie Jackson was a major exception in his time— solicit attention from the press. All enjoy it. Swoboda got an inordinate amount of press coverage, far in excess of his playing importance on the team. Ballplayers have never understood that the accessible, quotable players who talk to the press on good days and bad get the ink. It has nothing to do with batting average. It has more to do with Bartlett's average.

"I always enjoyed talking with the press. Maybe I was preparing for my later television job without knowing it. I think one thing you have to do if you want press attention is open up your psyche. I told the truth. I gave a lot of myself. I enjoyed the give and take."

In the spring of 1971 Swoboda was traded to the Montreal Expos for journeyman outfielder Don Hahn. A few months later he was traded to the Yankees. He was back in New York until he was released in 1973.

"I look back at it all now and I know I should have been a better player. I'm forty-four years old and there are nights I wake up from a deep sleep and I've been having this dream, a nightmare really, that I'm at the plate again and I'm facing some pitcher, Gibson or Carlton or Jenkins, only the best of them, and I'm still fooling with my hands, still moving the bat, still trying to get myself locked into a comfortable position at the plate. It occupies my mind a lot and I can't stop thinking about it. It's not that I miss the playing. That's gone and I have fully dealt with that. I think I miss most the opportunity to have been better. Can you understand that?"

Swoboda has had some dry periods during his television days. It is the nature of the profession, thirteen-week contracts after thirteen-week contracts and then nothing. More tapes, more interviews, more flights to other stations. Then the uprooting of the family again, Cecilia and the kids on the move, new schools, new homes, new friends, new pressures.

Through it all, Swoboda has maintained his poise, his charm, his laughter. He seems to have weathered all the turmoil of transition they all have faced. His situation in New Orleans now seems quite comfortable: the ratings are high, the surroundings are warm, the people are pleasant.

"I have this identification as an old ballplayer. That's something that I can always use. But what has changed here is that it doesn't mean as much. I'm here because they think I can do the job and I have. I had doubts when I went to the plate. There were days of much anguish. I don't have doubts when I do my television work. I know I'm good."

He arrived in New Orleans as the Saints had their finest season. It helped propel the ratings of his station and solidify his standing. He has no doubts that will continue. He does not expect to leave New Orleans now for many years.

"We're happy here. The kids are doing well. Cecilia has a good job. I think it has all settled down, finally. I enjoy the memories but I'm content with the present."

There would be only one job offer that could tempt Swoboda now after all those years of doing sports news and commentary on television.

"What if somebody came along and offered me a baseball play-by-play job? Would I listen? You bet I would. I don't know. It could happen. Maybe the Mets would want me back as their play-by-play man. That would be something, wouldn't it?"

The memories run deep. The ties between the right-handed right fielder of the 1969 Mets and the fans are unbreakable. This was a special man in a very special baseball season.

# 11

# *Men of Mobile*

August 27, 1969: Governor Nelson Rockefeller of New York, looking ahead to his reelection campaign next year, today urged more conservative spending programs for the state government. Observers at the Syracuse University speech said the governor was clearly attempting to shed a good part of his liberal image and move his political position further to the right. In Washington, a battle between the State Department and the Defense Department was shaping up over the deeds or misdeeds of North Vietnam. Officials from State suggested the North Vietnamese were decreasing their infiltration into the south. Defense officials revealed that captured documents indicated the North Vietnamese had added a hundred thousand soldiers in the south over the last six months. Casualty figures remained steady with the latest list including the names of 1st Lt. Peter Hinchman McMurray, twenty-four, of Duxbury, Massachusetts, killed in an aircraft crash, Sgt. Leroy Lemuel Bell, fifty-one, of Monticello, Florida, dead of multiple fragmentation wounds, and 1st Lt. Brian Andrew Hubis, twenty-two, of Beverly, Massachusetts, killed in a small-arms fire fight. In Washington, government researchers urged more study of the oral birth-control pills.

In San Diego, Jerry Koosman beat Clay Kirby and the Padres, 4–1. It gave the Mets 74 victories for the season. The 1968 team had finished at 73–89, best team record ever. The

'69 Mets had 36 games remaining; they would win 26 of them. Koosman would win 9 of his last 10 starts. Seaver would win 10 games in a row after his last loss of the season on August 5 against Cincinnati. The team would achieve this although their best hitter, Cleon Jones, was plagued with a series of injuries to his leg, hand, and rib cage and would miss 24 of their 44 games from mid-August on.

There were black schools in the South that fought integration almost as strongly as some white schools did in the turbulent 1960s. The black schools may not have been thinking of social factors. They were thinking of losing some of their finest athletes to integrated schools as a result of busing. Year in and year out, one of the powerhouses in all sports in Mobile, Alabama, was Mobile Training High, an all-black school that taught its students how to earn a living as automobile mechanics and carpenters, welders and sheet-metal workers, crane operators and masons.

The school had its finest years in baseball, football, basketball, and track and field in the early 1960s. The stars of the teams in all four sports would emerge as teammates later on the 1969 champion Mets. Born five days apart in 1942 and about a mile apart in the black areas of Mobile known as Plateau and Magnolia were Cleon Jones and Tommie Agee.

The finest athlete ever turned out by the school was Jones, with Agee just a tad behind. Both were exceptional baseball and football players, solid performers in basketball, and outstanding track and field stars. Both would make their fame in baseball and confess in later years that football was not only their favorite sport but their best sport.

"When I was playing I could throw a football sixty yards in the air," Jones once said, "and then run downfield and catch it."

It sounded a lot like the legends told by Negro League

baseball Hall of Famer Cool Papa Bell, who was so fast, the legends say, he could turn out the light in his room and be asleep before the room grew dark.

Jones scored 26 touchdowns in one record-breaking season, won a scholarship for his football prowess to Alabama A and M, an all-black college, and scored 17 touchdowns in his only season there.

Mets scout Julian Morgan had watched Jones in high school and had decided to sign the youngster. Jones was signed July 5, 1962, the first player signed as a free agent by the Mets after they began play. Jones possessed one of the most unique skills in baseball. He was a right-handed batter and a left-handed thrower. Left-handed batters who throw left or left-handed batters who throw right are the rule. When Jones finally came to the Mets hitting from the right side and throwing left-handed, old-timers could remember only one player, Johnny Cooney, an outfielder with the Boston Braves and Brooklyn Dodgers, who had similar credentials.

"When I was a kid growing up in Plateau," said Jones, "we used to play all our games on fields we put together ourselves. There was this one field that we put some old shirts down for bases. Behind right field there was this little creek and behind left field, well, man, it just went on and on for miles. We played our games there and after a couple of games I had lost four or five balls when I hit them left-handed into the water. We didn't have too many real baseballs so when the other guys came to me and said, 'You better stop doing that or we ain't got no more baseballs here' I just turned around. That's how I became a right-handed hitter. I just wanted to save those balls."

After the Mets signed him as a young outfielder, he played at Auburn, Raleigh, and even had six games with the Mets under Casey Stengel in 1963. Stengel took one look at the six-foot, two-hundred-pound perfectly muscled twenty-one-year-old and proclaimed him a future star.

Jones had the classic Southern black background. He had lived in a black area, attended black schools, associated only with other blacks. His first experience outside that environment was in professional baseball. "It just scared me to death," he said. He spoke only when spoken to, answered questions with his head down and his voice barely audible, and walked uncertainly through the Polo Grounds clubhouse. There were few black players on the Mets, and Jones felt so terribly alone. His inability to communicate with the all-white press of the day became a source of press-box humor, much of it tinted with old-fashioned racism.

The focus of many jokes about the Mets was catcher Choo Choo Coleman. His greetings consisted of "Hi, bub," and his answers to questions usually were either yes or no. Broadcaster Ralph Kiner once asked him his wife's name, and he answered, "She Mrs. Coleman, bub."

When Jones arrived he was as ill at ease as Coleman was in press relations. Years later, Jones would emerge as comfortable with the press, even a little outspoken, and always entertaining and friendly. Teammates considered him a fine fellow, a great player but not an intellectual wizard.

After strong seasons in Buffalo in 1964 and 1965, Jones was promoted to the Mets again. This time he would stay through 1975. He finished his career with the Chicago White Sox in 1986. He batted .281 over thirteen seasons and hit .340 in the championship season, the highest average ever compiled by a Met batter in the team's history.

Jones broke in with a strong rookie season in 1966. He batted .275, but slumped to .246 the next season. After Gil Hodges became the manager in 1968, Jones was platooned early in left field with left-handed–hitting Art Shamsky. He responded poorly. He didn't hit, he was lackluster in the field, and he complained to the press. "I ain't no platoon player and I can't hit like this." He soon was playing every day; he played in 147 games and batted .297. Hodges knew he had a talented player in Jones.

He was clearly the team's best hitter in 1969. Not only did he hit .340, he had 75 RBIs, hit 12 homers, scored 92 runs and stole 16 bases. He missed 25 games with assorted injuries but was the batter most feared by opposing pitchers, both left- and right-handers as he cracked line drives all around Shea and on the road.

He hit .429 in the playoff against Atlanta and .158 against Baltimore in the Series but was more remembered for being hit in the shoe with Dave McNally's bouncing curve ball. The Mets were down 3–0 in the sixth inning of the final Series game. McNally threw a slider, and Jones tried to get away as the ball came in on him. The baseball bounced away from the plate and rolled into the Mets dugout. Home plate umpire Lou DiMuro called it a ball. The baseball rolled down the step of the Mets dugout and was picked up by Hodges. He rolled it over in his hands and then began a slow march to the plate. Hodges showed the ball—clearly stained with shoe polish—to DiMuro. The umpire agreed it had come from Jones's shoe and he was awarded first on a hit-by-pitch. Donn Clendenon followed with a homer to cut the Baltimore margin to 3–2, Al Weis homered to tie it, and the Mets, behind Jerry Koosman, went on to win, 5–3. Do not mention this to Frank Cashen or Earl Weaver.

One other incident is often recalled from that season. In a game against Houston at Shea, a fly ball landed in front of Jones for a hit. Hodges walked toward the mound. He went past his pitcher and continued to short left field. Jones looked up to see him coming and walked in a few feet.

"I had a bad leg. Gil knew that. He asked me about it before the game. He came out there and told me to follow him in. He said if I was too hurt to run, I was too hurt to play. Sure I was embarrassed. Gil was tough. He did everything with a purpose. We had words after the game. Nobody likes that. I didn't hold a grudge. Gil was my man. He knew what was going on around that team. I don't think we could have won without him."

Jones was leading the league in hitting at the time. Hodges's message was clear. Everybody played hard or they didn't play. Jones stayed out of trouble until 1975. He had a bad knee that year and was left behind in Florida when the team headed north. A few weeks later, while training on his own in St. Petersburg, he was spotted in a van in the middle of the night. He and a woman were charged with indecent exposure. The case was never prosecuted because the Mets took care of a fine. Jones was ordered back to New York by the Mets.

In the most extraordinary public flogging any member of the press had seen, Jones was ordered to stand up at Shea Stadium and apologize for his actions to Mets fans. His wife, Angela, stood by his side. Mets board chairman M. Donald Grant stood by while Jones read his prepared apology. Members of the press who had to sit still for this humiliating charade were as embarrassed as Jones. Angela Jones's stoic face was the most significantly lasting memory of this episode.

In a foul mood the next weeks, Jones defied manager Yogi Berra when asked to play defense in one game. He refused to go in, and Berra ordered him suspended for insubordination. Grant refused to act, fearing repercussions from the baseball players union, then beginning to feel its power. Berra would not back down and he was soon fired.

Jones was allowed to leave gracefully at the end of the year, signed a free-agent contract with Bill Veeck's White Sox team, couldn't play because of his knees, and was soon released. He went home to Mobile.

After baseball, Jones tried several things. He ran a fast-food business which went bankrupt. He worked for a maintenance company. He got back into the game finally as a minor-league batting instructor for the Mets in the early 1980s. He was hired by farm director Chris Kager and fired by Steve Schryver when Schryver took over the post.

"I worked with Darryl Strawberry. I taught him a lot," says Jones. "Then Schryver came in and I was gone."

After some tough financial years, Jones went into com-
munity-service work a couple of years ago around Mobile.
"I work for the city, work with kids, work with the elderly.
I enjoy it. Sure I'd come back to baseball if they asked
me."

It is early spring in 1988. Cleon Joseph Jones is throwing
a football around with his son in the front yard of his pleasant
four-bedroom home in a quiet, integrated neighborhood of
Mobile. He is forty-six years old, still fairly trim, talking rapidly as always, smiling often, and enjoying the distant
memories.

"A couple of years ago I was having a baseball catch out
here. I was wearing my World Series ring. I made a throw
and then I noticed the ring was gone. I looked all around,
couldn't find it. Then about a month ago, this neighbor of
mine knocks on my door, holds out his hand, and says, 'This
yours?' He's got the ring. 'Where'd you get it?' He told me
he was digging and he just dug it up. I was happy to have it
back. It meant an awful lot.

"I don't want to rehash what happened. That's all old stuff
now. I just feel bad that I left with all those bad vibes. I didn't
deserve that kind of treatment."

Jones lived in an apartment in Jamaica, Queens, that summer and commuted to the ball park with buddy Tommie Agee
and, early in the season, rookie Amos Otis, who lasted with
the team until June 15.

"It was great to play with Tommie. We really helped each
other. He was my best friend, but I got along with everybody,
Koosman, Seaver, Grote, all of them. I never felt any problems over that black-white thing. It was a team that pulled
together. We spent time with each other on the road and we
got together a lot with our families when we were home. It
was all family on that team."

Jones said he remembered when the season turned. "I'd been there five or six years by then. The team wasn't very good. Then all of a sudden we get Seaver and Koosman and all those tough pitchers. I knew we had a chance. We played the Cubs and the Cards, and they weren't better than us. I was hitting the ball. I knew we had enough offense. We just got better together."

Jones gives a lot of credit to Agee for the success of the team.

"He was just a big-game player. He had come from a winning sports background and he didn't like losing. He was a key man on that team. When he made those catches in the World Series everybody got excited. Not me. I had seen him do that too many times in school. I think Gil helped him a lot. He took Tommie under his wing."

Jones said he was very happy to win with the Mets since he had been there so many years. "I remember when I first broke in at Auburn, New York, and Johnny Murphy (then the farm director) came down to see me for my first few pro games and he was really excited. 'You're going to help us win a pennant in a few years, young man.' That made me feel good. And then in 1964 I was in the big camp and Casey wanted to make me into a switch-hitter because I could run good. I told him I used to hit left as a kid but hadn't done it for years, and then I said I could do it if he wanted but I might not get to the big leagues as fast if I switched. He said he wanted to have me play for him so I didn't switch. I liked Casey a lot. I thought Casey was a funny guy."

Jones was injured a good part of the 1973 season when the Mets won again. He played well the last few weeks and had a big World Series against Oakland.

"I'm always talking to these groups of kids, teaching them baseball and all, and the parents come up to me afterwards. All they ever want to do is talk about '69. Nobody ever brings up '73. It's like that season never happened. But '69? Everybody remembers everything about that year. 'What was it like facing Gibson or Marichal or those other great pitchers?' I like to talk baseball with the older people because they remember that team. After all these years it's like my whole career came down to that one season. That isn't the way it was, but that's the way most people around here make it sound. It was just so exciting every day, and when we played those games against the Cubs down the stretch, well, that was the most noise I ever heard."

Jones said his life was comfortable now with Angela and the two children, a daughter in college and a son who is a throwback to his dad, a big, strong excellent athlete with potential in baseball and football.

"There have been some times I was in bad financial shape. Now I'm all right. I got a good job, I enjoy working with the kids and the old people in town. They all know me around here. I'm too old to play now anyway, and besides that my knees wouldn't hold up. Too many artificial surfaces in baseball now."

The 1969 Mets were clearly a pitchers' team. All the attention, all the success, all the emotion seemed to revolve around that wondrous young pitching staff. That pitching strength kept most games winnable because their guy on the mound didn't allow the other team six or seven runs. Still, they scored at least one more run than the other team a hundred times that year. The offense had to do a lot to earn that.

Few contributed more than Cleon Jones. He was a fine athlete with some shortcomings in dedication and discipline. It's a shame not to know how much better he could have been.


There were eleven children in Tommie Agee's family, including nine sisters, and with a family that large in Magnolia, a black community of Mobile, Alabama, the struggle to survive was evident. Like his friend Cleon Jones, Agee turned to athletics as a way out of that environment and into a better life. The Cleveland Indians thought so much of Agee's talents that they signed him off the campus of Grambling University to a bonus contract worth more than sixty-five thousand dollars in 1961.

After a resounding start with the Chicago White Sox as American League Rookie of the Year in 1966, Agee struggled through a couple of poor seasons.

He played for Eddie Stanky with the White Sox in 1967 and crumbled under Stanky's firm hand. The old Brooklyn Dodger and New York Giant second baseman was a stern fundamentalist and disciplinarian. He did not relate well to Agee, a sensitive, insecure, worrisome center fielder. "I felt under pressure at all times," Agee once said. "He was very difficult to play for. There was a lot of tension on that team."

The White Sox were in a tough pennant race with the Tigers and the Red Sox, the eventual winners in 1967, before things could be settled on the final weekend. That season left scars on Agee. He would come to the Mets under a cloud and spend more than a year with the team before he felt relaxed enough to engage in animated conversation with any player other than Jones or engage in a dialogue with Hodges.

"Finally Gil and Agee got very close," said a Met veteran who was close to the scene. "Agee would go into his office, close the door, and spill his guts with Gil. He was having a lot of personal problems. I think he was still a bachelor then, but he was involved with a woman who was having severe emotional problems. Agee was concerned about the lady's life and mental health and he needed somebody to talk all this through with, and Gil was always willing to listen."

Agee, the only 1969 Met who refused to be interviewed for this book, because, he said, he was doing his own book on the Mets, kept these personal matters private. Teammates did not know the extent of the problem, management was never made aware, and the press certainly didn't know. It made his 1969 performance even more remarkable. Agee's introduction to the Mets was a shocker. He had been obtained from the White Sox after the 1967 season in a deal involving Tommy Davis, then the team's best hitter. Hodges had seen Agee often in the American League, liked him very much as a hitter, and thought he would play well defensively with his exceptional speed. The Mets were always on the lookout for a center fielder and/or a third baseman. Agee, a big man—just under six feet tall and weighing two hundred pounds, with a thick neck, huge thighs, and broad shoulders— was still capable of explosive bursts of speed.

Agee began his Mets career in a most inauspicious way. He was beaned by Bob Gibson, the hard-throwing Cardinal Hall-of-Famer-to-be. Agee was removed to a St. Petersburg hospital after the spring-training incident, examined thoroughly, kept overnight, and released with instructions to rest for several days. He was soon back in the lineup, and by the end of spring training appeared to be swinging normally.

He got a few hits early and came into Houston with an impressive .313 average. On April 15, 1968, the Astros beat the Mets, 1–0. It took them only twenty-four innings to do it. Agee went oh for ten, and in that one game his average dropped 116 points, to .197. He then continued struggling until he was oh for thirty-four at bats, tying the Met record, set in 1962 by Don Zimmer.

"I hate to come to the ball park," he said during the slump. "I hate to put on my uniform. I want to come here, get in, get out, get away."

With a near-capacity crowd of over fifty thousand fans in the stands, Agee lined a single to left in the third inning. The crowd applauded him for three minutes.

"I stood there and I almost cried for him," said Tom Seaver.

Agee told the press later, "These people were wonderful, warm, marvelous. I had to do something for them."

The Mets had won the game, and with Agee getting a hit,

the clubhouse atmosphere was electric. Seaver was especially thrilled. He knew how valuable a successful center fielder would be to the future of this team: "For us to do anything he has to play well."

The rest of the season was a nightmare for Agee. He had some spurts and then would fall back. He experimented constantly with his stance, his swing, his bats, and his pitch selection. At times he was aggressive but would swing through pitches. At other times he would be unable to pull the trigger, as the players say, with the bat resting on his shoulder as strike three whizzed by the plate. Casey Stengel sang a diddy when another nonswinger, Jim Hickman of the Original 1962 Mets, would take endless third strikes. "Oh you can't improve your average with your bat upon your shoulder, tra la, tra la, tra la."

It would be one message Hodges would drive home forcefully on Agee in 1969. Hodges could handle swinging third strikes. After all he had plenty of them in his own career. It was third called strikes that upset him. Agee vowed to swing more often, more aggressively and to make more contact. How well he succeeded in 1969 can be measured by his career home-run total of 26 in 565 at bats.

Hodges felt, and rightfully so, that Agee was always a threat on the bases. He stole a dozen that year. More importantly, he could beat out slow rollers for hits. All this could be done only if he made contact. Agee had stolen forty-four bases for the 1967 White Sox but had gained some weight by 1969 and thereby lost a step. Also, in Hodges's system Mets could steal second base only under orders; they could, however, run from second to third on their own. Agee's judgment on that steal was sometimes faulty. In one close game, he barely escaped a tag as the Mets rallied to win when he stole third with two out. Hodges, asked if that was a wise play, said, "It's only wise when he makes it."

By mid-season Agee had gained his confidence and was

storming through the league. He was hitting the ball hard, fielding well, running well. He was also loosening up in the clubhouse, exchanging banter with his teammates in his squeaky, high voice and becoming a presence. He was especially well liked by most of his mates since they related to his 1968 struggles. Players who can fight off injury and frustration in baseball emerge as locker-room heroes to their mates. Athletes have a short professional life span. As some say, athletes die twice, once when their career goes and again when their body goes. If Agee was not the most important 1969 Met, none was more important.

His teammates also knew of the courage Agee had shown in coming back from the opening-day spring-training beaning by Bob Gibson. Conquering that fear of being hit by a baseball may well be the most important aspect in making it as a professional hitter, a skill Ted Williams has often described as the most difficult in sports.

When the Mets and Cubs engaged in one of their most bitter battles of the season, Chicago pitcher Bill Hands led off the game by hitting Agee. Jerry Koosman went to the mound and hit Ron Santo of the Cubs straight in the chest with a ninety-five-mile-per-hour fastball. "I would have done the same if any of our guys were hit," said Koosman. "It just meant a bit more because it was Agee and because he had gone through so much."

In the third game of the 1969 World Series Agee led off with a home run and made two remarkable lunging catches on drives hit by Elrod Hendricks and Paul Blair. It was the game that most identifies his career.

At the bar of a Westchester country club, where Agee has gone to help out teammate Ed Kranepool at his annual diabetes fund-raiser, he is besieged by older fans for further descriptions of the play. He repeats over and over again that he had both balls all the way. "I just ran them down the way I always did," he said.

He seems to enjoy discussing the plays and the past and the team. There is an edge to his voice when he is asked by some fans about the current state of baseball. "They don't play hard all the time because they have those big contracts," he said.

Agee always played hard. He put together three fine seasons between 1969 and 1971 with marks of .271 in 1969, .286 in 1970, and .285 in 1971. He was injured a good part of 1972, slipped to .227 that season, was traded to Houston, and finished up with the Cardinals.

Tommie Lee Agee is forty-six years old now, carrying far too much weight on his large frame, showing signs of wear and tear in his face. He has married comfortably for the second time now.

Agee and Cleon Jones had become partners in a bar and restaurant called Outfielders Lounge, near Shea Stadium, in the early 1970s. They each put in much time there and the establishment did well. With the end of their careers as Mets, they found their patrons drifting away, and by the late 1970s the lounge near Shea Stadium was sold.

Agee drifted in and out of recreational jobs, some for the city, others in private industry, never quite finding one that suited his personality or motivated him. He was between jobs in 1988.

"I think he'd like to get back in baseball," teammate Art Shamsky, who saw him often, suggested. "I don't know why somebody doesn't hire him. He knows a lot about the game."

For retired ballplayers who live modestly, the huge baseball pension—some three thousand dollars a month for a player of Agee's time in the game, a dozen years, and age—can suffice. There are paid appearances at clubs and organizations, an occasional product endorsement, a paid clinic, a fee picked up signing autographs at baseball-card shows. Agee has made his home in New York ever since he played for the Mets and is often seen at baseball events. Many of these events, however, are charity affairs that do not pay a fee.

There is, also, not quite the same job market for black retired athletes as there is for the white ones. Players such as Agee and Jones fall into a nebulous area. They were not quite big enough stars, not Willie Mays or Hank Aaron or Willie McCovey, to demand large fees for appearances. They were too big to be employed in better-paying but less prestigious positions that could use their skills if not their baseball identification. The association with the 1969 Mets helps these players in stroking their egos or getting them free lunch and free dinner at charity events but does not help them acquire a serious, solid, steady meaningful job outside the game.

"Most of us go from high school into baseball," Dr. Ron Taylor once said. "We are not qualified for anything but baseball. All of a sudden we are thirty-three or thirty-four years old and we are out on the street without a skill. It is fine for those players who decide to remain in the game. It is very difficult for those retired players who can't get a job in the game or simply don't want to."

It is rare and impressive when a former player, such as Taylor, can create a second (in his case a third) career as he approaches middle age. Neither Jones nor Agee could do that. For the years they played the game they each played it with exceptional skills, were popular performers on the Shea stage, and earned good salaries. The years beyond baseball were filled with some financial difficulties and some emotional adjustments. It is those early years away from the game that were most depressing. Both of them seem to have shaken off much of the restlessness they showed the first summers away from the game.

"I knew I wouldn't play forever," said Jones. "I'm happy now just watching my son play. A lot of the colleges down here are after him. He may turn out to be a better player than me. He might even play both sports, baseball and football, be another Bo Jackson. If that happens I'm going to be his agent. I want to keep him away from the sharks up in New York."

It was only fifteen years after Jackie Robinson when Agee and Jones played their first professional games. It was still a time of turmoil. They survived those early years, those burdens all young black baseball players carried. They were able to reach the full potential of their athletic skills and star on the most popular baseball team of all time. They each wear their World Series ring with pride.

"I'd make every year 1969 if I could," said Jones.

That can't be done. Cleon Jones and Tommie Agee helped make 1969 memorable. That was certainly done.

# 12

# *Sham and Rodney*

September 10, 1969: Four Israeli planes were downed in heavy fighting in the Sinai today as the battle between Egypt and Israel heated up. Sexy Alice Crimmins, convicted in the murders of her two small children in Queens, petitioned the courts to have the decision reversed on appeal. In the Bronx, District Attorney Burton Roberts called for abortion reform to stop "the butchering of desperate women" after arraignment of a nurse who performed an illegal abortion that resulted in the death of the woman. In Southeast Asia the Viet Cong blew up a club in Saigon. Three American servicemen were killed and more than a dozen were injured. Outside Saigon, fighting continued endlessly. Latest casualty lists included the names of Capt. Jerry Dean White, twenty-four, of De Queen, Arkansas, killed in an aircraft fire fight, Sfc. Lewis Edward Wood, twenty-nine, of Guntersville, Alabama, killed in a vehicle crash, and Pfc. David Thomas Fellows, twenty-three, of Caledonia, New York, dead of gunshot wounds.

Four young Mets, Bud Harrelson, Ron Swoboda, Tug McGraw, and Ed Kranepool, visited a Brooklyn winery, introduced themselves to the proprietor, and were given a dozen bottles of New York State champagne. They drove together to the ball park for the doubleheader against the Montreal Expos and told clubhouse man Nick Torman to put the champagne in a cool closet. "If we win the first game and we are ahead in the second game," said Kranepool, "put the champagne on ice. We'll be popping it."

Jerry Koosman had beaten Bill Hands and the Cubs, 3–2, on September 8. The Mets were a game and a half out of first. Tom Seaver had beaten Ferguson Jenkins, 7–1, on September 9. The Mets were a half game out of first. Ken Boswell singled in the twelfth inning of the first game of the September 10 doubleheader at Shea for a 3–2 win. As the winning run scored, publicity director Harold Weissman flashed a message on the huge electronic scoreboard: LOOK WHO'S NO. 1. The fans went wild. Nolan Ryan struck out eleven, pitched a three-hitter, and won the second game, 7–1. The Cubs lost in Philadelphia and the Mets were in first place by a full game. The miracle was coming true.

In the clubhouse after the doubleheader sweep, Agee, Harrelson, Swoboda, Kranepool, McGraw, Boswell, and the rest all drank champagne.

"You don't go into first place every day," said Harrelson. "This is a day that calls for champagne."

"We are a first-place team," shouted Agee. "First place teams drink champagne."

The Mets were joined in bars across the city, in the upper West Side and in Greenwich Village, in the blue-collar taverns in Queens and the black hangouts in the Bronx, along the neighborhoods in Brooklyn, in the outer borough of Staten Island and across the country—wherever New Yorkers or Mets fans assembled. For this moment, the country's racial strife, the poverty, the anguish, even the war in Vietnam, seemed to be forgotten.

Pete Hamill, the brilliant young columnist of the *New York Post*, would write, "Don't talk to me today about Biafra or Nixon or Vietnam or John Lindsay. The Mets are leading the league. Get out of the way and sing us no more sad songs. I'm going drinking. It's September and the Mets are leading the league."

Mets outfielder Art Shamsky offered me a swallow of champagne in the clubhouse after the doubleheader victory. "Imagine," he said, with a huge grin, "my mother wanted me to be a doctor."

On March 15, 1969, on a sunny day in St. Petersburg, Florida, Mets outfielder Art Shamsky, who also doubled as a first baseman, was taking ground balls off the bat of his buddy Ken Boswell. Boswell hit grounder after grounder at Shamsky as he worked on his quickness and agility around the bag. Boswell hit a ground ball. Shamsky bent down routinely. Shamsky stayed down. His back had gone south on him. At the age of twenty-seven, Shamsky had a major baseball injury. His career was in doubt as he remained in bed, under doctor's orders, swallowing pain-killers and fluids, barely able to move. It would be a week before he could get out of bed without excruciating back pain. It would be three weeks before he could attempt to swing the bat normally. A day before the Mets were to open the 1969 season at home, Shamsky attempted batting practice. He swung with little gusto. The pain was still there. The next morning he was called into Gil Hodges's office, two hours before the opener, and told he was being put on the disabled list. He would be shipped to the Mets Triple A farm team at Tidewater three weeks later. I met him as he was walking from the manager's office. His thin face was strained. His eyes seemed blurry. His body seemed limp. He was clearly in pain, emotional as well as physical, as he trudged toward his locker to pack his belongings. I asked what the problem was. He quickly explained he had been sent out to the minors. "If I can't play for the Mets, who can I play for?"

The statement would not sit well with the Mets front office. They were sending Shamsky out because they didn't think he was ready to play. Shamsky was only concerned that a ninth-place team couldn't find a place for him. It was typical of

Shamsky, a young man always worried about the state of his career, that his confidence would be shattered by this move. He truly believed he would disappear in Tidewater. He would not.

Shamsky returned to the Mets on May 13. The back problem was gone. He would prove to be one of the most productive offensive players on the team, the only .300 hitter other than Cleon Jones, the second leading home-run hitter with 14, behind Tommie Agee's club-leading 26, and a useful outfielder and first baseman. He was blazing hot in the playoffs, with 7 hits in 13 at bats against Atlanta, leading the club with an impressive .538 average. As Hodges switched to his right-handed hitters against the left-handed Baltimore staff, he started only one game in the Series, went hitless, failed in two pinch-hit attempts, and came out of the Series with no hits and a diamond Series ring.

"That's all anybody ever talks about with me, the 1969 Mets," says Shamsky. "I played professional baseball for thirteen years (eight in the big leagues) and that's all I ever hear. I wear the World Series ring. I show it to people and it's like magic. When kids see it at a Little League banquet their eyes light up."

Arthur Louis Shamsky was born in St. Louis, Missouri, on October 14, 1941. He has an older sister, now a psychologist in St. Louis. His father ran a small scrap-iron business. The Shamskys lived in the University City section of St. Louis, an area of mostly middle-class Jews. One of his closest friends as a youngster was Ken Holtzman, later a successful pitcher with the Chicago Cubs, Oakland, Baltimore, and the Yankees.

"We were Jewish but we weren't very religious. We observed the holidays but we didn't make a big thing of religion. About all I did as a player in recognizing the religion was take off the major Jewish holidays. I told the Mets when I joined them I couldn't play in the World Series on the day of the Yom Kippur game. That always got a big laugh. When I joined the Mets in 1968 nobody expected any World Series. One oddity of my career is that I finished up in Oakland with Holtzman and Mike Epstein. Has there ever been a big-league team with three Jews?"

As an outstanding basketball and baseball player at University City High, Shamsky was signed by the Cincinnati Reds in 1959. He was instructed to report to the Reds farm team at Geneva, New York. Neither of his parents was terribly excited about his choice of profession.

"My father would have preferred that I had gone on to business, but he was into baseball and I think he was thrilled when I signed. My mother certainly wanted me to go to college and become a doctor, of course. What else is a Jewish boy supposed to do?"

Shamsky played baseball as a kid every chance he got. "We used to put a quarter in the light machine at tennis courts just to hit some fungoes at night. We played every day, we played in the rain, we played every chance we got."

Six feet one, weighing a spindly 165 pounds, with brown hair and brown eyes, Shamsky arrived at the upstate New York town early in 1960 as one of the most promising Cincinnati prospects in years. He had a left-handed home-run swing and the Cincinnati scouts projected him as Crosley Field star. At eighteen, he was certainly more advanced than a couple of other kids on that Geneva team: Pete Rose, a talkative, cocky second baseman, and Tony Perez, a shy, introspective Cuban with no command of English.

"All three of us became very close," said Shamsky. "Nobody expected Pete to become the hitter he did, and not many of us thought Perez would make it, either. We were just kids. It's hard to see that kind of potential in eighteen-year-olds."

Shamsky's father was deeply involved in his career and would often call Rose to get an update on his son's performance.

"I guess I didn't want to give him too much information. Maybe he figured that Pete would tell him more."

Shamsky hit .271 as a Cincinnati rookie in Geneva, worked

his way up through the system, and joined the Reds in 1965. He hit three homers in one game against the Pirates, was benched the next day against a left-handed pitcher, and hit his fourth straight home run the next day against Vernon Law.

"People only know me for the 1969 Mets, but once in a while somebody points out that I hit four homers in a row for the Reds. That's a comforting thought."

After a sad 1967 season with a .197 average, Shamsky was traded to the Mets.

"I got a call from Bob Howsam, who was running the Reds. This was after the 1967 season. I had just been operated on for back trouble. The phone rang at home. It was Howsam and I thought he was checking up on my condition. I told him I felt fine. 'That's good because we just traded you to the Mets.' That was a shock because to me the Mets were a terrible team, they weren't going anywhere and I didn't feel I would play much. I also hated to leave the organization and my buddies, Pete, Tony, and Tommy Helms, guys I had grown up with. Then Bing Devine called. I knew Bing from St. Louis. He was thrilled to have me, and he said we would have a better team. That made me feel happy. The next day I picked up the paper and I read that Bing had left the Mets and gone back to St. Louis. I didn't know if he did it because he made a trade for me or what."

Shamsky was an instant success with the Mets. He hit .238, but a dozen home runs, and his power earned him attention. He also was soon identified as a Jewish player, a rare event in a city that has more Jews than any city in Israel. This ethnic identification was soon used even further as the *New York Post* hired Shamsky to write a ghosted column of doings inside the Mets clubhouse. I was his ghost. The column caused him some aggravation when players became jealous or angry at things he said, things they thought were secrets, but it, too, gained him recognition.

After the 1969 season, Shamsky had another good year in

1970 with a .293 average and eleven homers. His back gave out again in 1971—he hit only .185 in 68 games and was traded to St. Louis.

"I just didn't want to go there," he said. "There was simply too much pressure trying to play at home."

The players went on strike that spring of 1972, and when the strike ended, Shamsky was released by the Cards. He signed with the Cubs, got little chance to play behind Joe Pepitone, and was soon traded to Oakland, where he was released for the last time.

"This time I decided to quit. Three teams didn't want me. That was enough."

Shamsky had gone into the restaurant business with ex-Yankee Phil Linz a couple of years earlier. Now he went into it full-time, with some television work added, a few appearances, and assorted business deals. He was finished with baseball at the age of thirty. "At the age of twenty-seven I was on top of the world," he says. "At thirty I hit bottom."

Art Shamsky is sitting in the front of his new Manhattan restaurant, Champions, at 17 Murray Street. His partners are Mets pitcher Ron Darling, batting-practice pitcher Tony Ferrara, and former big-leaguer Jerry Casale.

He is forty-seven years old, a handsome, well-dressed man with a bristling mustache. His clothes are well fitting, and he could easily pass for a male model with his tall, dark, handsome look. He is eager to talk about the 1969 Mets.

"I think the 1986 Mets were a terrific team, but in five or ten years they will be forgotten. The 1969 Mets will be remembered forever. It was coming from behind, being so bad the year before, having so many great games, and the combination of personalities," he said.

Shamsky said he still retains friendships with the Mets around New York, Ed Kranepool, Tommie Agee, Ed Charles,

Bud Harrelson, a Mets coach, and Tom Seaver, who was pitching until 1987.

"Bos has invited me down to Texas to hunt but I've been too busy. I've invited him up here but he doesn't like New York. One of these days we'll get together. I saw Cleon two years ago. Tommie Agee was marrying Maxine in the summer, and Cleon was the best man. The wedding is about to start and he isn't there. Agee is getting upset. I told him I would be happy to be the best man. Just as the ceremony is getting ready to start, Cleon shows up. 'Where you been?' He seems puzzled Agee is upset. 'I knew what time it started. I just stopped off to get something to eat.' "

Shamsky's professional life after baseball has been similar to his life in baseball. He has had his ups and downs.

"I've done all right. I've had some good years and some bad ones. I have thought about moving someplace else, but I couldn't do any better anyplace else. I'm known here. Sometimes I walk down the street with Ron Darling and the kids recognize him, and the older people—the blue-collar people, the cabbies, the truck drivers, the laborers—all yell at me. Even young people who weren't born then remember the 1969 Mets. They've heard about us from their parents or their grandparents."

Shamsky lives alone in a fashionable West Side Manhattan apartment. It is large enough for his daughters to stay with him when they are in town. One recently graduated from college, and the second is a junior.

"When you talk about baseball marriages, it's hard to relate. I don't think baseball killed my marriage. We were just too young. I was twenty and in my third year of baseball and Randi was only seventeen when we got married. We were both too young. I met her in high school. She was my only girlfriend. I guess my problem with Randi was that I always thought of her as a seventeen-year-old."

Shamsky was married in 1963 and separated in 1977. They

were divorced in 1979. "We remained good friends. Randi remarried a guy in Philadelphia, and he is very good for her. My girls like him. I talk to her still about the girls. There is no bitterness. It's just that after I got out of the game I realized I didn't enjoy spending so much time with her. It wasn't that we grew apart. We were never really that close. Baseball just covered it up. I think if I had a regular nine-to-five job and came home every day we might not have lasted as long as we did."

Shamsky understood the adjustment that he and many of his teammates had to make after baseball. "You can't help but have to deal with those ego aspects of it. You put on that uniform and people are yelling at you and you are a big hero, and that seems to be the only thing that matters. Then your career is over and the yelling stops and you are just another guy on the street. The stars may have an even more difficult time than an average player. I don't know. There is just nothing that prepares you for it. It's just some sort of dream world, fantasy life, and then it is gone."

No one who has ever played the game on the big-league level can dispute Shamsky's contention that the pressures are greater but so are the joys.

"I was a kid growing up in St. Louis, listening to Harry Caray describe the games. Stan Musial was my big hero, and I slept with his picture under my pillow. Then I make it to the big leagues. Musial had finished playing by then but he was around the Cards and I met him and I told him about my feelings towards him and he just smiled. He must have heard that a million times. It is hard to describe that emotion of being a big-leaguer and it is hard to describe when they take that uniform away from you and now you are out there with everybody else trying to make a living."

Shamsky cannot remember any single hit or any single game that identifies the 1969 season for him. "There were just so many games, so many emotional nights, especially with the

Cubs. I remember Seaver's perfect game, of course [amazingly, most Mets describe it as "Seaver's perfect game," which it was for only twenty-five outs], and a lot of games I got key hits, and the hot playoffs. I also remember, after we got Clendenon, how much he helped us. He loved to get on guys. He kept people loose. God forbid you should make a mistake in a game. Would you hear about it from him!

"There were a lot of leaders on that team, a lot of guys that got after other guys. I think Grote was the least appreciated guy on the club by the fans. He was a great catcher, the best I ever saw. I lockered near him and I heard how he talked to the press and I always wondered why he did that. Seaver got the most attention but he deserved it. He did the most. What was satisfying to me was the playoffs. This had been a team that was dominated by the pitchers. Then came the playoffs against the Braves and the pitchers didn't pitch very well. The hitters got hot and won it. That was very rewarding."

Shamsky still bristles when asked about being sent out before the start of the 1969 season. "My back was all right by then. I only needed three or four days of batting practice. Richie Allen proved you don't need spring training. Gil and Johnny Murphy came to me before we left Florida for New York. They told me I was going to go on the disabled list and then I was sent to Tidewater three weeks later. I was really upset. That was my ego talking, of course, but I had seen too many guys go down and never come back. I thought I would disappear. Whitey Herzog was the farm director then and he saw me hit a home run down there opening day at Tidewater and he said, 'What the hell are you doing here?' I stayed ten days and then they brought me back. I got a pinch-hit the day I came back and I was all right the rest of the year."

He became close to Boswell and would pick him up by car each day and drive to Shea. There would be some discussion of the coming game, and both would feel tension as they arrived. "Then somebody would make a kidding remark about

Boswell's cowboy boots or get on me about an upcoming Jewish holiday and the tension would be broken. Remember the doubleheader when Koosman and Cardwell pitched 1–0 games? I missed that day because of Yom Kippur. Thank God we won. I got some hate mail, 'Jew this, Jew that for taking off.' But I got ten times as much mail supporting me for respecting my religion."

When Shamsky thinks back to 1969 his memories are always of the entire city and not just the twenty-five players on his team.

"Nothing ever mattered as much to so many people as that team. I think we helped the city, the civil rights situation, even made the pain of the Vietnam War go away for a while. There was so much about that year that contributed strongly to people's lives."

When it was over, comedian Phil Foster put an act together. Shamsky, Koosman, Kranepool, Agee, Jones, Seaver, Clendenon teamed up with Foster in a Las Vegas show. For two weeks, each player got twenty thousand dollars.

"It wasn't very good but it was fun. We ended the act by singing 'The Impossible Dream.' Cleon always forgot the words. He had cue cards in front of him but never read them. You know what I remembered most from Vegas? Every night, as we were going into the theater for the show, Clendenon would be paged by the hotel operator. I guess he just liked the sound of his name."

It was clearly the one season that changed Art Shamsky's life, the one year that moved his career from routine to memorable. Nothing he does today is not, in some way, connected to that summer.

"I have these strange memories. I don't think about a big home run or a big play in the field. I think about warming up in left field and looking out behind the stadium and seeing thousands of people rushing off the subway cars and down the station so they can get into the ball park for the first pitch, and then a few minutes later I am standing on the top step of the dugout just before the game starts and the national anthem is being played and I look up at the stands at Shea and every seat is filled. God, it was exciting."

The customers were filling up his restaurant now, the phones were ringing furiously, and the manager had problems that needed Shamsky's attention. He had to excuse himself from the past to operate in the present. He was asked now if he was a happy man.

"How can you be unhappy? I have my health, I have two beautiful daughters, I have a good business."

There was a large photograph of Shamsky on the restaurant wall. He was posing one 1969 day in his Mets uniform. His bat was cocked far behind his left ear. He had a determined look on his face. He would attack a fastball. It was of another time.

The day Art Shamsky's back went out during the 1969 Mets spring training, Rod Gaspar went in. It was the kind of fortuitous circumstance that has been going on in baseball for a hundred years. One man's bad fortune is the next man's golden opportunity. When Yankee first baseman Wally Pipp skipped his team's lineup in 1925 with a headache, manager Miller Huggins replaced him with youngster Lou Gehrig. It would be more than thirteen years before Gehrig would miss a game. That legendary scene would be repeated over and over as injured players excused themselves from the lineup only to see a youngster win their job.

Gaspar didn't win Shamsky's job. He simply won a place on the ball club as Gil Hodges's all-purpose player, sort of a latter-day Rod Kanehl, an Original Met who forced his way onto Casey Stengel's early teams. Gaspar was a five foot, eleven inch, one-hundred-and-seventy-pounder from Long Beach, California, with minimal big-league skills. He was a switch-hitter with little power. He hit only one home run, a line drive off San Francisco left-hander Mike McCormick on May 29, in 260 big-league at bats. He had only 54 big-league hits, but 49 of them came in that 1969 season and most of them seemed to have a bearing on a Mets win. He threw left-handed and did lead the club in assists, with 12. He also started 6 double plays from the outfield, a figure that led the entire National League. He stole 7 bases in 10 tries. More importantly, he was used as a pinch runner more than a dozen times and never once complained about the insult to his ego. He wound up hitting .228 that season. In 1970 he had fourteen big-league at bats without a hit after being shipped to the minor leagues and recalled in September. He got two more hits with San Diego in 1971 and his last three big-league hits with the Padres in 1974.

Despite supposedly unimpressive big-league credentials, Gaspar was a recognized name in the Mets scheme of things throughout the 1969 season and became a media pet prior to the World Series because Baltimore star Frank Robinson botched his name.

In attempting to downgrade the upstart Mets before the opener, the great outfielder of the Orioles indicated he didn't even know the name of many of his opponents. "Who should I be afraid of, Ron Gaspar?"

New York writers pointed out that Robinson, intentionally or unintentionally, had slurred Gaspar and Ron Swoboda by mixing up their first names. It would be ironic that both Gaspar and Swoboda would play vital roles in the winning of the pivotal fourth game of the Series.

Swoboda, of course, made that spectacular catch off Brooks Robinson's bat to hold the Orioles to a one-run inning before the Mets could win, 2–1, in the tenth. Gaspar—running for Jerry Grote, who had started the tenth with a fly-ball double—scored all the way from second base when J. C. ("I swelled up") Martin's bunt was fielded by left-hander Pete Richert, whose throw to first base struck Martin on the wrist.

The New York press made a point of reminding Frank Robinson in print over Gaspar's name and the fact that he scored the run that gave Tom Seaver and the Mets a victory.

Rodney Earl Gaspar was born April 3, 1946, in Long Beach, California. He is one of three sons. His father was an iron worker.

"My parents never had much money and whatever they did have they weren't able to save."

His bat control, running speed, and defensive skills won him a scholarship to California State. Believing he would grow, mature, and increase his power potential, the Mets drafted him in 1966. Gaspar decided to stay in school. No other club showed any interest in him, and when the Mets drafted him again in 1967 he signed with them. He was assigned to Williamsport, where he hit .260 and moved up to Memphis in 1968, where he hit .309.

"I had a real good spring in 1969. Shamsky got hurt and that gave me a chance to play more than I thought I would. Gil liked the fact that I could run and field, and he decided that I could be a contributor on that team. About three days before we were breaking camp, he told me I had made the club."

Gaspar, a sandy-haired twenty-three-year-old bachelor that season, roomed with Gary Gentry and was close to Ken Boswell, Wayne Garrett, and Shamsky.

"I was just a rookie but there wasn't a great division among the players. Of course, I never hung out with Seaver or Grote or some of the other experienced players."

He came to spring training in 1970, failed to make the big club but did get to meet his future wife. They now reside in Mission Viejo, California, with their five children.

Gaspar had been an active participant in the joys and hours of a big-league ballplayer. It all changed after his marriage when he became a Christian and devoted his life to the Lord.

"After I found God I never looked back. Now I had a conscience and I knew right from wrong. I was always directed to the right path."

Rod Gaspar runs his own insurance company now out of his handsome two-story, five-bedroom home in one of the prettier areas of southern California. His hair is still thick, and at the age of forty-two he remains remarkably trim.

"I've become a nationally ranked four-wall handball player," he said. "I travel to tournaments all over the country and I play almost every day. It keeps me in real good shape. I'm probably a little lighter now than when I played baseball."

His name remains recognizable for old baseball fans.

"Even out here in California people remember the 1969 Mets. I still wear the World Series ring and when I'm talking business, people can't miss that rock. It has been very helpful to me in business."

Gaspar admits he put in some long hours and enjoyed the night life when he played for the Mets.

"I was staying in Manhattan, I was young, I was single. That was a lot of fun. I stayed with Boswell or with Garrett, and we spent a lot of time together seeing the city life. I enjoyed every minute of it. I knew it wasn't going to last. Too many good outfielders on that team. I was there on a pass. Shamsky got hurt and they took me along on a road trip I was not scheduled for. I hit very well and when we got back to St. Petersburg I really felt I had a chance."

Gaspar's biggest thrill came Opening Day of 1969.

"There was just so much excitement coming to the park and when I got there one of the coaches told me I was starting in right field. I wasn't terribly nervous. I was a pretty cocky kid in those days and I felt real loose about it. I don't re-member much about the game except that we lost a wild one (11–10), but the experience of being out there will always be with me."

Like the earlier Rod—Kanehl—Gaspar quickly became a crowd favorite. He got into games, it seemed, only when they were close. His chores were limited, pinch-hit, pinch-run, steal a base, catch a fly ball, move to the plate as a switch-hitter to force the hand of the opposing manager. He always played with unbridled enthusiasm.

"I look back and I think that getting into as many games as I did [118] on a club that had Cleon Jones and Tommie Agee and Shamsky and Swoboda was quite a managerial feat. Gil Hodges really knew how to utilize his personnel. I always felt a part of the club. I knew I wasn't a star but I also knew I was a contributor. I think that was the best thing Hodges did with that team. He made every player feel a part of that unit and vitally important to the team's success. Sure, the big guys, Seaver, Koosman, Cleon, Agee, got a lot of attention, but the scrubs won a lot of games. You can't always say that about other winning teams."

Gaspar admits he was unhappy when his big-league career ended so suddenly in San Diego when he was twenty-eight.

"I went back to the minors and I felt sure I would be called back up by the Padres. It didn't happen. When I didn't get drafted by a big-league club in 1976 I decided to quit. I was only thirty but I had gotten into insurance, I had a growing family, and I could make that emotional adjustment."

Gaspar still gets questioned about that World Series play when somebody recognizes his name.

"I was well known before the Series started because of the Frank Robinson line. I gave a lot of interviews, especially to Baltimore writers who wanted to know who this Rod or Ron Gaspar that Robby was talking about was. I got a lot of clippings on it. Then the play with J.C. bunting the ball got me more attention because I scored from second and it ended the game.

"I was on second, Al Weis was on first, and J.C. put the ball down on the ground. My job was to get to third safely and I had a good lead. Then Richert picked up the ball and threw it towards first. I could see it hit and I just took off. Eddie Yost [the third base coach] told me later he was waving me in and screaming for me to go home, but to tell you the truth I never heard a thing. I just took off. The guys were all around home plate when I scored and there was a big fuss on the field about whether J.C. had run out of the base line but I didn't hang around to listen. I had scored the winning run in a World Series game and I wanted to go into the clubhouse and enjoy it."

There wasn't much to Gaspar's big-league career after that but he has no regrets.

"The most money I ever made was twenty thousand dollars. I've done all right in the insurance business and I have a wonderful family. God has been kind to me. I think back to those days and I am thrilled at the memories. We were a hundred-to-one shot and we won everything and it had to be some kind of a miracle. I would have liked to have played longer and I would have enjoyed being a big-league coach for a few years, but just being in New York in 1969 was wonderful."

Gaspar has married happily, raised a wonderful family, and built a successful business. He looks forward always to more joys and triumphs, looks back only with fond memories and no bitterness.

"There was something so special, so exciting about that 1969 team. The whole city, the entire country, seemed to get caught up in the doings of that team. I still get fan mail about that year and a lot of requests from collectors for my autograph. I know it is only because I was a part of the 1969 Mets. Nothing can ever replace that. I was in the minor leagues in 1973. The Mets won again. I hardly paid any attention to it. I don't know if anybody did outside of the two teams and the two towns. But everybody paid attention to the 1969 team."

Maybe some other player would have contributed as much

to the 1969 Mets in a utility role. Maybe not. The Mets of 1969 were a delicate balance of talent and personalities, molded and led by Hodges with managerial deftness that is rarely seen. The performance of Rod Gaspar that season, the small things he did, the victories to which his fielding, running, throwing, and switch-hitting contributed, make him as important as the big winners or the big hitters. Baseball, after all, is the ultimate team game.

"It is twenty years now and every time I look at that World Series ring on my finger I have to thank the Lord for my good fortune. What a wonderful summer."

The brashy bachelor of 1969 had changed dramatically into a soft-spoken, happy, fulfilled family man. "Say hello to all my friends in New York," said Gaspar, "and God bless you."

# 13

## A Boy Named Koo

October 16, 1969: Thousands of antiwar demonstrators in Washington, New York, Philadelphia, Los Angeles, and other American cities rallied today in heated opposition to the conflict in Vietnam. Blacks demonstrated alongside some of the antiwar protestors and shouted their opposition to the war and their demand for further action in the civil rights field. Militant leader Sam Brown promised this was just the beginning of marches.

In Moscow, the Soviet Union announced the safe landing of *Soyuz 6*, its latest moon-probe vehicle. At the White House, President Richard Nixon announced a plan to wean people off the welfare rolls. In Chicago, Yippie leader Abby Hoffman announced plans for mass demonstrations at the trial of the Chicago Seven, the civil rights demonstrators arrested at the 1968 Democratic convention. Jackie Kennedy Onassis became involved in a hassle with photographers outside her Fifth Avenue apartment. New York City mayor John Lindsay campaigned before enthusiastic crowds in the Hasidic section of Brooklyn. Singer Arlo Guthrie announced impending marriage plans to Jackie Hyde at Alice's Restaurant, in Stockbridge, Massachusetts.

In Southeast Asia, the fighting and the killing continued. The latest casualty lists included the names of S. Sgt. Michael Kenneth Sawyer, twenty-two, of Norfolk, Virginia, killed in an artillery-rocket attack, Cpl. Lawrence Lee Dwyer, Jr., nineteen, of San Antonio, Texas, killed in a grenade explosion, and Pfc. Leon Edward Goodman, eighteen, of Annapolis, Maryland, dead of malaria.

On September 24, the Mets had clinched the Eastern Division title with a 6–0 victory over the Cardinals. Gary Gentry pitched a four-hitter; Donn Clendenon hit two homers, and Ed Charles hit one. On October 6, the Mets won their first pennant in their eighth season with a sweep of the Atlanta Braves. The Mets won the first game in Atlanta, 9–5, behind Tom Seaver and Ron Taylor. They won the second game against Atlanta, 11–6, behind Jerry Koosman, Ron Taylor, and Tug McGraw. Tommie Agee, Ken Boswell and Cleon Jones each homered for the Mets. The final game was won, 7–4, with Gary Gentry starting and Nolan Ryan relieving in the third inning. Agee, Boswell, and Wayne Garrett hit home runs.

In the final World Series game the Mets won, 5–3. Davey Johnson, the Baltimore second baseman, ended the Series with a soft fly ball to left. Cleon Jones waited under it. "Come down, baby, c'mon down, I gotcha," Jones later told the press he was saying as the ball floated to him. He caught it and went down to one knee before coming up.

Jerry Koosman, who had pitched a commanding five-hitter for the fifth-game victory, turned around from the play in left field just in time to catch the leaping Jerry Grote in his strong arms. It was Koosman's second win of the Series. It made the Mets the only 1962 expansion team to ever win a World Series. The 1986 Mets, victors over Boston, would become the second.

He won 222 games and enjoyed every one of them in a sparkling career that lasted some twenty years through New York, Minnesota, Chicago, and Philadelphia. Ironically, Jerry Koosman's career was almost over before it began. A bad debt saved him.

Koosman was driving south to Florida after the 1965 rookie pro season at Greenville, South Carolina, and Williamsport, Pennsylvania, to play in a Mets winter-league program.

"We got as far as Macon, Georgia," he said. "One of the other players, Jerry Wald, was driving my car while I was taking a nap. He ran a stop sign in town and hit another car. We were taken by the police to the local station house, tried, and convicted. We had to put up one hundred and fifty dollars for the fine. We didn't have that kind of money. I called Joe McDonald, the Mets farm director, at his home and asked him to advance us the money. He was a little reluctant but when I said we would be in jail for a long time if he didn't come up with the dough, he agreed to wire it to us. We paid up and got out of there as fast as we could."

Koosman had been a struggling pitcher at Greenville with a 5–11 record and a 4.71 ERA. He didn't do much better at Williamsport with an 0–2 mark in two starts, and 11 walks in 12 innings. He did have 11 strikeouts there and 128 at Greenville to give the Mets pause.

"We didn't think he was a prospect, frankly," said McDonald, now with the Detroit Tigers. "He threw hard but he didn't have a breaking ball and his control wasn't much. But every time I thought about releasing him I also thought about my hundred and fifty dollars. I figured I would let him go on into the 1966 season and release him after I deducted my money from his paychecks."

Koosman pitched well in the winter league, picked up a slider to complement his good fastball, and won a dozen games against only seven losses for the Auburn, New York, Mets in a fast Class A league. McDonald got his money back and then some.

Jerry Martin Koosman, a big, strong farm boy out of Appleton, Minnesota, had been a slow starter and a late developer. All the Mets had to do was wait for him.

He was born on December 23, 1942, though most baseball

books listed his birthday as a year later. He fibbed about his age when he signed with the Mets late in 1964 because at the age of twenty-two in his first professional spring training in 1965 he would be surrounded by seventeen- and eighteen-year-old pitchers.

"I got that all straightened out when I retired," he said. "I was forty-three and I wanted my pension records to be correct."

He grew up on a large farm about one hundred and fifty miles north of Minneapolis. His father raised livestock and grew corn, oats, and barley. Koosman's day began and ended with farm chores—cleaning out barns, tending to the corn, repairing fences. He had been driving tractors almost as soon as he could see over the wheel. The school days were long, with more hours compressed into the winter season so that Koosman and the other farm kids would be available to help out with planting and harvesting chores in the spring and fall.

Temperatures in winter regularly dropped to twenty and thirty below zero, with an occasional reading of fifty below in some of the more bitter seasons.

"Every electric machine was attached to a battery so we could start it up. Our cars sometimes ran all night if we had something important to do. We couldn't always trust the batteries in the morning at fifty below zero."

There were two major activities for Koosman in the bitter-cold days of January, ice fishing and baseball pitching.

"We would go out to one of the frozen lakes nearby, set up our tents with heaters, cut a hole in the ice, and fish in our shirt sleeves. We would fill up a bucket of bass. Actually it was quite comfortable."

The winter baseball pitching was a little more tricky. Koosman and his older brother, Orville, used to play catch for hours in the hayloft of the family's big barn.

"We used to keep those things fairly warm for the livestock. We would climb up to the loft, where we stored the hay, clear a little mound, and start throwing. Sometimes I was the pitcher and sometimes I was the catcher."

By the time he was fifteen or sixteen, Koosman's pitching prowess was well known around the area. He spent a lot of time facing batters twice his age.

"We had these beer leagues around there, amateur leagues with guys who had played some college ball or even some professional baseball and played some tough games. The fields weren't all the best but we had a lot of fun. Each team would bring a keg of beer and when the game was over the winners would start draining that keg while the losers watched. That was painful. After a while the winners would break down and let the losers drink, too. We downed a lot of beer in those days."

After graduating from high school in 1962, Koosman joined the Army. He was uncertain about a career as a farmer, unknown to scouts as a baseball pitcher, and unsure about any alternate skills. He had soon grown to his full height of six feet, two inches, weighed a solid 210 pounds, and could throw hard. He played for a topnotch Army team at Fort Bliss, Texas. His catcher was a young man from Queens, New York, by the name of John Luchese. Without telling Koosman, Luchese wrote his father a letter about this big farm-boy pitcher that was mowing down Army batters. The senior Luchese worked as an usher at the newly opened Shea Stadium that summer of 1964. After receiving his son's letter, he discussed it with Joe McDonald. The Mets had never heard the name of Jerry Koosman.

"He had attended one of those regional high schools without much of a baseball program," McDonald said. "Our scout in that area never saw him. Few scouts showed up at those beer-league games. They were mostly for fun. Koosman had apparently fallen through the cracks of our scouting system."

On a gamble, McDonald assigned Red Murff, a Texas-area scout, to take a look at Koosman at his next scheduled game for his Army team. Murff drove over to Fort Bliss to see Koosman but had to wait three days since Army schedules were not written in stone. Finally, Koosman pitched and struck out a dozen. Murff approached him after the game and offered a two-thousand-dollar bonus if Koosman signed with the Mets. Koosman didn't want Murff to think he was getting an unsophisticated farmer so he asked for five thousand dollars. Murff said the Mets probably wouldn't be interested. He let Koosman sweat for a couple of days and came back for his next pitching outing. This time he offered Koosman only fifteen hundred dollars if he signed then and there.

"I figured I'd better take it or I'd owe them money," said the left-hander.

He fudged on his age, signed the contract, and reported to the Greenville club the next spring after his Army discharge. He moved through the system quickly from Greenville to Williamsport to Auburn, where he led the New York-Penn League in ERA with a 1.38 mark after finding the slider, and then to the Mets in 1967. He made the team that spring, pitched in a couple of games before being optioned out in the middle of May, and returned on September 1. He would last eleven memorable seasons with the Mets before being traded to Minnesota after the 1978 season.

Koosman, a handsome, heavily muscled young man with dark eyes and dark hair, married a beautiful young woman from his hometown. Lavonne and Jerry Koosman and their three attractive children now make their home in a large plot of land not far from where he grew up in the town of Chaska. The two older Koosman children are college students.

Koosman was 19–10 with the 1968 Mets and lost the Rookie of the Year award to a young Cincinnati catcher, Johnny Bench. It would have given the Mets two back-to-back award-winning rookie pitchers. Tom Seaver won it in 1967. Koosman, overcoming several serious injuries in 1969, including a severe burning from boiling popcorn spilled on his hand and a dead arm suffered in a cold April game, was 17–9. He pitched the first Mets opening win ever with a 3–0 1968 victory over the Giants, had a 2.08 ERA that year, and a 2.28 with six shutouts in 1969.

Koosman, clearly the Met best liked and most admired by his teammates, was also the press favorite. He was warm, accessible, helpful, and cooperative. One occasion, before a getaway day game against Houston, I explained that I had terrible deadline pressures in writing my story after the game and still making the plane home. I would have no time to visit the clubhouse for postgame quotes, but as I represented an afternoon paper, quotes from the pitcher were essential to my story.

"OK, got your pencil? This is what I will say if I win, and this is what I will say if I lose."

He did, in fact, lose and I used his pregame quotes in my postgame story. We kidded about it later on the team bus.

"Save those winning quotes," he said. "You'll need them for my next start."

Koosman's Met career ended on a sour note. He was 3–15 in 1978 with a dreadful team. He had been 21–10 for the 1976 Mets and followed that with an 8–20 season when the bottom fell out of the team. With free agency exploding on the baseball scene, Koosman was anguished that the Mets refused to bid for available players to improve the club. He criticized management and asked to be traded. He was sent home to Minnesota. He was a twenty-game winner for the Twins in 1979, his second twenty-game season.

He was 6–4 with the Phillies in 1985, underwent knee surgery, was released, and later spurned a Cardinal offer for a free-agent spring-training chance. "It was time to go home."

An amateur pilot, a wonderful golfer, a skilled fisherman, an expert with automobiles, Koosman had plenty to do. In 1986 he began a national amateur-baseball program, aimed at showing off young players—players who had fallen through the cracks of the big-league scouting systems as he had—for possible college scholarships and future pro careers. The program is called America's Best, and he runs it out of an office in his home. Several ex–Major Leaguers—including former teammates Don Cardwell, J. C. Martin, and Joe Pignatano; Tom Tresh, Wayne Twitchell, and Don Kessinger—work with him in this program.

Jerry Koosman is at home in Chaska. He is forty-six years old ("That's my honest age, not my baseball age," he says) and busy at work with the amateur-baseball program. His hair is full and thick and there is some extra girth around the middle. He has paid the price for those beer leagues and for being a teammate of Don Cardwell, Ron Taylor, and Tug McGraw.

"What a wonderful year, what a bunch of great guys. I think the two guys who mattered most that year were Rube Walker and Gil Hodges. Rube was just so much fun to be around and we kidded him unmercifully. He was our punching bag, the guy you could use to let off steam. If things weren't going well, he was our crying towel."

Koosman said that Hodges controlled every aspect of that team's operation but did it with a soft hand.

"He was a gentleman's gentleman. He could get on you, correct you, but he never did it in a way that embarrassed you."

Koosman remembered losing a game to the San Diego Padres. Clarence (Cito) Gaston homered to beat him in the ninth inning. Hodges, very upset, asked, "What did you throw him?"

"A fastball," said Koosman.

"Why would you throw him a fastball when you know he can't hit a curve ball?"

"Grote called for a fastball."

"Aren't you the pitcher?"

Koosman told me, "I really learned something from that. A pitcher has to control his own game. It was a lesson I always stayed with."

Actually, the 1969 season started out unpleasantly for Koosman. Hodges and Walker ordered him to stop throwing his slider.

"I had won nineteen ball games in 1968 with the slider. Now they wanted me to throw a curve. They were concerned about my arm. I was very upset. Soon I had arm trouble. But my arm came back, I had a good year and I threw curves. They must have been right. It was a couple of years later before I started throwing the slider again."

The Mets stayed close to the Cubs through the first three months. They proved their worth in two big series against Chicago. Koosman was a key factor each time. Some think the pennant was won when Koosman hit Ron Santo in the chest with a fastball.

"Bill Hands had knocked Agee down. I went to the mound and I knew what I had to do. Nobody was going to intimidate us. That was one of the turning points of the season. There were a lot of turning points. One time somebody slid into Grote and sent him flying. This was against Montreal, and the next inning Cleon came home and he sent their catcher, Ron Brand, halfway to the dugout with a hard slide. We protected each other. We were like family."

Unlike many of his mates, Koosman had a close relationship with Tom Seaver. He respected Seaver's professionalism and was also able to bring out some of the boyish laughter Seaver often showed.

"I loved to kid Tom. You know how serious he could be, especially about his pitching. Well, this one day he was getting ready to start against Houston. I came up with this idea that we would announce that Tom had been traded to see how he would react. Jack Simon, who was our radio producer, hooked up a microphone that came out of Seaver's radio. Seaver kept the radio above his locker and listened to music before a game. Well, Jack could imitate Howard Cosell's voice pretty good. He goes off to the back room and all of a sudden we hear over Seaver's radio, 'Here is a sports bulletin. Howard Cosell reporting. The New York Mets have just traded Tom Seaver to the Houston Astros.' We threw in the names of a couple of other guys to make it sound legitimate and then we all started moving towards Seaver's locker to see if he had heard it. He heard it, all right, and you could see his face was white. We really had him going for a while and he was very upset. He immediately figured I had something to do with it. I denied it but he kept saying, 'I'll get you, Koo, I'll get you for this.' He never did."

The night before Seaver was traded to the Reds in 1977, after some bitter contract negotiations and some unpleasant statements, the two pitchers were joined by Bud Harrelson in a farewell dinner and some late-night drinking. They knew an era was ending for the Mets. Harrelson would be gone at that season's end, and Koosman would be traded away after one more Mets year.

While they were together, for some ten years, Seaver and Koosman may have been as good a pitching pair as the game has ever seen. Seaver won three Cy Young awards but many of the Mets still believe it was Koosman who was clearly the one irreplaceable player on the 1969 and 1973 National League championship teams. Trying not to nitpick in a choice between two brilliant pitchers, some Mets point to the 1973 World Series. Koosman won the fifth game with a 2–0 victory over Oakland with strong relief by Tug McGraw. It gave the Mets a 3–2 Series lead before they flew west to Oakland for the last two games. Seaver lost the sixth game, 3–1, with Reggie Jackson hitting two run-scoring doubles, and Jon Matlack was beaten the next day with Jackson hitting another two-run homer.

Koosman minces no words. "Tom Seaver was the best pitcher I ever saw."

Koosman enjoyed watching the world-champion Minnesota Twins from afar in 1987. "They were a lot like us. They were a close bunch of guys and they won close games. Heck, when we got two runs in 1969 we thought we had a laugher. When you look back at how few runs we scored that year it was a miracle to win a hundred games. Let's face it, as young as most of us were, and coming off a bad year, the entire season was a miracle."

Only Seaver, who tried to pitch for the Mets in 1987, and Nolan Ryan, who was still going strong in 1988, lasted longer in baseball among members of the 1969 team than Koosman did. It was a happy ride for the upbeat left-hander from Minnesota.

"I played with a lot of teams, but the 1969 team had to be my favorite. When you win it all it is just so satisfying. We had a closeness, we knew how to play, and we were successful. Gil was the guy who gave us backbone in that tough pennant race through his leadership. I doubt if we would have won it with another manager. He was perfect for us and I guess, in a way, we were perfect for him."

Koosman seems to be one of only a few of the 1969 Mets who can look back with unbridled joy and ahead with unmitigated confidence. He had come out of the Minnesota beer leagues a little shaky, picked up his slider, learned to master his popping fastball, earned respect, and enjoyed much success. He was a hero of the fans, and with a warm smile and a cold beer won over all of his teammates. He has combined a successful career with a marvelously close family life. He is as unpretentious today in his advancing middle age as he was as the left-handed half of that dynamic duo that pulled the Mets from also-ran status into world champions. There clearly seems more to the Koosman story than just some brilliantly pitched games and some very important 1969 wins. There is some certainty that many of the youngsters he helps through America's Best will carry forward his solid values. There just wasn't a better person on the 1969 Mets.

In the annual New York Baseball Writers show held after the 1969 season, there was a parody of a popular song with the names of the Mets substituted for the real words of the song. The ditty ended with some twenty-five baseball writers on stage raising their voices loudly, if not melodically, in the final phrasing with the words ". . . and Jack DiLauro." It earned a big laugh from the huge audience.

Jack Edward DiLauro, a left-handed pitcher, won exactly one game for the 1969 Mets. He pitched in a total of 23 games that year, with 4 starts. He played with the Mets from May 14 through the end of the season, was sent to Tidewater a week after the World Series ended, and played one more big-league season in Houston in 1970. He also won a game there.

No player can be considered unimportant on a championship team, but DiLauro was probably the least known of the 1969 Mets. The first game he started in the big leagues may have been the game that convinced the Mets they were a contending team.

DiLauro had been in the Detroit organization for more than a half dozen years when he was purchased by the Mets for their minor-league club at Tidewater. He did not throw hard, and on a team with the likes of Seaver, Koosman, Gentry, Ryan, Cardwell, McAndrew, and McGraw, that lack of speed showed up dramatically.

Ryan, bothered with blistered fingers, a rough military-reserve schedule, and finally a severe groin pull, was forced to miss several turns.

"They called me up in the middle of May, I got a couple of relief appearances and then I started against the Dodgers," said DiLauro. "I pitched nine shutout innings and we won, 1–0, in the fifteenth. I remember going out for the ninth inning and more than thirty thousand people at Shea stood up and gave me a standing ovation. I just stood at the mound, my head was down and I was crying. It was the most emotional moment of my life. It was worth all those years of beating my head in the ground in the minors in the Detroit organization without hopes of making it."

DiLauro, a six foot, two inch, 185-pounder from Canton, Ohio, suffered from one of baseball's oldest prejudices. He was discriminated against because he didn't throw hard.

"I was never appreciated as a pitcher no matter how well I did. They were always looking for the guys who threw hard. I always relied on the other eight guys on my team."

DiLauro got his only Mets win on July 20 in the second game of a doubleheader in Montreal after Gary Gentry was beaten in the first game.

"That was just after the moon landing. I used to say, 'One small step for man, one giant win for DiLauro.' Guys used to kid me about getting my second win when man walked on Mars."

He went to Houston after playing with the Mets and never could get along with manager Harry Walker.

"It was a personality thing. He just didn't like me. That club was more interested in silly discipline than in winning. One time the general manager, Spec Richardson, had a sign posted in the clubhouse that every player had to wear his hat on the field. When I did my running I liked to take it off because I sweated so much into it. This one time I was running without my hat. I ran to the other side of the field and a lot of my teammates were sitting along the foul line. They pointed to my head because I didn't have my hat on and they knew Richardson was watching. I yelled as loud as I could, 'Screw the hat.' I didn't see Harry Walker sitting there. Everybody knew his nickname was the Hat because he wore these fancy fedoras all the time. He thought I was yelling 'Screw the Hat,' meaning him. I guess that finished me with him."

He bounced around the minors for a couple more seasons

after that and then quit baseball. He went back to Ohio, divorced his wife, Diane, in 1973, met and married a woman with two children and now lives in Malvern, Ohio, with Jane and two grown sons. He manages a sporting goods store in a Malvern shopping center.

It is early afternoon and Jack DiLauro, forty-five years old, is in his office. He appears a little heavier than he did twenty years ago but still is athletic-looking.

"I left baseball with a bitter taste. I guess I think about those days too much. I was used. They needed me for a few games and then discarded me at the end of that season. I was only twenty-nine when I was finished with baseball. I didn't have anything to do, anyplace to go, any training for anything else. I never made any money in baseball so it was all very hard for me. I got this job and became the manager a few years back. We are all right now. I have a nice house on a lakefront site. We're comfortable."

DiLauro was a cocky kid and seemed hardly awed when he joined the Mets.

"I was no green rookie. I had been around baseball six or seven years by then. I felt if I pitched well I would get a chance to make a career. I pitched well (a 2.40 ERA in 63 innings) but it didn't matter. I wasn't very comfortable with Gil Hodges there. He just never talked to me. I don't think he talked to anybody other than his coaches. I don't think there was a single player on that team who had a one-to-one relationship with Gil."

DiLauro said there was some sort of class distinction on the Mets.

"I hung out with the other rinky-dinks on the team, Gaspar, Bobby Pfeil, after he came up from Tidewater, a couple of the other scrubs. I got close to Nolan Ryan. He was very unhappy there. He never got along with Hodges. He was not used properly. Anybody could see the greatness in him. Somehow or other he was never used in turn, something would come up, a rainout, an injury, anything to disrupt his schedule. They never explained anything to him. Nolan never talked negatively about anybody, but you could see he was unhappy. He grumbled once in a while about being stuck on that team. But he could throw smoke. Wow. I think he was lucky to be traded away when he was. He might not have achieved all those things if he stayed in New York."

DiLauro is still proud of the connection with the 1969 Mets and wears his World Series ring all the time.

"It's good for business. This is a sporting goods store and people know about the 1969 Mets and they know me around here. They know I was connected to that team. It's good for my ego."

DiLauro has not been to a big-league game since he last played. He just does not find it worth his trouble.

"The game has gotten boring, all the big salaries, all the talk about money. We played because we loved it. I knew I was never going to make a lot of money. I knew I wasn't that good but I enjoyed the game and I enjoyed the guys. Just sitting in the bullpen with McGraw and Taylor and Piggy out there could be as much fun as actually pitching in the game. That's what I missed the most when I left."

DiLauro played baseball and football in high school, won a scholarship to the University of Akron, played another year of baseball, pitched in a good summer amateur league and signed with the Tigers for a fifteen-thousand-dollar bonus. Then he bounced around the Detroit organization for a half dozen years.

"I played in eight towns in six seasons and I never really got a serious chance to make the ball club. 'He doesn't throw hard enough.' I heard that all the time. Then Whitey Herzog saw me pitch a couple of games in the minors. He recommended the Mets get me. He really understood pitching. He liked those hard throwers—Seaver, Koosman, Ryan—but he also seemed to know that a guy could win without throwing the ball through a wall. I owe him a lot for that chance."

DiLauro was glad to escape the minor-league life. He found it difficult. "I had this apartment in Queens when I joined the Mets. I was a new groom and my wife enjoyed the life in New York. After I stopped playing ball and I was struggling with my life, we just grew apart. We were divorced in 1973. I married Jane in 1977. One of our boys is an art student and the other one is trying to decide on a career now."

DiLauro cites his game against the Dodgers as his most emotional experience in the big leagues. Only one other day can rival it. "I was in Tidewater when they told me they wanted me in New York right away. I got dressed, raced to the airport, and missed the plane. I had to wait for the next one and didn't get there until the fourth or fifth inning of the game that night. The Mets were playing the Atlanta Braves. I got to the clubhouse, got dressed, and walked onto the bench. I knew some of the guys from spring training. I just looked up on the scoreboard and saw that Phil Niekro was pitching a no-hitter for the Braves. That would have been some debut for me. Anyway the Mets went on to get some hits and win the game. When it was over I just went to the top step of the dugout and stared out at the huge stadium as the people filtered out. It was just an incredible sight seeing all those people in that ball park. It is hard to describe the thrill of just being in a big-league park."

DiLauro enjoys the sporting goods business, still plays a good game of golf, is active in a couple of bowling leagues, and spends some time fishing in the summertime.

"I guess I'm just upset that my career wasn't longer, that somebody didn't take a chance on me. Maybe I was ahead of my time as a pitcher. I see a lot of guys now who are winning and making big money without throwing hard."

His career was short and hardly significant. But he did have that one win, he did contribute, he did sit in the bullpen on a World Series team.

"I wanted more of the game. I didn't want to leave so early. I wished I could have gotten along better with the managers and the front-office people. It's twenty years now and hardly a day goes by that I don't think about something relating to the Mets of 1969. I guess I always will."

All of them contributed to that 1969 dream season, Seaver, Koosman, Grote, Jones, Agee . . . "and Jack DiLauro."

# 14

# Hall of Fame Pair

November 20, 1969: *Apollo 12* rocketed off the moon today with astronauts Charles (Pete) Conrad and Alan Bean on board to link up with the orbiting mother ship. In Hyannis Port, Massachusetts, Joseph Kennedy, Sr., the patriarch of the political family, was buried in a driving rain. His sole surviving son, Senator Edward Kennedy, quietly read several essays at the gravesite. In Los Angeles, investigators performed microscopic tests on a pair of tinted sunglasses found at the site of the murder of actress Sharon Tate. The glasses were described by police as "the first workable clue" in the brutal killings of the actress and several friends.

In Washington, photos were released documenting the My Lai massacre of March 16, 1968. Lt. William L. Calley, platoon leader of Company C, First Battalion, 20th Infantry Regiment, 11th Light Infantry Brigade, had been formally charged with the murder of civilians in the South Vietnamese village. Casualties continued unabated in Southeast Asia. Among the latest names released by the Pentagon were Pfc. William Arthur Duncan, twenty, of St. Louis, Missouri, Sgt. Leslie Tobias Hammack, twenty-two, of Mooresville, Indiana, and Captain Harvey Paul Kelley, thirty-one, of Omaha, Nebraska, all dead of fragmentation wounds.

In New York, the Baseball Writers Association released results of the National League Most Valuable Player voting.

San Francisco first baseman Willie McCovey, who led the league with 45 home runs and 126 runs batted in while hitting .320, was the winner in a tight vote against New York Mets pitcher and NL Cy Young award-winner Tom Seaver. The right-hander, who was 25–7 with a 2.21 ERA for the world champions, collected 243 votes in the national balloting among the writers to McCovey's 265. The vote immediately set off a furor among fans and the press as they argued the relative merits of awarding the MVP title to a pitcher as against an everyday player. To many, Seaver was an everyday player. His influence on the team was enormous. On the bench, in the clubhouse, on the road, and while pitching, Tom Seaver had more impact on the image, style, and success of the 1969 Mets than any other player.

As I drove up the Merritt Parkway to his sprawling Greenwich, Connecticut, home on a snow-covered winter morning, my impressions of Tom Seaver were clear. He was simply the best of them. There would have been no miracle without him. *Time* magazine had asked that summer of 1969 on a cover, "Is God Dead?" When that question was posed to Seaver facetiously after an important win, the strikingly handsome twenty-four-year-old pitcher had replied, "No, he's alive and well and living in an apartment in Queens." Seaver had been a baseball miracle of sorts. A skinny kid pitcher in Fresno, California, he had matured into a husky hard-thrower after a six-month tour of duty with the Marines. Signed by Atlanta, he had wound up as a Met after the commissioner's hat trick. Joining a team with little pitching talent, he had been thrust immediately into the starting rotation and responded in 1967 with a Rookie of the Year season. He was even better in 1968 and clearly the best pitcher in baseball in the championship season with the 25–7 record and a 2.21 ERA. His ERA would not rise above 3 runs a game until an injury-filled 11–11 season in 1974. He won 20 games or more five times. He finished his career after the 1986 season, despite an aborted attempt at coming back with the Mets again in 1987, with a lifetime mark of 311–205. Only eleven pitchers in all of baseball history have won more.

His influence in the clubhouse was enormous. He was always first among equals. He got more personal attention from management. His blond wife, Nancy, wearing those ever-present tam-o'-shanter hats, was photographed and filmed more than the wives of all the other players put together. His nicknames, Tom Terrific and The Franchise, summed up his standing. He was serious when he pitched and prepared, a clubhouse comic in freer moments. His laugh would sometimes be a loud cackling sound, amusing or annoying his teammates depending on the mood of the moment. He was close to Harrelson, Koosman, and Grote, comfortable with most others, strained with a few, notably Kranepool and Swoboda, whom he derided as not serious enough students of the game, squanderers of their time and talent.

In 1977, as the team declined dramatically and free agency rocketed salaries upward, he was traded to Cincinnati. He had asked for a contract extension and Board Chairman M. Donald Grant had dug in and fought. This would be the stand that would set the tone on free agency around the Mets. *Daily News* columnist Dick Young would carry Grant's sword. The coup de gras would be felt when Young suggested in print that Seaver wanted more money because his wife, Nancy, was jealous of the money Nolan Ryan and his wife, Ruth, were now enjoying in California. It would force Seaver's hand. He told GM Joe McDonald he now must be traded. The deal was consummated with the Reds by phone and announced in a sweltering Atlanta Stadium clubhouse. Seaver would break down in tears the next day as he bid farewell to the press in front of his locker at Shea.

Seaver enjoyed continued success in Cincinnati until he

returned to the Mets, now under new management, in 1983. He was 9–14 that year. Shockingly, he was lost to the team the following season when claimed by the White Sox in the compensation pool, a move frought with rumors of skulduggery. He stayed in Chicago until June 29, 1986, when he was traded to Boston. He helped them win the pennant that year but injured his knee in September. It would keep him out of the playoffs and World Series. Ironically, his last appearance as a player (except for the unhappy attempt at a Met return in 1987) would be on the bench of the Red Sox in the sixth game of the losing 1986 World Series at Shea.

He sat out the rest of 1987, and in 1988 considered various opportunities in baseball management, broadcasting, and private business.

His magnificent, reconstructed old Greenwich barn on a breathtaking site loomed over the hill now. A workman finished clearing the snow from his circular driveway, and Seaver pulled up in his van. He had taken his daughters to school, Nancy was busy with her chores, and the retired pitcher could talk of those wondrous days.

"I was tired of the travel, the bus rides, the late nights, being away from my family," Seaver said. "There was nothing more to achieve. I could have hung on with the Mets. They would have paid me a lot of money to keep trying. I couldn't compete any longer."

The conversation quickly turned from the present to the past, from the aching knee and fleshier form to that hard, well-muscled boyish leader of the 1969 Mets.

"We pass over 1968 too quickly. That was the season the executive people were getting the pieces together, getting the club in position, getting Agee to play center field, bringing Grote along as the catcher, getting the pitching staff together. They could see that there was a Seaver, Ryan, Koosman,

Grote, Harrelson and getting Gil Hodges. Gil stayed with Agee after he had a tough year in 1968, and Agee got his feet on the ground. That hole was filled. Gil established that he was the boss, the person who made decisions, that he would be the person of strength and everybody understood that."

Seaver leaned back in his chair and tried to reconstruct the building of that team.

"You could see they cleaned out the guys who were there before, guys who were just filling positions, the Hal Reniffs, the Bob Shaws, the guys whose careers were over and they were going with the young people, the McGraws, the Seavers, the Koosmans, the Gentrys, and we were all too young and naive to know just how good we were. It would be interesting to pick Gil's mind at this point and see what he thought at that time."

The Mets could hardly know, coming off a ninth-place finish, what wonders lay ahead for them.

"Only Grote seemed to know. He said repeatedly that spring that we could win, we were good enough to compete with anybody, we had the best team in the league," Seaver said. "I thought we could be a .500 team. Had we had six or seven years together, seen these players together, Seaver, McGraw, Koosman, Gentry, Harrelson, maybe I would have said we could win."

Seaver never envisioned that spring a season of such dominance after winning sixteen games each of his first two seasons. "You never think that. If you want to win twenty games you have to start out trying to win one. Every year you go to spring training and you start out with zero. You take each start as it comes. That was always my approach."

Seaver said the offense fed on the pitching and the pitchers knew the offense was better than people suggested, especially after Donn Clendenon joined the team in June.

"But if you ask me why did we win I would have to say the pitching and the defense, especially up the middle with Grote,

Harrelson, and Boswell, and Agee in center field. Harrelson was exceptional, very competitive, a very smart player, knew each individual player and knew how to play."

In early May the Mets were in fourth place, 6 games behind the Cubs, making no particular dent on the National League East race. Seaver remembers a weekend in Chicago. "We are facing Durocher's Cubs Friday, Saturday, and a doubleheader Sunday. Durocher is throwing at our black guys, Agee and Jones, knocking them down, intimidating them, really playing hardball, and they win the first two games of the series. We are eight games out of first place. Saturday night I'm out with my sister, Katie, who has come down from her home in Northern Michigan, just the two of us, and I'm pitching the next day. 'Watch what happens when Santo comes up tomorrow,' I tell her. 'It's going to be interesting.'

"So the next day I get the first three hitters out. Santo comes up leading off the second. I throw a slider down and away. The next pitch I throw right between his helmet and his head. He goes down flat on his back. Wham. Nobody told me what to do. Gil didn't tell me to do it. It was just something that had to be done. Koosman would have done it, Gentry would have done it—especially after losing two games. Santo on the day went oh for eight and struck out about six times. We were just about ready to be taken and now I win that game, 3–2, and McGraw wins the second game, 3–2, and we come out of Chicago .500 for the series after losing the first two games."

Seaver smiled broadly and then he became very animated. "I got an addendum to that story. Years later I was playing for Cincinnati and I come down to the coffee shop for breakfast in Chicago. Johnny Bench is having breakfast with a guy and I recognize that he is with Santo, who has now been out of baseball for years. Bench and Santo had been good friends. I walk over to say hello and he says, 'You remember that day you knocked me down? I was so damn mad.' We laughed about it but he still remembered it. We had some hard throwers on our team and when they started throwing at us they got it pretty hard. Later on, Koosman hit Santo. That was the series where Bill Hands hit me on the wrist. I went in after the inning and Gil said, 'You hit him. I don't care if it takes four pitches; hit him.' I finally hit him on the leg. The message was delivered. That was the game Grote got so angry he started firing the ball back at me. He threw one back and it really stung. I had to call him out and tell him to take it easy on me. My left wrist was killing me. He just got so emotional sometimes, he couldn't control himself."

The excitement began building in late May and early June as the Mets won eleven games in a row for the first time and did it against the West Coast clubs, especially the hated Giants and Dodgers and the new San Diego Padres. They were now beating good teams regularly and doing it in tough games. One of the big wins came against Los Angeles on June 4.

"Everybody on the team might have a different game but for me," Seaver said. "I came to the realization we could win after a game against the Dodgers at Shea. We were in a scoreless game into the fifteenth inning. Then Garrett hit a ball up the middle with a man on second. There was going to be a close play at the plate. Willie Davis came charging in and the ball went under his glove. The winning run scored. There was real electricity. I remember going into the clubhouse and making eye contact with Grote. It was like an electrical charge. That was the last ounce on the scale that tipped me over into believing we could win."

By July 8 the Mets had cut the Chicago lead to four games. Seaver was facing Ken Holtzman the next night at Shea. The Mets believed and the fans believed that this miracle season was truly building to a thrilling finish. All doubts would be removed that night. It was Seaver's almost perfect game, witnessed by some fifty-eight thousand people.

"My father had come from California on a business trip and

he was at the game. Nancy had picked him up at the airport and now they were there, and by the fifth or sixth inning I knew I had great stuff. It was a fabulous game. It was as good a game as I ever pitched. Emotionally, I was totally aware of what was going on. I came to bat and I got this incredible standing ovation. I felt as if I was almost levitating. It took great discipline not to get too emotional.

"Nancy was in tears after that game. Just the way she was after I won my three hundredth game at Yankee Stadium. There is just no physical outlet for that emotion. I saw her in the runway after the game, coming from Kiner's Korner, and she was in tears and I asked her why she was crying. She could hardly answer. Mrs. Payson was there, too, to congratulate me, I remember that."

Through the first twenty-five outs, Ron Santo hit a long ball to center for an out and Jimmy Qualls, a rookie, hit a hard grounder to first base and a long fly to right, the only hard-hit balls of the night.

"Qualls hit the ball sharply both times, and when I faced him the third time I told myself if anybody gets a hit tonight, it would be this guy. I didn't know him and I had faced him twice, pitched him inside and he hit the ball sharply both times. I decided now I'd better go outside. He hit the ball sharply to left field. A clean base hit. No dying quail. I've seen the pictures of myself after that hit and I try to read my emotions. I don't know if it's relief or disappointment or what. I know it was one of my best games, better than my no-hitter with Cincinnati. That was just a fun game. I really didn't have very good stuff that day. I was lucky. Joe Morgan made a couple of good plays and all the balls were hit at somebody."

In remembering the game, I could only think of the noise in that ball park at that significant instant in Mets history. Seaver stood at the mound, his body almost limp, his shoulders sagging, his eyes focused on the dirt of the pitching mound as more than fifty thousand people applauded him. It was clearly a moment that most identified the 1969 season. "I have always been an athlete who could get right back to work. I prided myself on that. That's what I did. I got the next two hitters out and we won the game, 4–0. It was pivotal for us because it showed the Cubs how good we were. If a young pitcher could get within a couple of outs of a perfect game and then the next day another young pitcher would give them more trouble, they had to know winning this pennant would not be a walk in the park."

As it turned out, the Cubs salvaged the series the next day by beating Gentry, 6–2. They left Shea with a shaky 4-game lead which they built back up to 9½ games by August 13, after the Mets lost three in Houston. By September, the Cubs had nothing left and the Mets roared past them for the title.

"We weren't concerned after losing three in Houston. We just couldn't play there. When the schedule came out we looked at those games and said 'OK, that's three straight losses.' We move on from there."

Gary Nolan would beat Seaver in Cincinnati on August 5. The right-hander would then win ten straight games as the Mets rallied to win the crown despite that 3-game loss in Houston and the fall to 9½ games back.

"That's when Gil made his most important contribution. As we were too young in the spring to realize we could win we were too young in August to realize we should lose now. He just handled that club brilliantly over the last six weeks."

There were some who said Seaver never said anything to the press without first weighing the impact of his chosen words. Bright and articulate, he understood that there was more to language than just filling out the spaces in the *Times* crossword puzzle he did regularly. He was asked about Hodges. He spoke carefully, the words coming after much thought.

"I loved Gil. He had more influence on me as a professional than anyone else I ever came in contact with. He was extremely strong, quiet and strong. He was aloof, sometimes to the degree that you had no idea what he was thinking, how he thought of you. You always knew what his objectives were. He was uncommunicative in those early days of 1968, but he changed a great deal after his heart attack. He became a lot warmer.

"He ran the ship. You talked to those guys on the old Brooklyn Dodgers, and they would tell you he was one of the warmest, nicest guys they had ever met. He was very intimidating around us. He was also a lot smarter than people gave him credit for. Intellectually, he managed exactly the way he could get it done. He looked at managing and realized, with his lack of education, he couldn't manage with an open door, easygoing policy. He managed like the Marine he was. He understood that was the best way for him. He was the platoon leader. We were the privates. This is the way we do it. Nobody argued with him. He was the sergeant. He was the boss. We're going to take the beachhead and if you try to do it your way you will get your butt blown off. We're going to do it my way, not our way."

Seaver had prospered in his short stay in the Marines and he knew of Hodges's heroic Marine war record. He respected him for it. He respected many of his teammates for bringing that same sense of character and intensity to the game. Nobody was more intense than Grote.

"I understood Grote. I got along with him well. He loved to get on people, needle people, pull practical jokes. He just didn't like the same things done to him. So I didn't needle him. The only fun of needling is see a guy react in a funny way. Jerry just didn't take it very well. Koosy and McGraw were the best in giving and taking."

Seaver said he also had a strong relationship with Jones and Agee. "I don't think black or white mattered on that team. I felt close to Agee and Jones and I didn't feel very close to Clendenon. It wasn't race, it was age, and the fact that I didn't know him very well since he only joined us that very season. I liked everybody on that team."

The pennant was won and the celebrations were held and twenty years later Seaver looks back with some degree of regret. "The best celebration was after the division. We celebrated with our own guys, the players, and the press guys that had been there from the beginning. That's the way it should be. It got too big after that. When we won the pennant and the Series and won the pennant again in 1973 it was just a sea of people in the clubhouse. It took all the joy out of it."

Seaver was on a division-winning team in Cincinnati during 1979 but saw his team lose the pennant to the Pirates.

He was on a pennant-winning team in Boston in 1986. He was ineligible for postseason play because of a knee injury.

On June 22, 1987, he officially announced his retirement after failing to get in good-enough shape to pitch for the Mets.

"I tried. I have no regrets about that," he said. "I came home and took the summer off and was able to be with my family and go to picnics and enjoy a lot of free time. I'm still enjoying it."

Seaver was never a free agent so even though his salary escalated to well over a million dollars in his final season of 1986, he never reached the salary level achieved by so many others not nearly in his class.

It was time to leave and as we walked through his living room I admired his high wood-beamed ceiling and his handsome modern furniture and the flowers that seemed to thrive in the open, airy house. There was one side wall that caught my eye. It held three huge plaques: the Cy Young award as the most valuable pitcher in the National League for the seasons of 1969, 1973, and 1975. There was room for several more plaques, and he was clearly robbed of the award in 1981 when a Los Angeles publicity campaign helped steer it to newcomer Fernando Valenzuela, with a 13–7 season against Seaver's 14–2 in a strike-shortened year. Only Steve Carlton has ever won it four times.

For Seaver, at the age of forty-four, there would be the retirement of his uniform number, 47, by the Mets in 1988, the certain Hall of Fame induction in 1992, and some impressive career on or off the ball field to go with his standing as one of the game's finest pitchers ever when the time was right for him.

Now he would settle into a second stage of his professional life with as much indication of success as he found throwing baseballs. He would not be perfect, of course. He would simply be better than almost anybody else around at whatever he did. It was as good a reason as any for so many people being made uncomfortable by Tom Seaver without ever really being able to answer why.

Maybe Walter Johnson threw harder. Maybe Bob Feller or Sandy Koufax or Lefty Grove did. Just maybe. For hundreds of baseball players and millions of baseball fans, the standard of high heat for more than two decades was a handsome soft-spoken Texan by the name of Lynn Nolan Ryan. Ryan had been mechanically timed at 100.3 miles per hour on his fastball and no sophisticated timing device could adequately measure any of the others.

Baseball is a game of numbers. Ryan has the numbers. He entered the 1988 season, his twenty-first in the big leagues, with 4,547 strikeouts, more than one strikeout an inning for twenty-one seasons, surely the most incredible measure of strikeout pitching consistency in the history of the game. He is the only man to pitch five no-hitters and got close to a sixth early in 1988 until Mike Schmidt of the Phillies singled off him. His record into 1988 was 261–242, numbers that are a constant source of argument when Ryan's Hall of Fame credentials are discussed. "He is little more than a .500 pitcher," detractors would say. He has played on one pennant winner, the 1969 Mets, and three division winners, the 1979 Angels and the 1980 and 1986 Astros. He has won 20 games only twice. Yet, his peers hold him in such high esteem that most of them consider a long foul ball a good day against him.

As he entered the 1988 season, he was three months past his forty-first birthday. He threw as hard as he did in 1969, one of the major miracles of Ryan's brilliant career.

"I watch him now," said St. Louis scout Rube Walker, a 1969 Mets pitching coach, "and I see no difference in his velocity from then." Says Ryan, "On any given pitch I can throw as hard as I ever did. I just don't have too many of them in me for a single game."

Despite the fact that he is often criticized for lack of control, his strikeouts nearly double his walks, a ratio old baseball thinker Branch Rickey, the impressario of the old Brooklyn Dodgers, would have clearly admired. Rickey, who ran the Dodgers, had a pitcher who probably threw as hard as Ryan, one Rex Barney. He could never learn the strike zone. No pitcher with five no-hitters and twenty-one successful seasons can be judged not to have known the strike zone.

While all in baseball admire Ryan for his speed, few speak of him with the same sense of pitching awe reserved for Koufax in his prime, Tom Seaver, Bob Gibson, Feller, Grove, Johnson, a few others. There has always been this sub rosa sense that with that incredible speed and that God-given pitching power, Ryan has been an underachiever, a pitcher who should have set as many records for winning as he has for strikeouts. It galls Ryan. "It takes more than a pitcher to win games," he says.

If he fails to win 300 games—he might continue pitching two more seasons to make it—Ryan should still be a unanimous Hall of Fame selection. No pitcher intimidated hitters as Ryan does.

"I don't go out to intimidate people. Because of the type of pitcher I am and the state of mind I have to be in to be effective, I think it tends to that at times."

Ryan was born January 31, 1947, in Refugio, Texas, some

twenty miles outside of Houston. He was raised on a ranch in the nearby town of Alvin and now owns a spread of some seven thousand acres not far from where he was brought up. His wife, Ruth, the loveliest of the 1969 Met family and still as strikingly beautiful at forty-one as she was at twenty-one, was a high school sweetheart. They have three children, Reid, Reese—named after California Angels coach, Jimmie Reese, a dear old friend—and Wendy. The oldest, Reid, a handsome young man, was nearly killed about ten years ago when he was struck by a car in front of their Anaheim home.

Ryan was thin and gawky when he first began playing baseball at Alvin High School. New York Mets scout Red Murff began watching him when Ryan was barely fifteen.

"I liked him but I thought he was just too skinny to have a chance at being a big-leaguer," Murff once related. "I saw him pitch two or three times. He threw so dang hard. He had to be worth a chance. I kept thinking about him when he turned eighteen, just before the draft that year in 1965. I decided to visit his house. This big, burly man answered the door. I identified myself and he identified himself as Ryan's father. I asked him how he was built when he was Nolan's age. 'Oh, just about the same as Nolan is today.' That was good enough. I decided to take a chance."

Murff recommended Ryan and the Mets decided to gamble. They weren't too excited by the prospect as evidenced by Ryan's selection after 614 other players were picked in that first free-agent draft in 1965.

He was assigned to Marion, Virginia, where he was only 3–6 but struck out 115 hitters in 78 innings. He was 17–2 with 272 strikeouts the next season at Greenville, South Carolina, before being moved up to Williamsport and then to the Mets at the end of the year for a couple of games.

With injuries and reserve duty, he pitched little in 1967 at Winter Haven and Jacksonville. Gil Hodges kept him with the Mets in 1968 after he got a good look at his arm. "I wanted that boy near me," Hodges said. "I didn't want anybody tampering with him."

He started 18 games in 1968, was 6–9, struck out 133 in 134 innings, and frustrated Hodges. "Gil wanted us to take care of his arm," says Walker. "He wanted us to take care of the arms of all the young pitchers. Nolan didn't pitch as much as some of them because he kept breaking down."

He pulled groin muscles, had elbow problems, lost time again with military duty, and struggled with blisters. Trainer Gus Mauch finally helped him. "When I was with the Yankees we had a few young pitchers who had blister problems," the trainer once said. "I went to this delicatessen near the Stadium and bought a jar of pickles. I threw away the pickles and had the pitchers soak their blistered fingers in the brine. It toughened the skin."

Ryan would often be seen sleeping in the back of the Mets plane on long flights with his right index finger, the one that blistered the most, soaked in pickle juice. He often smelled like a delicatessen. "I don't know if that toughened the skin or it just got stronger as I pitched more," Ryan says. "I know it worked, whatever it was."

Ryan was 6–3 in the 1969 championship season, locked up the playoffs by relieving Gary Gentry and striking out Rico Carty in an emotional seven-inning performance. He relieved Gentry again in the seventh inning of the fourth Series game, was saved by Tommie Agee's great lunging catch, and preserved the shutout.

On a staff with Seaver, Jerry Koosman, Gentry, Jim McAndrew, Tug McGraw, and some veterans, Ryan's pitching turn often was swallowed up. He became discouraged in 1970 and 1971. He won 7 and then 10 games but showed little consistency. He also felt uncomfortable in New York, a small-town Texas boy in the big, bad city.

Devoted to his wife, Ruth, Ryan was especially unhappy when he was on the road with the team and his wife was alone in their Bayside, Queens, apartment. By the middle of 1971 he yearned for a trade. The Mets, recognizing his speed but concerned about his consistency and repeated injuries, decided to give him up for Angel infielder Jim Fregosi. Ryan went to California and Fregosi joined the Mets. In his first spring workout, Fregosi missed the hop on a fungo hit by Gil Hodges, and the ball broke his finger. Ryan moved on to his Hall of Fame pitching career.

The big right-hander broke Sandy Koufax's strikeout record of 382 by one in the first year of the designated hitter, 1973. He was the league strikeout leader seven times. After the 1979 season, he signed with Houston as a free agent. He was making one million dollars a year, a bargain, when he visited Shea with the Astros in 1988.

Nolan Ryan is still a very handsome man. His hair is thinner now, but his face is smooth and his body is relatively lean and hard. As he sits in the visitor's dugout at Shea, he still seems boyish, brutally honest, and idealistically decent. Ruth still often travels to New York with him to visit with friends they knew as Mets years ago.

"I guess I have to be very surprised that I'm here and still pitching," Ryan says. "I really never expected to pitch this long, especially being a power pitcher. I guess my legs have helped me go on this long. I do a lot of walking and a lot of outdoor work on the ranch every winter."

Ryan has no special feelings at Shea anymore. It is just another visiting ball park. "Everything has changed. The ball park looks different. The people are all different. I really have very little relationship to the Mets. I guess the only guys I still know from the old days here are Arthur Richman [the traveling secretary for the Mets] and a few of the sportswriters. Even they have changed."

There were some doubts about his career when he was a

Met. Much of it revolved around Gil Hodges. "My only disagreement with Gil was in the way he used me. I understood the situation with the reserve obligations and the other pitchers, but I just wanted to pitch more. It was very difficult when you are trying to establish your career and you pitch one day and sit for two weeks before you pitch again."

When the trade was made to the Angels, a player strike was in progress. Ryan was working out privately with a few teammates. His money was running low.

"I considered packing it all in and going home. I was glad for the opportunity with the Angels after being used in and out with the Mets. But I wasn't sure I could afford the housing until we started getting paid."

Coach Jimmie Reese took him in. The bond between the young pitcher and the old coach, who had been a 1930 Yankee teammate of Babe Ruth, was one of the most touching in sports.

Ryan soon established himself with the Angels, broke the strikeout record the next season, in 1973, and has been a baseball marquee name ever since.

"I don't think anybody would have thought that I would last this long or be as successful as I have been back in 1969. Some of it was God-given talent, but I have also worked awfully hard."

Ryan was close to Seaver, to Jerry Grote and Ken Boswell, and a few of his other teammates. As a continuous competitor over the last two decades, he has missed most of the Mets reunions and social situations. He is usually too busy pitching.

"I'm not too terribly aware of records. I know I have five no-hitters and I kept track of the strikeouts for a while but mostly I just enjoy pitching. It was the same then. I just didn't have the opportunity to pitch as much as I wanted to. I knew I never would be the pitcher I could be if I didn't."

Ryan has to know that the trade to California turned his career around. In New York he might have become a second

Rex Barney, a hard thrower of legendary proportions who just quite didn't make it.

"I enjoyed pitching for the Mets. I had a lot of friends. I got my start. I guess I didn't love pitching in New York. I'm a small-town guy. New York was a little intimidating for me. Also, I was what?—twenty-two, twenty-three years old then. Maybe it would have been the same in Houston or California at that age. Maybe I'd be more comfortable pitching here now at forty-one."

Ryan enjoyed working with Rube Walker. "I don't think anybody on that staff ever had a bad word for Rube. He was really like a second father to all of us."

It is time for another game in the long career of Nolan Ryan. He is wearing the orange and yellow uniform shirt of the Astros. As he stands up and shakes hands, I can see that same handsome young face I saw when he wore a Mets uniform over twenty years ago. Time has been very kind to Nolan Ryan.

# 15

# *Mostly Memories*

Some of them were called back to Shea in the summer of 1988 for the retirement of Tom Seaver's uniform number, 41, and the celebration of the Mets' twenty-five seasons in the Flushing ball park. All of them received an invitation for the 1989 Old-Timers' Day—twenty years after their memorable championship season—to once again hear that joyous noise of thundering hands.

They are middle-aged men now, some far too heavy, others surprisingly bald—all of them showing the passage of two decades on their faces. No matter. They are bonded eternally in the season of 1969.

It had been such a momentous summer. They had come together from California and Carolina, from Baltimore and the Bronx, from other organizations and from the Met farms to achieve this baseball immortality.

For a few of them the years afterward have not been kind. There have been too many divorces among them, too much frustration, too many years of looking back. It seems, finally, as they gather together again that enough time has now passed. They want desperately to accept their present.

Their names are locked into the life and history of the city. They had brought so much goodwill, so much triumph, so many hours, weeks, and months of reflected glory for all the thousands who lived this dream vicariously. It was not simply a victory in baseball. It was for each observer an elevation of his own worth.

Through their athletic talents, these 1969 New York Mets provided hope for all. How often through the years would people suggest that if the 1969 Mets could overcome so could they. The significance of the Mets' deeds has only grown with time. The world around them seemed to glow brighter in the wake of their triumph. It was not true that the war in Vietnam stood still in 1969 or the civil rights demonstrations ended or college kids wore suits and ties and respected authority. It was true that through that triumph the Mets had made a hard year easier.

There were some sad events to follow that season of 1969. A week after the World Series, Ed Charles would be released and Jack DiLauro returned to the minors again. In some few months, January 14, 1970, the general manager of the championship team, Johnny Murphy, would collapse and die of a heart attack.

The event that caused the true shock, the one most significant emotional blow to the team, would occur in West Palm Beach, Florida, on April 2, 1972, when Gil Hodges, returning from a golf course, fell over backwards onto a concrete hotel walk and died of heart failure at the age of forty-seven.

Don Grant would surprise the press, the players, and the public by naming Yogi Berra the team manager. Berra would win a pennant in 1973, with many of Hodges's players, but the team would go into serious decline after that. It would be thirteen years, in 1986, before the Mets could win another pennant, now under new ownership, with new players, and under the leadership of a tough manager named Davey Johnson, the same man who ended the 1969 World Series as a Baltimore second baseman and who seemed to many very similar in tone and character to Hodges.

Many of the 1969 Mets would serve military reserve obligations, a factor in the maneuvering of the season. None would be forced to serve in Vietnam though three of them—Ron Taylor, Ron Swoboda, and Tug McGraw—made goodwill visits.

The war in Southeast Asia would grind on until the fall of Saigon in 1975. The official casualty list included the names of 58,130 Americans, starting with Capt. Harry G. Cramer, who died on October 21, 1957, and ending with Col. Winfield Wade Sisson, who died September 8, 1983, of injuries sustained earlier. The anguish of the war spread across the country, and the hurt is still felt these many years later. Some soothing would finally begin with the construction of a memorial to these fallen warriors in a park in Washington across from the Lincoln Memorial, with all of those names carved into a marble wall. The communists would rename Saigon, the city so many of these Americans died defending, Ho Chi Minh City.

Mrs. Joan Whitney Payson, the team owner, and Casey Stengel, the team's first manager, died within weeks of each other in the fall of 1975.

The Mets drifted backwards in the late 1970s, were sold to the Doubleday group in January of 1980, and reached their dream in the fall of 1986 with the franchise's second World Series triumph. There are new heroes for the next generation of fans, a hard-throwing youngster from Florida named Dwight Gooden, a stylish first baseman named Keith Hernandez, a classy catcher named Gary Carter, an enigmatic outfielder named Darryl Strawberry. That 1986 team compiled a marvelous record of 108–54, winning the division title by 21½ games. Only a few old sportswriters knew how far the Mets had come from their 40–120 start of 1962, when they finished 60½ games out of first place.

The future for the team looks bright. Under the leadership of Frank Cashen, the former Baltimore boss, the Mets have prospered and produced winners. It seems logical to believe they will be among baseball's best well into the twenty-first century.

As the 1969 Mets gathered again at Shea, their presence evoked so many sweet memories. They have gone off in their own life directions, and now, twenty years later, they came together for a Shea day. They were not so old yet, not so out of shape, that even young observers could not see the athletic excellence in them, their pride and their presence. The glistening World Series rings many wore proudly to this reunion reflected their shared glory.

If there were some disappointments in their years after 1969, some unrest, some frustration, it was only natural. What they taught us, what we probably always knew, was that every season comes to an end. Even a season as glorious as 1969 must slip back into the memory of each man as summers pass.

"What was at once humbling and invigorating about baseball," Tom Seaver once said, "is that each season you begin with a 0–0 record."

In their middle years the seasons come faster, the summers run into fall, the winters blend into spring, the triumphs of their youth become less important in the measure of their total years.

In 1969 the Beatles recorded their final number together as a group. It was called "Let It Be." The 1969 Mets would hear that dirge for the rest of their lives.

# Index